# THE EVERYTHING
## Guide to Writing Copy

Dear Reader,

I became a copywriter by accident. During an earlier sales career, I was asked by my boss to take a stab at writing a new product brochure. At the time, I didn't know a thing about persuasive writing. But I gave it my best shot.

To my surprise, I found copywriting fascinating, challenging, and fun. Soon I was reading everything I could get my hands on about the subject and picking the brains of some of the top experts in the field. I had stumbled upon a new passion—and a new career.

That was fifteen years ago. The most important lesson I've learned during that time is that effective copywriting focuses on the customer. So this book is structured with you—the customer—in mind. Whether your task is to create a sales letter that sizzles, a Web site that converts, an advertisement that jumps off the page, or any other promotional piece, you'll find the help you need in these chapters.

And if you're interested in making copywriting your business or career, this book includes advice on making that happen, too.

Persuasively yours!

# The EVERYTHING® Series

## Editorial

| | |
|---|---|
| Publisher | Gary M. Krebs |
| Director of Product Development | Paula Munier |
| Managing Editor | Laura M. Daly |
| Executive Editor, Series Books | Brielle K. Matson |
| Associate Copy Chief | Sheila Zwiebel |
| Acquisitions Editor | Lisa Laing |
| Development Editor | Brett Palana-Shanahan |
| Production Editor | Casey Ebert |

## Production

| | |
|---|---|
| Director of Manufacturing | Susan Beale |
| Production Project Manager | Michelle Roy Kelly |
| Prepress | Erick DaCosta |
| | Matt LeBlanc |
| Interior Layout | Heather Barrett |
| | Brewster Brownville |
| | Colleen Cunningham |
| | Jennifer Oliveira |
| Cover Design | Erin Alexander |
| | Stephanie Chrusz |
| | Frank Rivera |

Visit the entire Everything® Series at *www.everything.com*

# THE
# EVERYTHING®
# GUIDE TO
# WRITING COPY

From ads and press releases to on-air and
online promos—all you need to create copy that sells!

Steve Slaunwhite

**Δ**

Adams Media
Avon, Massachusetts

*To my daughter, Erin. The most fascinating person on the planet.*

An Everything® Series Book.
Everything® and everything.com® are registered trademarks of F+W Publications, Inc.

Published by Adams Media, an F+W Publications Company
57 Littlefield Street, Avon, MA 02322 U.S.A.

*www.adamsmedia.com*

ISBN-10: 1-59869-251-8
ISBN-13: 978-1-59869-251-8
Printed in the United States of America.

J   I   H   G   F   E   D   C   B   A

**Library of Congress Cataloging-in-Publication Data**

Slaunwhite, Steve.
The everything guide to writing copy / Steve Slaunwhite.
p. cm. – (The everything series)
Includes index.
ISBN-13: 978-1-59869-251-8 (pbk.)
ISBN-10: 1-59869-251-8 (pbk.)
1. Advertising copy.  I. Title.

HF5825.S63 2007
659.13'2–dc22
2007010848

Sales letter sample on page 137 used with permission of Ivan Levison & Associates
Sales brochure excerpt on page 173 used with permission of Kudzu Graphics
Copywriter sales letter on page 285 used with permission of Pam Magnuson

*This book is available at quantity discounts for bulk purchases.*
*For information, please call 1-800-289-0963.*

# Contents

## Writing Internet Copy / 151

## Writing Sales Communications Copy / 169

## Writing PR Copy / 185

## Writing Customer Communications Copy / 199

## Writing Marketing Communications Copy / 211

## Writing Branding Copy / 225

# Acknowledgments

I'd like to thank Lisa Laing, my sage and very patient acquisitions editor.

The following copywriters and other experts kindly contributed samples to this book: Michael Huggins, Ivan Levison, Pam Magnuson, Ed Gandia, Diane Autey, Neil Sagebiel, Oliver Sutherns, and Dianna Huff. Shannon Diederich provided invaluable assistance on some key chapters.

A big thank-you to my family for putting up with me during my marathon writing sessions.

And, finally, special thanks to Colleen Sell for recommending me for this project. (I owe you one, pal!)

# The Top Ten Traits of Killer Copy

1. It has an attention-grabbing headline that instantly resonates with the people reading it (your target market).

2. It lets readers know you "get" them by telling a compelling story that is relevant to their world.

3. It promises a benefit to the reader that is unique to the product being promoted—or that puts a unique spin on a benefit shared by, but not being touted by, competitors.

4. It speaks to readers rather than about products (or whatever is being promoted) and uses specifics to show how the product satisfies a desire or solves a problem of the reader.

5. It is written in a conversational tone.

6. It uses simple, meaningful, lively, and sincere language.

7. It has a rhythm and a logical flow of information so as to guide the reader seamlessly through the text from the first word to the last.

8. It inspires and instructs the reader to act—by using words that appeal to the readers' emotions and including a directive that tells them what you want them to do: "Give us a try!", "Call today!", "Order now!"

9. It is clean and polished—free of typos, improper typographical treatments (bold, italics, oversized type, fancy fonts), and errors in grammar, punctuation, and spelling.

10. It compliments and plays off of the graphic elements of the piece.

# Introduction

▶ ONE OF THE GREATEST COPYWRITERS OF ALL TIME was P.T. Barnum. He's the guy who made the Barnum and Bailey Circus such an enduring success and created such memorable slogans as "The greatest show on earth." In 1850, he took an unknown Swedish singer and, purely through the effectiveness of the ads and posters he wrote, caused a sensation when she arrived in America. More than 30,000 cheering fans—who had never heard her sing a note!—met her ship at New York harbor.

Perhaps better than anyone else in his time, P.T. Barnum knew how to unlock the selling power of words. In fact, many of the copywriting techniques he pioneered are still being used today.

Copywriting is indeed a powerful tool. From sales to marketing to public relations, every field of persuasive communications without exception relies on it.

You may not realize it, but copywriting plays a big role in your day-to-day life. And it's not just because of all the ads! The words on the side of a cereal box are copy. So are the words on a restaurant menu, catalog, coupon, and even the back cover of this book. Effective copy is meant to educate you on the product, get you excited about it, and, hopefully, motivate you to buy it.

So how do you write effective copy? The "trade secrets" aren't just for ad agency scribes sipping cappuccinos in their Madison Avenue offices. Many people can benefit from learning how to write great copy—a manager who needs to send out a press release, a freelance writer struggling to craft a client brochure, a self-employed professional promoting her own business, or a dad trying to sell his baseball card collection on eBay.

The good news is copywriting basics are relatively easy to master. How do you craft a powerful headline? How do you write tantalizing body copy? What are the best words and phrases to use? How do you decide what to say, and how to say it? What are the proven formulas for creating a killer sales letter, ad, or Web page? All these questions and more are answered in this book

But that's not all. This book also features many of the cutting-edge tips, tricks, and strategies used by the top copywriters in the world.

Of course, the information in these pages won't make you a super-star copywriter. Only practice can do that. (Don't clear space on your mantle for all your ECHO and Caples awards just yet!) But if you follow this book closely, your copy will be more effective, and you'll reach and persuade more people with your words. That's a promise.

*The Everything Guide to Writing Copy* is divided into two basic parts. The first part guides you through the craft of copywriting—the rules, techniques, and strategies. The second part looks closely at more than fifty typical copywriting projects and provides you with tips and formulas on how to complete them successfully. Need to write a powerful ad? A knockout Web site? A sizzling sales letter? It's all here.

In addition, we also cover how to make a living as a copywriter, either on staff at an agency or company or on your own as a freelancer.

Copywriting is as fun to learn as it is to write. You get to be creative and play with words and ideas. Sure, it can be challenging, too. But that's part of the appeal. Even when writing copy is hard work, it's often worth the effort. There are few things more satisfying than having the words you so carefully crafted work so well in a sales, marketing, or public relations piece.

Ready to get started? To borrow another famous line by P.T. Barnum, "Ladies, gentleman, children of all ages," welcome to the world of copywriting!

Chapter 1

# What Every Copywriter Needs to Know

There's no mystery to copywriting. Some people say it's just good clear writing. Others say that great copywriting requires special talents and little-known techniques. The truth, of course, lies somewhere in the middle. Yes, it takes certain skills and knowledge to craft copy that does its job—sell. But with just a few key strategies and tools, even the novice can write an effective sales, marketing, or PR piece.

## What Is Copywriting?

When copywriters first began plying their trade in the mid-1800s, the profession was very easy to define. Copywriters wrote ads. Period. Print advertising was the primary way companies promoted their products and services back then. There was no television or radio. Certainly no Internet.

Today, of course, things have changed dramatically. Copywriting has a much broader definition and can be difficult to nail down. Obviously, the text in an advertisement is copy. But so are the words in a press release, in a salesperson's PowerPoint presentation, in the dialogue of a radio commercial, or even on a restaurant menu.

Technically, copywriting is writing the words that are printed, spoken, or displayed in any type of advertising, marketing, sales, and publicity piece. It encompasses all communications media—print, broadcast, Internet. And it includes all the written elements of a promotion, including the headline, the body of the text, slogans, photo captions, spoken dialogue, and even stage directions (in the case of scripts for video and television).

**ALERT!**

Do not confuse copywriting with copyright. These two aren't even distant cousins! A copyright protects the ownership of original works, such as books, songs, photographs, and screenplays. It is usually denoted by the © symbol. Copywriting, however, is a form of writing and has nothing to do with creative rights, trademarks, and patents. (You can, of course, get your copywriting copyrighted.)

It's almost impossible to get through the day without being influenced, at least to some degree, by copywriting. It's in the ads you see in magazines, in the banners on the Web sites you visit, and on the billboards you notice as you drive to work. It's a big part of your life, whether you like it or not.

There's no doubt that you have been persuaded to buy something because of the copy. Perhaps a direct-mail letter persuaded you to subscribe to a magazine at a special discount. Or a catalog description prompted you to visit a Web site and place an order. Or a television commercial motivated you to test-drive a new car.

Copy is used to promote just about every product or service sold on the planet. It's also used to promote schools, hospitals, arts groups, religious organizations, and charities. Copy is even used to promote people (such as politicians), ideas (such as global warming), and ideals (such as equal rights).

**FACT**

About one-third of all copywriters are self-employed. In the trade, these people are referred to as freelancers. About 40,000 copywriters in the United States hold staff positions in advertising, marketing communications, and public relations firms. And many more times that number hold staff positions within the marketing and publicity departments of corporations and nonprofit organizations.

With all those "buy me" messages coming at people from all directions in both their personal and professional lives, is it any wonder that only the best copy gains attention and gets results? That's why it is so important not to take the task of writing an ad, Web page, sales letter, or any other promotional piece lightly. There are proven formats and techniques that are required in order to create copy that breaks through the clutter and persuades people to take action. All these formats and techniques are covered in this book.

## Are Copywriting and Business Writing the Same?

There are a lot of similarities between copywriting and business writing. Business writing is all about conveying business-oriented information in a clear and compelling way. That could be in an internal proposal, newsletter article, memo to staff, or product documentation.

Many copywriters also do business writing, and often do it well. However, many good business writers are bad copywriters. Business writing requires the ability to organize and articulate information in a logical and clear way. Copywriting requires those skills plus the ability to write words that engage readers (or "prospects," as they are called in marketing lingo) on an emotional level and convince them to believe or do something.

Here is a typical example: You want to write an ad that persuades novice welders to adhere to a particular safety guideline. A business writer might write the following headline:

Turn on the acetylene valve before turning on the oxygen.
Otherwise, an explosion may occur.

That line certainly conveys the information accurately and clearly. But take a look at what happens when a skilled copywriter takes a stab at crafting the headline:

"A" before "O"—or up you'll go!

Both present the same information. But which one is more memorable and impactful? Which one surprises, triggers your emotions, and paints a vivid picture you won't soon forget? The answer is obvious.

Good copy appeals to the prospects' intellects and to their belief systems. While the main job of business writing is to explain and inform, the main job of copywriting is to *sell*.

## You Might Be a Copywriter if...

Look around and you'll probably notice something with copy on it—an ad, a brochure, an e-mail, a Web site. Now ask yourself who wrote it. Was it written by a crack copywriter working at a trendy Madison Avenue ad agency? Or a busy marketing manager at a major corporation? Or a small business owner wearing, among many, the copywriter's hat? Or a freelance writer living just down the street?

The answer could very easily be any of the above.

Agency copywriters—those who work at advertising, marketing, or public relations agencies or media or content development companies—often scribe the mass campaigns you see in glossy magazines or on television. Smaller agencies may only have one or two copywriters on staff, but the larger ones can have a whole team of copywriters headed by a copy chief or director of copywriting. At a very small agency, dual responsibilities are common. So someone could be both the resident copywriter and the account executive.

The writing can also be done by someone within the media company itself—the newspaper, radio or television station, or Web site company. Radio stations often have a copywriter/producer on staff who creates the ads for local advertisers. Newspapers, too, usually have someone who assists their small-business clients in putting together an effective ad.

And a lot of copy is written by freelancers. In fact, freelancing is one of the fastest growing segments in the marketing and public relations industry. Freelancers are independent contractors who are hired by agencies, businesses, or nonprofits to write copy for specific projects. These self-employed professionals often work out of their homes, but they can sometimes work on site at their client's location as well.

Copy can also be written by someone within the company or organization that needs it. For example, if a company requires a new product description for a Web site, someone in its own marketing department might be asked to write it to save the trouble and expense of hiring a freelancer or agency.

Finally, many independent professionals and small-business owners write copy to promote themselves or their own products and services. They may hire a graphic designer to create their Web sites and brochures but often can't afford the services of a professional copywriter. So they do the job themselves.

## A Copywriter by any Other Name

Copywriters don't always have the word "copywriter" in their job titles. In fact, the vast majority of people who write copy don't have this skill reflected on their business cards at all. A copywriter might be known as:

- Advertorial scriptwriter
- Audio-visual (AV) or multimedia writer
- Direct-mail or direct-response writer
- Jingle writer
- Online marketing writer
- Marketing or marketing communications (marcom) writer
- Multimedia developer
- Newsletter writer
- Public relations writer
- Web advertising writer

Remember, too, that many copywriters do other forms of commercial writing in addition to or instead of copywriting. The field of commercial writing includes:

- Ghost bloggers
- Content developers or providers
- Corporate communications or business writers
- Employee communications writers
- Newsletter writers
- Speech writers
- Technical writers

Finally, insiders at a company may be copywriters—at least some of the time—but have something different on their business cards:

- Marketing manager
- PR manager
- Marketing coordinator
- Communications manager
- Publicity manager
- Marketing intern
- Product manager

In fact, just about everyone is a copywriter at some point in their lives. We all need to persuade other people with our words, whether it's in a resume to get a job, an e-mail to a friend to encourage them to come to a house party, or a classified ad to sell a used car. Whenever you need to carefully structure and present your words to motivate someone to do something, you're a copywriter. Welcome to the club!

## Skills You Will Need

There are a lot of myths about what it takes to be a copywriter. Some say it requires a way with words that rivals Hemingway. Others insist that you need the marketing savvy of a Madison Avenue superstar. Still others claim that it takes a creative genus who can dream up catchy slogans and tantalizing headlines at the drop of a hat—the writing equivalent of Picasso.

Becoming an effective copywriter isn't that much of a rarity. Of course, you do need some talent for using words and how to convey a message effectively to a target audience. But much of what you need to know—the techniques, formats, skills, best practices—can be learned. Even a rocket scientist, at some point in his or her career, couldn't tell the difference between propulsion fuel and a cooling tank.

**ALERT!**

Although copywriters are part of a team—designers, illustrators, strategists, production coordinators—they often work in solitude, even when working within an agency or company. This makes it challenging to coordinate efforts with others. Consequently, copywriters need to be self-motivated and work well independently with little direction.

Copywriters are not journalists. Nor are they creative writers. Although they possess many of the same skills required of those professionals, copywriters are primarily business people who work closely with clients and other members of a project team to produce a promotional piece that fulfills a strategic objective. Consequently, copywriters need many of the same capabilities that any businessperson needs: interpersonal, organizational, presentation, and strategic thinking skills.

## Passion for Information

Like a tireless journalist, a good copywriter will be relentless in her pursuit of the facts. She won't quit until she understands the product or service she is writing about completely and the target audience she is trying to persuade.

The most successful salespeople know their products, customers, and competitors inside and out. They can identify and articulate how their product solves an important problem or satisfies a chief need or desire of the customer in a way that is distinctive from or superior to the competition. That is also the key to writing persuasive copy: knowing the target market's hot buttons and how to push them with words.

A copywriter will dig through all the background information, read all the boring stuff—the technical documentation, the memos, the product development presentations—and do additional research. She will also study the competition and look for opportunities to say things that they aren't saying to gain an advantage.

**FACT**

In the late 1960s, a talented copywriter at BBDO—the ad agency at the time for Wisk detergent—noticed that no other detergent was saying anything about that nasty grime that builds up on shirt collars. The subsequent "ring around the collar" ad campaign became one of the most successful in history. This is a great example of saying what the competition isn't saying.

Also like a journalist, copywriters must be great interviewers. They need to be able to ask the right questions, in the right way, to pull out all the salient facts. That's because the background information provided on a product or target audience doesn't always tell the full story.

## Ability to Write Well

This skill may seem like a no-brainer. But it's amazing how many people think that mastery of the written word is not all that important in copywriting. That, of course, is nonsense.

In the absence of language know-how, imitators are rarely able to adapt and expand their skills to suit different products, markets, and media. Consequently, their copy tends to be not only stale and unoriginal, but also irrelevant and unclear. Copy that doesn't relate and doesn't make sense to prospects falls flat.

People who don't know the first thing about composition, grammar, punctuation, vocabulary, literary devices, and other mechanics of language can sometimes mimic certain copywriting techniques. But the end result is usually formulaic.

In fact, one of the challenges of writing copy is to convey the key messages in a clear, concise manner. The biggest mistake that copywriters make—and it's astonishing how often they make it—is to focus on being clever to the detriment of clarity. Think about it. How many brochures or Web sites have you read where there is no clear idea of what's in it for you? As advertising legend David Ogilvy once said, "If it doesn't sell, it's not creative."

As a copywriter, words are your bricks and mortar. How skillfully you put them together in phrases, sentences, and paragraphs will determine the strength of the persuasive case you are building. If your writing is weak, your promotional piece will fall down like a house of cards, regardless of how compelling the messages are. But if your writing is strong, your promotion has a much greater chance of standing up to the scrutiny of even the most skeptical prospect.

## Creative Intelligence

Ask 100 people what creativity is and you'll probably get 100 different definitions. Ask 100 copywriting pros whether creativity is essential to great copy, and you'll probably get an even mix of "yes," "no," "usually," and "sometimes" answers. Yet if those same people were asked to point out the most creative copy in a lineup of several comparable examples, the majority would likely pick the same piece.

Though hard to define, creativity is easy to recognize. When you see it, or read it, you immediately know it. And deep in their hearts, everyone with something to promote or sell wants creative copy. What they don't always recognize, though, is the difference between creative copy that titillates and creative copy that motivates. And if copy doesn't trigger the right response, it doesn't matter how exciting it is.

Writing copy that is both unique and useful requires creative intelligence—the ability to come up with innovative solutions to practical problems.

People who possess a high degree of creative intelligence typically:

- Think both creatively and strategically
- Easily draw analogies, associations, and connections between ideas and things
- Recognize the differences and similarities between related and unrelated ideas and things
- Have broad attention spans and can process multiple thoughts simultaneously
- Mentally collate, organize, and assimilate vast amounts of information
- Adeptly process divergent thoughts and converge them into a single unique concept
- Focus on the process and on solving problems rather than just trying to impress
- Are curious, investigative, reflective, and examine things from several angles
- Have self-confidence, pride in their work, and a desire to excel
- Are self-motivated, self-directed, and dedicated, willing, and able to put concentrated effort and considerable energy into their work
- Are flexible—open to ambiguity, experimentation, new ideas, risk, and external evaluation
- Are independent spirits and freethinkers—unrestrained by convention

With copywriters, creative intelligence manifests itself linguistically—in using words creatively for a practical purpose.

## *Savvy Salesmanship*

Copywriting is selling. When you think about selling skills, forget everything you've learned from those pesky telemarketing calls you receive at dinnertime or those hard-driving used-car salespeople. Hype and pressure have nothing to do with genuine selling.

Selling is all about empathizing with the prospect, clearly understanding his problems, needs, and desires, and positioning your product or service to address those issues. It's also about encouraging people to try the product or service, and giving them sound reasons to do so.

The most important selling skill you can cultivate as a copywriter is the ability to walk a mile in the prospect's shoes. Indeed, empathy is the master skill of successful selling. You need to develop a real sense of the prospect's problems, needs, and desires.

One of the biggest blunders that beginners make is coming on too strong in their copy. They mistakenly think they have to twist the prospect's arm and get him to sign on the dotted line. But remember, you're not in a room alone with the prospect. He's not sitting across your desk squirming for an opportunity to get up and walk away. Instead, he's reading your ad, listening to your radio commercial, or viewing your Web site. He can walk away anytime.

That's why the key to selling on paper (and on screen) is authenticity. You have to be truthful, genuine, trustworthy, and have information that is truly meaningful and impactful to the prospect.

## Computer Skills

Computer skills are among the most practical skills that every copywriter must master. You won't get very far—even if you're writing copy for yourself or your own business—if you don't know how to use a computer.

Today, all working copywriters need to be computer literate and Internet savvy. At a minimum, you must know how to use word processing software (such as Microsoft Word), how to send and receive e-mail, and how to search the Web for research purposes.

Most copywriters will also need to have at least some familiarity with the following applications software:

- Page layout programs, such as Quark XPress and Adobe InDesign
- Presentation packages, such as Microsoft PowerPoint, Adobe Persuasion, and Corel Presentations
- Electronic portfolios for storing, organizing, and displaying your work samples
- Web authoring and editing tools for creating and converting text to HTML, XML, JavaScript
- Document sharing programs, such as Adobe Acrobat (Adobe PDF—Portable Document Format—is the standard for sharing and reviewing design concepts)

If you plan to make copywriting your career, then typing skills are also very important. Hunting and pecking letters on the keyboard with just one or two fingers will severely reduce your productivity, no matter how proficient you get at it. Fortunately, there are many software programs that can teach you to type well in just a few weeks.

## Where Do You Learn This Stuff?

Most copywriters acquire this broad range of knowledge through a combination of formal (college, university, vocational school) and informal training. Informal training might involve taking courses, attending seminars, reading books, reading trade journals, doing an internship, hooking up with a mentor, hiring a writing coach, or working in an entry-level position in an agency or in-house marketing department. On-the-job training and self-study are arguably the best ways to learn and develop good copywriting skills.

## *Traits of Successful Copywriters*

People who write copy need much more than just great writing and savvy selling skills. They also need to work under tight deadlines and with an assortment of personalities involved in a project: clients, marketing managers, creative directors, graphic designers, account executives, editors, and many others. Copywriters must be creative on demand while simultaneously producing copy that consistently achieves objectives.

Not surprisingly, then, the top two traits of successful copywriters are:

- The ability to work well under pressure
- The ability to work both independently and collaboratively

Successful copywriters tend to be:

- Imaginative
- Aesthetically inclined, visually as well as verbally
- Enterprising
- Detail oriented
- Good researchers
- Keen listeners and observers
- Multitaskers
- Efficient time managers
- Well read, with interests in many areas

Nevertheless, anyone who hires, manages, or works with copywriters will expect them to know the fundamentals of copywriting and how copy fits into the grand scheme of things. It's also helpful if you know:

- The rules of proper English
- The writing style conventions specific to copywriting

- The different elements of copy—headlines, lead lines, taglines, captions—and how to use them
- Proofreaders' marks
- Proper manuscript format (which depends on the type of piece being produced)
- Computer proficiency, including word processing and online editing programs (such as Microsoft Word's Track Changes feature)
- Working knowledge of media production: graphic design, typography, and layout
- Working knowledge of the media for which the promotional piece is being written: publication, broadcast, Internet, interactive, audiovisual (multimedia)
- The basic principles and practices of advertising, marketing, and public relations
- Standard business and client relations protocol
- Familiarity with the market and industry for which the promotional piece is being created

And if all that isn't enough, if you aspire to be a freelance copywriter you'll also need to be:

- Well organized
- Goal oriented
- A savvy self-promoter
- A good negotiator (because you'll be pricing and quoting a lot of projects)
- Disciplined

Wow. It sounds like a lot. Does every copywriter have all these traits? Rarely they do. Some are strong in some and weaker in others, as with any profession. However, the more skilled you become in each of these areas, the better equipped you will be to succeed in this fascinating and rewarding field.

# Chapter 2

# A Sales, Marketing, and Public Relations Primer

Does someone need to be persuaded? Enter the copywriter! There are many specialties within the broader field of business communications that rely on effective copy. However, their borders are not always clearly drawn. What one person might call "public relations" another may refer to as "marketing communications." It's better to think of these specialties as circles on a page, each one unique yet overlapping the others to some degree.

## *What Is Sales Communications?*

Of all the terms used to describe how companies reach out to prospects and customers—marketing, PR, customer relations—sales communications is the least used. This area of business communications is often lumped in, perhaps unfairly, with general marketing communications. In fact, it's often marketing managers, not sales managers, who are most often involved in the brochures, presentations, and other materials created in this area.

However, this is changing, albeit slowly. In recent years, many corporations have been creating positions, such as sales communications manager, to recognize the specialized skills and knowledge required for this unique type of communications.

So what is sales communications? Simply put, it is all the materials created to help salespeople do their jobs faster and better. It helps them reach out to prospects and customers, identify sales opportunities, make persuasive presentations, follow up effectively, and close sales.

**FACT**

Sales communications materials are also referred to as sales literature or sales collateral. They are essentially any materials created to assist salespeople in doing what they do best: sell. If you are tasked with writing for sales communications, arrange to speak with one or two salespeople directly. This will give you the perspective you need to create these materials effectively.

Sales communications typically includes:

- Brochures
- Sell sheets
- Presentations
- Model letters and e-mails
- Model proposals
- Case studies

These materials are usually produced in print, but electronic versions are becoming increasingly popular. Salespeople, especially those who pound the pavement in the business-to-business sector, often make presentations using their laptop computers. Instead of showing the prospect a printed brochure, they display the online version. In some cases, a salesperson can even customize an electronic brochure with unique copy and visuals tailored to each presentation—something you can't do with a print version.

Writing effective sales communications is one of the most common tasks for a copywriter, or anyone else who writes copy for a company. It's like being the assistant salesperson. Your job is to help win the sale.

## What Is Marketing Communications?

Marketing communications is one of the most common specialties within business communications, yet the most difficult to define. Technically, it can mean anything that the marketing department produces to reach out to prospects and customers, whether that be a press release, sales brochure, or advertisement.

Why such a broad, fuzzy definition? In smaller companies, marketing communications is a catchall category. Often there is no public relations or advertising department, so any persuasive piece that needs to be produced falls by default under the marketing communications umbrella. That's why marketing managers at smaller companies usually write the press releases.

In larger companies, however, the function becomes more clearly defined. Marketing communications is more focused on creating materials, as required, to help build brand awareness, generate leads, increase Web site traffic, attract shoppers, and achieve other objectives related to promoting products and service.

To complete their many projects and campaigns, marketing communications managers will often work with ad agencies, design firms, and freelancers—in addition to their own in-house staff.

Marketing communications includes the following materials:

- Ads
- Annual Reports

- Brochures
- Exhibits
- Flyers
- Packaging
- Pamphlets
- Point-of-sale (POS) displays
- Signage
- Slogans
- Taglines
- Web sites

However, there is a lot of crossover into other fields. It's not uncommon, even at a large corporation, for a marketing communications manager to also be involved in putting together a media kit or writing model letters for the sales staff.

Marketing communications is also known by the acronym marcom. In fact, some professionals in this field have job titles like marcom manager or marcom director.

**ESSENTIAL**

In business-to-business marketing, one of the most important tasks of marketing communications managers is to create campaigns that generate leads. A lead is simply the name and contact information for a prospect who has expressed an interest in a product or service. For example, people who fill out a form on a Web site to download a brochure have a higher likelihood of buying the product.

## What Is Mass Advertising?

Mass advertising can easily fit under the heading of marketing communications. However, it's included in this separate section for one important reason: it is often created and managed by advertising agencies.

Mass advertising is what most people imagine when they think about marketing. It's the commercials you see on TV, the spots you hear on the radio, and the glossy ads that captivate you in national magazines.

While a company might create its own advertisement for a trade magazine or a specialty publication, it is unlikely to rely on in-house staff to produce a commercial for airing during the Super Bowl. Why risk the expense and the potentially amateurish result? A company is more likely to turn to an ad agency that has an impressive track record in TV work and knows how to handle such details as scripting, casting, shooting, and negotiating the best time slots.

**FACT**

Mass advertising—in both print and broadcast formats—is perhaps the one thing that advertising agencies do best. They know how to create advertising that is memorable, generates buzz, and builds brand awareness and preference. And they know how to get these ads into the right media (newspapers, magazines, radio, television).

Mass advertising usually refers to national campaigns where there is a lot of visibility. However, more focused regional campaigns, for a citywide pizza delivery service for example, may also be included in this category.

Mass advertising typically includes:

- Print ads
- Radio ads
- Television ads
- Other associated materials, such as brochures and Web pages

Most of the glamorous writing jobs in mass advertising are handled by the agency's own in-house writers or freelancers. However, sometimes a company staff writer or marketing manager gets involved in the copywriting process, especially when the products involved are complex or technical.

## *What Is Public Relations?*

Public relations is a huge, multifaceted field. Technically, it's all about communicating with the various "publics" of an organization—customers, shareholders, journalists, editors, government legislators, and the general public. This book is going to focus on the most common application of public relations for a company: generating publicity for its products and services.

The field of public relations originated in the United States where it was initially used to promote the railroad industry. The actual term "public relations" was first seen in the *1897 Year Book of Railway Literature*.

Obviously, getting a trade magazine or television show to talk about your product or service is a huge advantage. Publicity is more credible than advertising and other forms of marketing communications. People have a built-in skepticism for promotional materials but will often believe almost anything they read or hear in the press.

Public relations managers in a company spend much of their time building relationships with editors and journalists, and preparing a range of materials to provide information and pitch story ideas to this group.

Typical PR writing projects include:

- Articles
- Backgrounders
- Fact sheets
- Media advisories
- Media kits
- Presentations
- Press releases
- Speeches
- Spokesperson's materials

Public relations managers will also utilize materials produced for other areas of business communications, such as sales brochures and case studies.

Midsized and larger companies often have a public relations manager or department, or they retain a public relations agency. Smaller companies will tend to use an independent PR consultant. Some freelance copywriters provide PR consulting as an additional service to their clients.

## What Is Customer Communications?

As the term implies, customer communications is all about staying in touch with customers. Despite the lack of service you may have experienced dealing with some organizations, companies really do take customer satisfaction seriously. They want you to be happy! But not just for altruistic reasons. A customer who is delighted with a company's products and services is good for the bottom line.

Companies know that a loyal customer will buy from them again and again, and perhaps spread the word to friends and colleagues.

**FACT**

There's a term in the customer relations field called *customer lifetime value*. It refers to how much sales can be expected from a loyal customer over his or her lifetime. For example, if you love a particular brand of shampoo, you may buy $512 worth of this product over the years. Companies really do pull out a calculator and figure this stuff out.

So what role does persuasive communications play here? Companies produce a range of materials designed to motivate customers to become and remain loyal to its products and services. There are also strategies (cross-selling and up-selling, discussed in Chapter 14) that are used to persuade you to buy even more.

Typical copywriting projects include:

- Brochures
- E-mails
- Flyers
- Letters
- Loyalty or incentive materials
- Newsletters
- Telephone call scripts
- Support information

Customer communications is a bit of an orphan in the sales, marketing, and public relations fields. It doesn't have a home. Usually, it's the marketing department that handles the production of any needed brochures, newsletters, and other materials in this area. Increasingly, however, companies are dedicating resources to this function. It's not uncommon for a corporate manager to have a title like customer communications manager or even director of customer satisfaction.

## What Is Direct Marketing?

Direct marketing can ignite a lot of passion in people. You either love it or hate it.

Everyone, it seems, complains about the junk mail that clogs their mailboxes, or the pesky telemarketing calls that interrupt dinner, or the infomercials that take over the airwaves in the middle of the night.

**FACT**

Direct marketing is also referred to as direct-response marketing or direct-response advertising. "Response" refers to the primary purpose of direct marketing: to motivate the prospect to take some specific action, an action that usually leads to making a purchase.

However, the companies that sell products via direct marketing wouldn't bother to do so if this technique didn't work. In fact, direct marketing, when done properly, can be an extremely profitable way to generate orders for a wide range of products, from magazine subscriptions to kitchen gadgets to exercise equipment and more.

You may be one of those people who claim to dislike direct-marketing methods. However, chances are you've purchased at least one product—perhaps even more—through mail order, telephone solicitation, e-mail promotion, or television infomercial.

## *Just a Little Respect*

Compared to other forms of marketing communications that build brand awareness or simply convey information, direct marketing has a much tougher job to do: sell the product or service.

It's for this reason that copywriters enjoy a lot of respect in the direct-marketing industry. They are the salespeople—the ones who use their well-crafted messages to bring in the orders. Copywriters make direct marketers money.

Direct marketers produce a lot of written materials, including:

- Advertising
- Direct-mail packages
- Infomercial scripts
- Landing pages
- Micro sites
- Postcards and other self-mailers
- Radio ads
- Telemarketing scripts
- Web sites

Direct marketers are relentless testers. They are constantly tweaking, revising, and changing their communications to determine what works and what doesn't. Buyer response rates, rather than aesthetics, is the most important consideration. If a rotting banana peel with copy written on it gets a higher response rate than a letter, then that's what a direct marketer will put in the mail.

Many of the world's largest companies run direct-marketing campaigns to complement their other sales and marketing efforts. Some even have specialized direct-marketing departments. There are also agencies that specialize in direct marketing. However, freelancers and consultants tend to rule this industry. So if you're a freelance copywriter in direct marketing—and you're good at what you do—the future looks bright.

## *What Is a Campaign?*

"We're having a sales campaign in the fall." "The public relations campaign generated a lot of buzz for us." "Let's launch the new product with an aggressive marketing campaign." Okay, so what the heck is a campaign anyway?

In the sales, marketing, and PR worlds, a campaign is simply a special effort to accomplish a specific goal. That might be to increase sales for a particular gizmo, introduce a new brand of chewing gum to bubble-blowing enthusiasts, or get users of a software product to upgrade to the latest version.

Campaigns typically have a set beginning and end, and they usually fall outside the normal day-to-day activities of a sales, marketing, or PR department. It's extra work.

Here's an example: You're a copywriter for the marketing department of a travel company. Your everyday responsibilities might include writing Web site copy, e-mails to prospects and customers, destination brochures, and more. Then, your marketing manager announces, "The Christmas holiday period is coming fast. Let's do a promotion to motivate our customers to book their vacations early. We'll offer discounts and a chance to win a special mystery prize. We'll use e-mail and direct mail as our communications channels." Welcome to a new campaign!

Campaigns can be exciting to work on. But that's not the only payoff. A successful campaign can really be a feather in your cap; something you can take pride in and add to your resume and credentials. "I wrote the copy for the Gizmo Plus ad campaign that successfully increased market share by 22 percent." That's a career milestone worth bragging about.

# How a Promotional Piece Is Created

You're flipping through your favorite magazine and an advertisement catches your eye. It's for a new kind a hiking shoes. The picture of the happy family ambling cheerfully along a hiking path, against a spectacular mountain background, captivates you. The copy of the ad emphasizes comfort and safety, which further convinces you to rush to your local sportswear store and try on a pair.

The ad did its job. But how was it created? What were the steps taken by the company between "We need to sell more hiking shoes" to placing the finished advertisement in the magazine?

Communications projects go through a relatively predictable series of steps. Whether you're a small-business owner doing it all yourself or part of a larger marketing team at a corporation or ad agency, the general process is relatively the same. (The only real difference is the amount of cooks in the kitchen.)

Imagine you are the staff writer for that hiking shoes manufacturer. Where did you fit into the overall process? What happened before and after you wrote your masterpiece of advertising copy?

## What's the Problem?

Most communications projects are initiated by a problem, challenge, or desire. For example, a company may need to increase sales of a new product, drive more visitors to its Web site, or attract more buyers into its stores.

In the case of our hiking manufacturer, there is a new brand of shoes to launch. Buyers have to be made aware of the new product and be presented with good reasons to purchase it. Otherwise, the shoes might languish on the store shelves and not sell very quickly. Or, worse, the retailers might return them.

## Deciding on the Solution

Once the problem is identified, deciding on the solution is the most important step in the process. The marketing team at the company must determine what it is they need to produce. A brochure? A flyer? A special Web site? A television commercial? It's never an easy decision.

At larger companies or ad agencies, members of the marketing team may get together to brainstorm ideas. At smaller companies, there may be just one marketing manager or business owner involved, sitting at a desk staring at the ceiling, hoping to come up with an answer. The question always is: What is the most effective means of reaching and persuading the target audience?

For our hiking manufacturer, the target market is active families. So the company decided that ads in family-oriented magazines—especially those that focus on family vacations, adventures, and sports—would be the best strategy.

## Bringing Ideas to Life

At this stage, the project is defined. It's a full-page advertisement.

The next thing a marketing department or ad agency might do is prepare a creative brief. (This is explained in more detail in Chapter 3.) This document guides the writers, designers, illustrators, photographers, and others involved in actually creating the ad.

At a smaller company there may not be a creative brief. So the process is often less formal. The marketing manager or business owner might simply describe what is needed to his freelance designer or design firm by phone or e-mail.

As the staff writer for our hiking manufacturer, you will likely work closely with a designer to develop some initial ideas for the ad. These are often referred to as concepts. A concept might include two or three headline ideas and associated visuals. These may be mocked up and presented to others involved in the project so that the best idea can be selected.

**FACT**

A mockup of a concept can be as simple as a rough pencil sketch or as elaborate as a full-color layout that's nearly a finished piece.

Once the concept is chosen, you get to work writing the copy. The project leader—the marketing manager or creative director—may also need to assign a photographer, illustrator, and other creative professionals to the job. That, of course, depends on the requirements of the ad.

## Dealing with Approvals

Once the ad is completed in draft form, it gets reviewed and approved by the powers that be. In a larger company, this is usually the senior managers involved in the project. This can lead to a lot of conflicting opinions and ideas. The larger the approval committee, the longer the approval process tends to be.

In a smaller company things are a lot simpler. Typically it's the marketing manager or business owner who approves the ad. He or she either likes it as is, hates it and sends the whole thing back to the drawing board, or requests that revisions be made. It's the third scenario that occurs most often.

Requests for revisions are common when creating a promotional piece. Don't take them personally. Everyone wants to make sure that the final piece is the most effective it can be. No matter how perfect you thought your first draft was, a revision—even when you complete it grudgingly—often makes the copy even better.

## Putting on the Finishing Touches

Once the copy and design is approved, your job as the copywriter is essentially over. But that doesn't mean the work on the promotional piece is finished. Far from it. The project now enters the stage where it has to be prepared for its intended media.

The computer files for a print ad—or any print piece—need to be carefully prepared for commercial printing. This is often called prepress or the mechanicals. It involves such issues as crop markings, color codes, and color separations.

If a promotional piece is destined for the Internet—a Web page, for example—then the computer code, usually HTML, needs to be carefully checked to ensure that everything displays and works correctly (often called preflight). The last thing you want are dead links or images that don't appear.

## Measuring Results

Finally, the ad is completed, sent to the magazine, and appears as scheduled in the upcoming issue. Does that mean the project is finished? Put to bed? Done? Not entirely.

The final step in the process is evaluating results. Did the ad work? Did it solve the problem that prompted its creation? It's not always easy to measure the effectiveness of a promotional piece. But when it is possible, the information can be used to make the next ad, brochure, or Web page even better.

Chapter 3

# Planning a Copywriting Project

An archer would never draw a bow without first clearly seeing the target and determining how best to hit it. The same holds true for copywriting. Before you write a single word, you have to determine the goal of the piece you are writing and ensure you have all the facts you need at your fingertips to hit the bull's-eye. Otherwise, you're certain to miss. Planning is key.

3

# How Copywriting Projects Are Initiated

How does a copywriting project hit your desk? If you own your own business, the answer is obvious. If you need a new sales letter, Web page, or presentation written to help promote your products and services, you give the assignment to yourself.

**E ALERT!**

When writing copy for your own business, the toughest part of the job is discipline. There is no one else to crack the whip. You're the boss! You have to motivate yourself to sit down and put pen to paper (or fingers on the keyboard).

If you work at a larger company as a staff writer—or as a sales, marketing, or PR manager—copywriting tasks are typically initiated in one of two ways.

First, the project might be anticipated. You might have known for awhile that you'll be writing copy for an upcoming ad or articles for the next customer newsletter. This gives you a chance to plan ahead and schedule your time accordingly.

Second, copywriting projects can come unexpectedly. The company might have decided at the last minute to participate at a trade show. Suddenly, letters and handouts need to be written—and fast.

If you're a writer at an ad agency, every project seems to be a rush. Even those based on established marketing plans with clients are often done at the last minute, with the entire creative team scrambling and working late. This is part of the agency culture. It's fast paced. You rarely get a chance to catch your breath. It's five o'clock and the account executive comes to your desk and sheepishly asks, "The client needs a new banner ad written. Can you get the copy done by tomorrow at 9 A.M.?"

Whether you're a copywriter at an ad agency or a staff writer at a company, the amount of information you receive to begin the project varies widely. You might get a detailed creative brief (explained later in this chapter) describing everything you need to know to write the copy. Welcome to Nirvana! More likely, however, the information you receive will be incomplete and you'll have to fill in the gaps somehow. That's why dogged research is such an important part of the copywriting planning process.

# Digging for the Facts

Imagine if someone dropped a computer CD on your desk and said, "This is our new software product. Please write a Web page to promote it to our prospects and customers." Then he walked away.

Chances are you would chase after him, shouting questions. "Hey, what is this product? What does it do? How much does it cost? Who is the target audience? Why would they buy it?" There would be no practical way to begin writing copy without at least having rudimentary answers to these questions first.

Getting all the facts—or at least as much of them as you can—is the first step in planning a successful copywriting project. You have to act the part of a determined investigative reporter and dig for information and insights into the product and its potential buyers.

Here is a worksheet that can help guide you in getting the information you need to get started on a copywriting project.

**Copywriting Information Worksheet**
- What exactly needs to be written?
- What is the scope of the project? (You need an estimate of size or length: a four-panel brochure, a nine-page Web site, a quarter-page print advertisement.)
- What is the objective of the piece? (To generate sales leads? Get orders? Build brand awareness and preference? Convey product information?)
- What is the product or service being promoted?
- What does the product look like? (Is a demo available? Is a sample available?)
- What are its features, benefits, and advantages?
- What are the different styles, sizes, versions, makes, models available?

- How does the product or service differ from similar competing products? (What does it have or do that the competition either doesn't do as well or not at all?)
- How is the product positioned in terms of price? (Cheap? Expensive?)
- Is there a guarantee? If so, what is it?
- Are there any product reviews, customer testimonials, and other third-party endorsements available?
- Who is the target audience? (Corporate CFOs? Working moms? Tradespeople? Gaming enthusiasts?)
- What factors would motivate someone to buy the product?
- If there was just one reason why a customer would purchase this product, what would that be?
- What is the deal? Is there a special price? A money-back guarantee? Some extras thrown in?

**ALERT!**

Sometimes the piece you're writing is part of a larger campaign. You might be crafting the sales letter, for example, but other writers may be involved in creating ads, radio commercials, and Web pages, all tied together by a common theme. Make sure you learn what the campaign theme and creative guidelines are so you can integrate these into your copy.

Unfortunately, most projects have such tight deadlines these days that writing copy without first having all the facts has become the norm. Do the best you can. The more information you can get your hands on about the piece you're writing, the more effective your copy will be. It will be faster and easier to write, too.

## Becoming the Product Expert

You have to thoroughly understand the product you're writing about. You have to become a product expert. If you don't, you won't be able to write authoritatively about it to the target audience. And if you can't do that, you don't stand a chance of persuading them to buy it.

As consumers ourselves, it's relatively easy to understand everyday products such as hairspray, computer games, and even mortgages. But what if you're writing copy to promote a new logistics tracking software? Or a management training program? Or a marine propeller shaft bearing system? These complex business-to-business products and services require a lot of research for a novice to understand. (See the Complex Products section in Chapter 17 for tips on how to climb the learning curve quickly.)

If you don't fully understand a product, don't be afraid to ask questions. Talk to your client or boss, the product development team that created the product, or the salespeople that sell the product. Get the answers you need.

Learn how the product works. Make a complete list of its features and benefits. It's also important to understand the advantages. What qualities or features does the product have that makes it stand out from competitors? What does it do or have that is unique? An interior house paint might be odorless and therefore perfect for a child's room. A courier service might provide overnight delivery before 8:00 A.M., earlier than anyone else. Those are examples of advantages.

## Get the Background Materials

Background materials are those things that have already been written about the product or service. So your first step in any copywriting task is to collect as much of this information as possible. After all, there may be well-written explanations, sentences, paragraphs, headlines, turns of phrase, and other existing text and ideas you may be able to use in your new copy.

Here is a list of common materials to ask or look for:

- Advertisements
- Articles
- Brochures
- Case studies
- Catalogs
- Transcripts of speeches
- Online demos
- Letters and e-mails to prospects and customers
- Flyers
- Sales presentations
- Internal presentations
- Market research reports
- Marketing plans
- Memos
- Press releases
- Media kits
- Teleselling scripts
- Product reviews
- Product specifications
- User manuals
- Promotional or how-to videos
- Sales training materials
- Sales letters and direct mailings
- Sell sheets
- Technical reports
- Web pages
- White papers

Not every item on the above list will be available or even exist. Try to collect as much information as you can. This is your first step in educating yourself on the product or service, and its potential buyers.

# *Understand the Audience*

The target audience is the most important part of a copywriting project. After all, these are the people you're attempting to persuade! If you don't captivate them with your carefully chosen words, your copy will fail totally—no matter how well-written you think it is.

Think you already know enough about the target audience? You might be in for a surprise. Imagine you're writing a sales training brochure targeting sales managers. It will be used for a trade show to be held in November. You decide on the following headline:

It's Not Too Late to Make This Year's Quota

You assume that this headline will touch a nerve—addressing the number one concern of these managers.

Good guess. But you're wrong. If you really researched this group thoroughly, you'd understand that by November and December sales managers already know how the year will end. Sales training isn't going to turn things around within the next few weeks. What this group is really concerned about is forecasting. Upper management is pressuring them to predict next year's sales. Knowing this, a headline like the following is likely to be more successful:

Forecast a Better Year by Factoring an Extra 9% Increase in Sales, Guaranteed

The lesson? You can never learn enough about your target audience.

Job titles can help you understand more about your target audience. With a little research, you'll discover that marketing VPs travel a lot, human resources managers don't feel appreciated by upper management, and IT managers are overworked. These may be generalizations, but they are helpful to know when crafting persuasive copy.

In the background materials you receive on the project, you might be provided with market research, demographic, psychographic, and other types of reports that will give you valuable insights into the target audience. Study these documents thoroughly.

## *Get Inside the Head of the Buyer*

You should understand your target audience to a point where you empathize with their problems, needs, and interests. You can never truly walk a mile in someone else's moccasins. But you can come pretty close—with research.

The problem is there isn't always a lot of time available. You might be asked to write an advertisement targeting librarians—a group you know little about—and have just a couple of days to do it. How are you going to get inside their heads to understand how they make buying decisions? Here are some fast-track tips that will help.

- *Read what your prospect reads.* Just about every group—accountants, seniors, even shuffleboard enthusiasts—have Web sites, newsletters, and other publications that target their interests. Find out what they are and review a few issues. This will give you insights into the target audience and what the style and tone of your copy should be, too.
- *Haunt the blogs and forums.* Want to find out what the hot issues are with a target audience? Blogs, discussion boards, and forums are a great way to find out.
- *Seminar descriptions.* Seminar descriptions often address the most important concerns of a target audience. If they didn't, the seminar wouldn't sell! Professional associations—such as the American Association for Certified Public Accountants—as well as magazines and other publications, often run seminars. You can also do a search for seminars on the Internet.
- *Speak to the sales reps.* Salespeople are a terrific source of information on a target audience. After all, these are the folks who deal with prospects and customers every day. They can often provide you with insights you won't find anywhere else.

- *Meet your target audience.* Sometimes it's possible to talk to a prospect or customer directly. If so, this is ideal. Alternatively, your company or client may have commissioned a survey of the target audience and has a summary of their thoughts and opinions. Ask if this information is available.
- *Attend trade shows.* There is a trade show for just about every professional and personal interest. These are a hub of activity where sellers and buyers meet to discuss new products, services, and ideas. You can learn a lot here from hanging around the exhibits and listening to the questions asked and the issues raised. It's an education.

You can't always get all the answers, but try to create as clear a picture as you can of your target audience. Even little differences can be significant. A thirty-five-year-old homeowner raising kids and building a career does not have the same buying criteria as a fifty-five-year-old planning for retirement. You need to know these differences before you can write an effective brochure pitching an investment advisory service.

## *Project Chitchats*

"I want to discuss a new project with you," your boss or client announces. "Let's schedule a phone appointment for 3:00 P.M. this afternoon."

Chances are this will be one of the most important discussions you'll have about a new copywriting project. You'll learn what background materials are available, who to contact when you have questions, the scope of the project, and much more. So don't take this kind of meeting lightly. You'll need to listen closely and ask questions to ensure you get all the information you need to write the most effective copy possible.

**FACT**

Project briefings by phone or in person are common at ad agencies and at corporate marketing and PR departments. It's the customary way to kick things off to make sure everyone hits the ground running.

If you're new to the process, take good notes, ask questions, and don't be afraid to speak up if you don't understand something. There are no dumb questions at a project meeting. Everyone—especially the person in charge of the project—wants to make sure that everyone else is on the same page and thoroughly understands what's expected of them.

## Interview Smarts

Another common way that copywriters research the product and target audience is through interviews. Just like an investigative reporter, you may have to, "stick a microphone" in front of your boss or client, a product expert, a salesperson, or even a customer, and ask questions.

Usually these interviews are conducted on the phone, but they can also be handled in person. Follow these tips:

- *Always make an appointment.* Never just call and start asking questions. Schedule a day and time that is convenient for both of you. This gives you both an opportunity to prepare.
- *Do your research first.* The contact will appreciate that you've done your homework and learned all you can about the product and the target audience before the interview.
- *Prepare a list of questions.* This helps to ensure you get all the answers you need. (Use the Copywriting Information Worksheet featured earlier in this chapter.)
- *Take good notes.* It's embarrassing if you have to call back and ask a question again just because you didn't write the answer down.
- *Ask if you can follow up.* You may have questions later on. Ask the interviewee if he or she is available for follow-up questions. Some people prefer that this be handled by e-mail.
- *Use a tape recorder if you have one.* When you record a phone conversation, always inform the other party. It's not just a courtesy. In some jurisdictions, it's the law.

## *Teleconference Tips*

Teleconferencing is popular to say the least. There is probably a teleconference unit on every boardroom table in America! As a copywriter, you will no doubt be invited to one of these group telephone meetings to discuss projects and brainstorm ideas. That's because it's so difficult these days for corporate managers, agency personnel, and others involved in a project to be in the same room at the same time. Virtual meetings have become the norm.

**QUESTION?**

### What is a teleconference?

It's simply a meeting held over the phone for three or more people. Typically, you're given a special dial-in phone number and access code, along with the date and time of the teleconference. Sometimes you're also provided with a special Web address where you can view visuals during the meeting and make notes on a virtual blackboard that everyone can see.

Here are some useful teleconference meeting tips:

- As people introduce themselves, write down their names on a piece of paper. This will help you keep track of who's saying what during the discussions.
- If you do lose track and need to know where a comment or piece of information came from, simply ask the speaker to identify himself again. For example: "Who said that? Was that you, John?"
- If you're one of the first few people to "arrive" at the teleconference, it's normal to chat before the other participants call in. But be careful what you say! Avoid negative talk about people who haven't arrived on the call yet. They could be there already, quietly listening to every word you say!
- Teleconferences can sometimes drag on, but stay tuned in. Don't do anything that is distracting, such as surfing the Internet, doodling,

or working on other projects. You want to be able to give a good answer when you're called on for an opinion.

- Ask if you can be added to the e-mail list of anyone who is taking notes. And take good notes yourself, too. Don't assume that you will automatically receive a summary of the call. You may not.

During a teleconference, or any type of project meeting for that matter, you might be put on the spot by someone asking you for some initial ideas: "Hey, Karen. What sort of headline do you think would work best in this ad?" Unless you're the kind of person who can come up with great ideas on the fly, it's best to say that you need time to absorb the information: "I'll get back to later."

## What Is a Creative Brief?

A creative brief is simply a document that provides a detailed overview of the project. It often includes such information as:

- The goal of the project or campaign
- What needs to be created
- The product or service featured and its top features and benefits
- Details on special offers, pricing, or incentives
- Insights into the target audience
- An analysis of the competition
- The project schedule

Creative briefs can run the gamut from a simple one-page overview to a multipage tome containing detailed instructions regarding the writing style, tone, and formats—even suggested headlines!

**FACT**

A creative brief can also be known by many other names. Copy brief, project plan, copy platform, project brief, scope document, creative plan, and project worksheet are just a few names you might run into.

These documents are typically prepared by the creative director or marketing manager. However, you as the copywriter may also be involved.

If you work for an ad agency, design firm, or public relations agency, there is little doubt that you will be given a creative brief. It's the standard way these firms communicate project details to staff and freelancers.

If you're writing copy for yourself or your own company, you should prepare your own creative brief. It will keep your copywriting on track and help you coordinate more effectively with others involved in the project, such as your graphic designer.

Here is a sample of a very simple one-page creative brief.

Creative Brief for ACME Freezers brochure
Objective: To help our salespeople present the benefits of ACME *Freezers*.
Target audience: Independent restaurant owners.
To be created: A four-panel brochure.

**Key messages:**
- ACME Freezers are more expensive than other comparable walk-in freezers.
- They use less energy—saving 10%–20% on electricity charges compared to other walk-in freezers.
- The battery backup will maintain the temperature for 24 hours in the event of a power failure, reducing the risk of food spoilage.
- Comes with a full 7 year warranty—two years more than the competition.

**Characteristics of a typical buyer:**
- Restaurant owners who have recently expressed an interest in walk-in freezers.
- They want to save money. (Profit margins can be slim in the restaurant business.)
- They also want to comply with health and safety regulations.
- They also take pride in having modern kitchen facilities. (Their restaurant is like a second home to them. And, in fact, they spend more time there than their own homes.)

Timelines: Copy outline due ____.                    Final copy due ____.

Chapter 4

# Get Writing

Every copywriting project starts with a blank screen or sheet of paper. Even if you've done all the background work or have a creative brief in hand, there are still a few things you need to determine before you put words on the page. What writing style will you use? How long will your copy need to be? How will you structure the key messages? Which tactics will you employ to persuade the reader to act? This chapter helps you find the answers.

4

# *Determine the Writing Style*

Read a thriller novel and the style is fast paced and loaded with action. Cozy up with a romance and you're spellbound by a budding relationship that struggles to grow and blossom. Review an academic paper and you expect to find an intelligent argument based on solid research and analytical thinking. Every writing genre has its own unique style, and copywriting is no different.

So what exactly is style? In a nutshell, it concerns your choice of words, how you structure your sentences, and the basic tone and personality of your writing. Style also speaks to the pace of the writing. Is it fast? Slow? Methodical? And even voice plays a role. Who's doing the talking? A helpful expert? A friendly advisor? A slick salesperson? A cautious committee? The detached bureaucracy of a major corporation?

There is a lot of misinformation about copywriting style. There are some who insist that sales copy should reach out and grab the prospect by the shirt collar and then, with Ginsu knife precision, overpower him with hard-selling words and phrases. Others balk at this approach, saying that great copywriting is really about being clever and creative, with catchy slogans and an inventive use of language. There are still others—especially in the business-to-business sector—who claim that copy should be formal and businesslike, so the reader will be impressed.

So what's the truth? Yes, copy should be attention grabbing, creative, impressive, catchy, inventive, and employ the elements of effective salesmanship. But that doesn't necessarily mean it needs to be aggressive, clever, or businesslike. The best writing style is one that elicits the best audience response. And how do you determine that? Ask your audience!

It's the target audience—all those prospects and customers you are trying to persuade—that is the best source of information on how to weave your words.

Sometimes it's easy. For example, if the market for your promotion is IT professionals, then you can expect your copy style to be explanatory, technically detailed, in-depth, and expansive. People in the IT professions like a lot of solid information, with minimal use of expressive prose.

If you're writing a brochure aimed at teenagers who love computer games, you might guess that your writing style should be adventurous, fast paced, and fun. And you'd be right.

In just about any kind of promotion, copy that sounds like it has been written by a human being works better than text that seems like it has been churned out by a machine or vetted relentlessly by a committee. Copy that speaks to the reader engages the reader. Copy that speaks at the reader accomplishes nothing.

## What Does the Prospect Read?

It's not always easy to guess which copywriting style and tone will work best for a particular target audience. What if you're writing a sales letter to be sent to accountants? Or working moms? Or retirees? Or entrepreneurs? How do you determine how to reach them persuasively with the right words, sentences, and paragraphs?

The most effective—and fortunately the easiest—way to determine your ideal writing style is to read what your audience reads. Every professional, business, and special-interest group—from plumbers to high-school students to middle-aged tennis enthusiasts—has publications that are dedicated to their needs. If you want to write copy that persuades retired travelers, then *Travel 50 & Beyond* magazine should be something you should review. Study the magazines, newsletters, and Web sites that your target audience is already reading. Then use a similar style in your own copy.

Here's another great tip that makes this process even faster. Find a magazine that your target audience reads, and then read the opening letter from the editor. It's typically located within the first few pages. Editors know how to speak to their readers in a style and language that works best.

### Beware of Corporatespeak

Corporatespeak is the stiff formality that some copywriting suffers from, especially in business-to-business communications. This is the result of a writer thinking that the copy should be written this way, or a company review committee scrutinizing every word. What gets lost is a genuine connection to the prospect.

## Long Copy or Short?

A client asks you, "How long should my sales letter be?" How would you answer this question? "One page? Four? Ten?"

The answer is not easy. Determining the length of your copy is one of the toughest decisions you have to make when writing a promotional piece.

Contrary to what you may read and hear from so-called experts, there is no absolute rule. Sometimes long copy in a sales letter or on a Web page works very well. Sometimes it doesn't. How do you make that determination? There are a number of factors that influence how long your promotional copy should be, whether you define that as the number of words, screens, panels, or pages.

**ALERT!**

A major factor in determining writing style is the type of promotion you're creating. Sales letters, for example, require a casual, friendly approach because you're speaking one-to-one with the prospect. A press release, by contrast, is more news–oriented, while a brochure may require an informational tone. So be sure your writing style meets the requirements of the promotional piece.

### Determine Ideal Copy Length

A great way to use the following list is to rank each item that relates to your promotion on a range from low to high then add up the results. Of course, figuring out ideal copy length isn't an exact science. But this technique will give you a much clearer idea. And it's better than simply guessing, which is, unfortunately, what most copywriters do.

### Factors That Influence Copy Length

- *Standard formats.* The promotional piece you're writing may have a standard format that influences how much copy you have to work with. For example, a press release is often no more than two pages. So 750 words would be a maximum.
- *Planned layout.* The promotional piece may already be conceived and designed to some degree. If you're asked to write a four-panel brochure, and there are already some pictures and other visual elements in place, your copy will have to be written to fit.
- *Action required.* What are you asking the reader to do? If the purpose of the promotional piece is to generate a lead—by persuading the prospect to request a free information kit, for example—then you may not need much copy. However, if you're asking for an *order*, it's going to take more copy to convince the reader to pull out his credit card!
- *Emotion.* How much of the buying decision is emotional rather than practical? Purchasing a lawnmower is a practical decision for most people, usually requiring just a persuasive explanation of the features and benefits. An exotic vacation, however, may be highly emotional, with dreams of fun and family and adventure, and would require longer, more descriptive copy.
- *Dependence.* How much is the prospect dependent on your copy to get all the facts and information he needs to make a purchasing decision? If you want to motivate someone to order a $950 software program with your direct-mail letter, you may need several pages to make a convincing argument. However, if the prospect is buying a new fridge, he'll get a lot of the information he requires at the store by talking with the salesperson.
- *Price.* The rule of thumb is: The bigger the price tag, the longer the copy. If you are promoting a one-day seminar for $99, you may be able to get away with a four-panel brochure. But you'll need a lot more copy than that to convince someone to invest in a $3,500 weekend boot camp.

- *Brand power.* How well-known is the product or service you're promoting? If you're writing a direct-mail letter to sell subscriptions for *Forbes* magazine, you may not need too many pages. People are already familiar with and trust that publication. However, if the company or product is unfamiliar to the reader, you will have some credibility building to do. And that will take more copy.
- *Readership.* If the audience is highly interested or enthusiastic about the topic your product or service represents, then they will read a lot of copy. For example, people who love to cook will be willing to read several pages describing a new Professionals Series frying pan with technologically advanced nonstick coating.

The most important question to ask yourself is: "How much copy do I need to convince the target audience to take action?" That action may be to fill out an online form, call for a free consultation, visit a store, take advantage of a special discount, place an order, or any number of other objectives.

## Organize the Key Messages

Ideally, you have compiled a lot of information on the product or service and the target audience of your promotion based on your review of all the background information, additional research, and interviews of key contacts. What do you do with all that information?

Your next step is to go through everything and pull out the key messages you want to feature in your promotion. There are three lists you need to create:

- Features and benefits
- Proofs and other evidence
- Audience characteristics

Make your list of features and benefits as comprehensive as possible. Divide your page into two columns. On the left write down all the features, and on the right list all the corresponding benefits. Here's an example:

### Time Management Seminar Features and Benefits List

| Feature | Benefit |
| --- | --- |
| One day seminar | Learn effective time management in just one day. Save time. |
| Free time management software | Nothing more to buy. |
| Learn how to gain one hour per day | More time for personal life. |
| Learn stress-free techniques for getting things done on time | Reduce stress. Accomplish more. |

On another page, create a list of evidence and other proofs. These are the support for all the claims and promises you can make about the product or service you're promoting.

### Proofs and Other Evidence List

- Proof: Time-management system endorsed by the American Association of Professional Organizers.
- Proof: Instructor is recognized expert in the field.
- Proof: A dozen testimonials of seminar participants, along with permissions to use full names.
- Proof: Money-back guarantee. "If this program doesn't boost your productivity by at least one hour per day, you're seminar fee will be refunded."
- Proof: Picture of free software, along with several screen shots clearly illustrating the features.

Your final list is all about the prospect. Ask yourself: "What does the prospect care about?" If you've done your research into the target audience, you'll be able to list several characteristics, needs, hopes, ambitions, problems, issues, and other traits of the people you're trying to sell the seminar to. Put yourself firmly in their shoes.

**Audience Characteristics List**

- Finance and accounting professionals working for midsized companies
- Highly educated
- Responds to well-articulated business case based on facts
- Busy professionals who are often swamped with work
- Need for accuracy and precision in what they do
- Appreciate systems and procedures that generate predictable results
- Works primarily at a computer
- Are driven to improve what they do and how they do it

The great thing about making these three lists is that they become an excellent source of ideas. You'll generate plenty as you go through this process.

# How to Generate Great Ideas

Few people can accurately define what an idea is. Yet just about everybody knows when they have one. An idea is simply a thought that results in a new opinion, suggestion, impression, plan, or objective. It doesn't have to be original. It doesn't even have to be new. In the copywriting field, an idea just has to be something that makes you think, "Hey, this might work!"

**ALERT!**

Don't confuse ideas with being creative. The two are not always the same. A great idea for a brochure, for example, might simply be to convey the information in a clear, straightforward manner. Now that may not sound all that exciting or creative, but it sure is a great idea.

There is no mystery to generating ideas. You get them all the time. Your brain is hard-wired as a powerful idea factory that is generating these wonders continuously. All you have to do is feed that factory with the right raw materials and be sure to capture those ideas so you don't forget them.

The raw materials come from your background research on the product and the audience, the objective of the promotional piece you're attempting to create, and your current understanding of what works and what doesn't. Raw materials—or inspiration—for great ideas can also come from the creative brief (if there is one), your swipe file (which is a collection of particularly effective marketing pieces for other products and services), competitor's materials, and even information that is not associated with the project at all, like the last great novel you read.

## Ideas Are Fleeting

Fortunately, copywriters usually have no shortage of good ideas. The problem is in capturing them. If you're working on the lead paragraph for a sales letter, you might get a great idea for a different part of the promotion, such as the brochure, reply card, or envelope. You might even get ideas for an entirely different project! When you do, don't rely on your memory. Write it down! Keep a separate page open on your computer or notepad where you can jot down ideas as they arise. That way an idea will never fall through the cracks of your memory.

## Getting Unstuck

One of the toughest challenges in generating ideas is doing so on demand. You may be working on a headline, a difficult paragraph, or creative concepts for an advertisement and just can't wait for inspiration to strike. You need a darn good idea. And you need it now!

What do you do? Following are some tips for shifting the idea factory in your head into high gear.

### Get Away from the Computer

Staring at a blank screen or confronting a difficult passage for too long can make things worse. What you may need is a new place to work on the problem. So get out a pencil and notepad and go somewhere quiet. Often a change of scenery is all you need to get those ideas flowing again.

### Don't Judge Too Quickly

Ever get an idea and then disqualify it almost immediately? It's like having an idea guy on one shoulder and a pessimist on the other. Well, flick that pessimist off your shoulder! Write down any idea, no matter how bad it may seem, and see where it takes you.

### Take a Break

Go for a walk. Make yourself a cup of coffee. Play a game of tennis. Or switch gears completely and work on an entirely different project. Get your mind off the problem so your subconscious can work on it for awhile. When you get back to writing your promotion, you'll be surprised how quickly the ideas will come.

### Brainstorm

This is a process of pouring all your ideas onto the screen or page, no matter how absurd they may first seem. Some copywriters like to brainstorm by jotting ideas onto sticky notes on a wall and then standing back and seeing how some ideas fit with others. Often a combination of poor ideas can add up to a great one.

### Try a Mind Map

This is a great technique for generating ideas very quickly. Put the product name in the middle of a page. Then draw lines connecting words that are associated with it. For example, if you are writing a promotion for a scheduling software for home-improvement contractors, the words and phrases you might connect with that product are "time management," "truck," "mobile," "time wasted picking up parts," "job estimations," "dealing with the trades," and "time is money." This map of related words can be a great source of ideas.

If all else fails, go back to the well. Revisit all the background materials, interview notes, and other research you have done on the project, as well as any strategic documents such as the creative brief. Doing this will often get you looking at the same information in a new way, which could be just the idea you were looking for.

# *Outline*

It was said that Mozart could write an entire symphony in his mind. Then, when he was ready, he simply picked up a quill and wrote it all down. His first draft was often his final draft.

**ALERT!**

Creating an outline for a boss or client to review is like having a second writing project. Writing and presenting the outline can add up to 50 percent more time than would normally be required to complete the project. So take this into account when you quote the job and schedule the work.

That was nice for Mozart. But the rest of us mortals typically write in layers, starting from some rough notes and ideas and then progressing through several drafts until we arrive at something that appears to be final. In other words, we revise, revise, and then revise some more.

The first step in the writing process is often the outline. This is similar to the rough pencil sketch that an artist makes before putting paint to canvas. An outline can serve two purposes:

- *A step in the approval process.* Sometimes you'll need to show your boss or client an outline and have him or her approve it before you proceed to the writing stage. This is common for long copy assignments, such as multipage brochures, Web sites, and direct-mail packages.
- *A guide to writing.* An outline can make the writing process faster and less painful. You don't have to think about what comes next. However, it can be restrictive. What if you develop better ideas as you're writing the piece?

How detailed should your outline be? That depends. If you're the kind of writer who needs a solid framework to work within, then your outline will need to be fairly organized and detailed. On the other extreme, there are many copywriters who can get their fingers dancing on the computer keyboard with just a few notes in front of them. If you don't have to show it to anyone, write just as much of an outline as you need to feel comfortable and confident as you begin to write.

Your outline might require a lot of detail if it needs to be shown to your boss or client. She is going to need to be able to understand how you plan to approach the promotional piece: how it will begin, how the various text elements will be put together, the key messages, the writing style.

An outline should have the following elements:

- The main headline and other headers
- The opening paragraph or first few sentences
- Copy points listed as bullets (note that the copy points are a list of what you're going to say in your copy, not how you're going to say it)
- Indications of any text boxes, starbursts, sidebars, and other text elements you foresee

Here's an example:

### Print Advertisement for Checkup Toothpaste – Copy Outline
Headline: Show Us Your Smile!
Copy Points:
- Safe for the whole family, even young children.
- Completely organic. No harmful chemicals added.
- Tastes great. (Most organic toothpastes have a plain or sour taste.)
- Fluoride free.
- Gets rid of bad breath.
- Makes your mouth feel clean and refreshed.
- Brightens your teeth.

Make sure your outline isn't carved in stone. You don't want it to restrict you from using a good idea that might come up later in the writing process. An effective outline should be detailed enough to guide your writing yet flexible enough to accommodate changes, additions, and deletions as required.

# Proven Copywriting Formulas

Is there a secret formula to copywriting? Like a chemist in a lab, can you take 20 mgs. of *credibility*, mix it with 50 mgs. of *product benefits*, and get *killer copy* to come to life in the beaker?

That may seem a little oversimplified. However, there are proven writing formulas for producing great copy. None of these will guarantee that your promotion will be effective, but they are extremely helpful in keeping you on the right track.

## AIDA—the Master Formula of Marketing

AIDA is the granddaddy of all copywriting formulas, and perhaps the best-known in the advertising industry. The acronym stands for:

**A**ttention
**I**nterest
**D**esire
**A**ction

The amazing thing about this formula is that it almost always works. If you gain attention, get interest, build desire, and ask for action, you are going to get results with your promotional piece. There really is no doubt about it.

The weakness of this formula is in applying it. The first and last steps are easy enough to understand. But exactly how do you get interest and build desire? These two steps merely describe the events. They don't give you the strategies.

The AIDA formula is most useful when reviewing your copy. If the words you crafted guide the reader through the four steps, you can rest assured that you are definitely on your way to a winner. However, if your promotion merely piques interest yet fails to build desire, then you have some revising to do.

## *Motivating Sequence*

Popularized by Robert Bly, a well-known copywriter and consultant, the motivating sequence is very similar to AIDA, however, it's much easier to use while you're crafting your promotional piece. Each step is practical and relatively straightforward to apply. The motivating sequence is an ideal model for planning, outlining, and writing your copy.

- Get attention
- Identify the problem or need
- Position your product as the solution or answer
- Prove your product is the best solution or answer
- Invite the reader to take action

The last step includes any action that you are trying to persuade the prospect to take, whether that is placing an order, filling out an online form, requesting a free information kit, or visiting a special Web site.

**FACT**

The motivating sequence was developed by copywriting expert Bob Bly and writing instructor Gary Blake, Ph.D. It is amazingly versatile. You can use this simple formula to write sales letters, ads, Web pages, product descriptions—just about any kind of marketing or publicity piece.

Here is an excerpt from a sales letter written using the motivating sequence formula. Notice how it follows all the steps, from getting attention with the multiple headlines, to positioning the product as the only solution, to offering a proof (the testimonial), and asking for action.

*Sales letter excerpt:*
- Bogged down by employee management "paperwork"?
- Tired of juggling word docs, spreadsheets, and scribbled notes?
- Frustrated by administrative tasks that consume up to 30% of your schedule?

If so, you need an Assistant. And here's one every manager can afford…

Dear Manager,

Take a look at your schedule over the next few days. How much time will you spend monitoring employee performance, tracking attendance, and documenting incidents?

If the answer is, "Too much!" then you'll want to try ManagerAssistant 2.0. It's the only solution that simplifies and automates your employment management tasks so you spend less time on administration—and more time on real management.

Joan Smith of ABC Company says, "I really do think this is the best management tool out there."

For a FREE 30-Day Use version of this remarkable solution, please visit *www.ManagerAssistant.com* today, or call 1-905-XXX-XXXX.

What is ManagerAssistant 2.0? It's an innovative software that lets you…

## Bob Stone's Gem

The word "gem" isn't used here just to be complimentary. This formula is so respected that "Bob Stone's Gem" has become part of the vernacular for copywriting and marketing professionals.

As the name implies, this technique was created by Bob Stone, a legend in the industry and the author of the classic *Successful Direct Marketing Methods*. His formula was originally meant for sales letters and direct-response advertising, but it's useful in dozens of other types of promotions as well.

1. Begin with your strongest benefit
2. Expand on the most important benefit
3. Tell exactly and in detail what they are going to get, including all the features and benefits
4. Back up your statements with support copy
5. Tell them what they'll lose if they don't act
6. Sum up the most important benefits
7. Make your call to action. Tell them to "reply now" and give a good, logical reason why they should.

Bob's formula is very easy to follow. You should be able to walk through the steps without much problem. And when you do, you'll have written a potentially very effective promotion.

## The Approach Formula

Here is a formula that is especially useful in direct-mail letters. It can also be handy in telemarketing scripts as well since it does not use a hard-sell approach, which can be a turnoff for many prospects. It emphasizes making the right impression and following a logical step toward the sale.

Arrive
Propose
Persuade
Reassure
Orchestrate an opportune opportunity
Ask for the order (or response)

Here's how it works. You *arrive* by making the right impression, either with your headline or opening sentence or paragraph. Then you don't waste any time. You say right away what the promotion is about and what's in it for them (*propose*). Next you *persuade* by listing your most important benefits. You follow that up by proving (*reassure*) all your claims. In step five, you make your compelling offer (the *opportune opportunity*). Finally, you ask for action.

Chapter 5

# Ingredients of Highly Successful Copy

Writing copy is a lot like making pancakes. You have to make sure you have all the right ingredients! If you miss the baking powder or oil, for example, your pancakes will be flat and tasteless. Copywriting is similar. If you forget to bring the benefits to life or build belief, your copy just won't work. That's why it's important to mix all the right ingredients, in just the right proportions, to create a winning advertisement, brochure, Web page, flyer, or other persuasive piece.

## Gain Attention

By the time you get out of bed, scan the newspaper while sipping a morning coffee, drive to work listening to the radio, turn on the computer and check your e-mail, you're exposed to dozens—perhaps hundreds—of marketing messages. All before 9:00 A.M.!

There's no avoiding them. Advertising, sales, marketing and other persuasive messages are everywhere—on radio and television, in magazines and newspapers, all over the Internet, in e-mail inboxes, on posters and billboards, and in the mailbox.

The competition for the hearts and minds (and wallets) of customers is stiff. So if you want your copy to break through the clutter and get noticed, you have to make sure it gains attention.

**ESSENTIAL**

Think about it. If the advertisement or sales letter you're writing doesn't get noticed, customers won't read it. And if customers don't read it, they won't be persuaded by the message you so painstakingly crafted.

So how do you make sure your copy gains attention? Following are the most common ways to accomplish this.

### A Great Headline

An effective headline is the copywriter's number one secret weapon. It is by far the simplest and most effective way to gain attention in just about any form of advertising, sales, marketing, or public relations communications.

A headline is that big block of bold text at the top of an advertisement. But you'll also see headlines at work in sales letters, flyers, catalogs, Web sites, trade-show exhibits, e-mail promotions, and even in blogs.

How do headlines work? Imagine flipping through your favorite magazine. Your decision whether to read a particular article depends, at least in part, on the article's title (which is a lot like a headline). If you want to plant a vegetable garden, for example, then an article with the headline "Grow Veggies That Make Your Grocer Green With Envy" will likely get your attention.

**ALERT!**

Make sure the headline matches the message. If your headline reads "Your Hair Is On Fire!" it will certainly gain attention. But if the ad is actually about photocopiers and has nothing to do with a head in flames, then potential customers will just get annoyed. They'll feel duped and may actually decide not to buy the product.

Advertisements use the same technique. Headlines are like article titles, striving to capture your interest. Have trouble with acne? Then the headline "Reduce Acme Blemishes—Overnight" will seem like it's jumping off the page. Want to be a published author? Then your eyes will lock on the ad that reads "Get a Book Contract in 90 Days." Planning on buying some new clothes? You might even clip the ad that reads "One Day Only: Save 25% on Cashmere Sweaters."

As you can see, headlines are an important tool in the copywriting trade. They're fun to write, too. How do you develop a great headline? You'll learn dozens of proven techniques in Chapter 7.

## An Eye-Catching Visual

You don't always need a headline to gain attention. Sometimes a clever, fascinating, or even shocking visual can work just as well.

On your way to work you notice a billboard with a huge picture of a duck staring right at you. His feathers are ruffled. He looks panicked. He seems to be struggling to say something—to you! It's such a beguiling image that you take notice. And as a result, the billboard ad takes hold. Before you know it, you're reading the line of copy adjacent to the picture, encouraging you to donate to a much-needed bird sanctuary.

The picture did all the work. No headline required.

But pictures and other images are not the only way to create an attention-grabbing visual. Imagine receiving a direct-mail piece that looks like a child's puzzle box. Or coming across a magazine advertisement that folds open into a poster. Or picking up a brochure and discovering that it opens into an elaborate unexpected shape.

Sometimes a very simple idea can be extremely effective. For example, a collections agency once sent a sales letter to potential clients. It had no headline, just a small stone glued to the upper right-hand corner. The letter began as follows:

In ancient Greece, business owners would attempt to collect on overdue accounts by throwing stones at the customers. This forced a customer to choose between a daily bruising and paying up. Today, things are more civilized. But debt collection is no less frustrating…

There are many creative ways to gain attention with the visual presentation of your promotional piece. The possibilities are limited only by your imagination and, of course, your—or your client's—budget.

You don't have to be an artist. When you come up with a visual idea for a promotion, make a rough drawing. It doesn't have to be a work of art. Stick men are fine! In most cases, the designer or art director will be able to interpret even the most amateurish of scribbles.

## A Combination of Headline and Visual

Often you will need a headline to work with a specific visual to gain attention. In print advertisements, headlines and visuals often work in tandem. Take away one or the other and the impact, and in some cases even the meaning, diminishes.

Consider this headline:

Look What Happens When Salespeople Follow The Power Prospecting Method.

Alone this headline doesn't make much sense. Look at what?

However, when you put this line of copy next to its intended visual—a salesperson's weekly calendar filled with appointments for presentations with hot prospects—then the meaning is clear. Any sales professional or sales manager who comes across this ad will want to learn more and, therefore, read the body copy.

## *Focus on the Customer*

Perhaps the biggest mistake that people make when writing copy is focusing primarily on the product. "But wait a minute," you might be asking. "Isn't that what I'm supposed to do? After all, I'm writing a flyer to sell fitness club memberships. Isn't the fitness club the topic of the flyer?"

Yes it is, to some degree. You definitely should highlight all the great equipment, amenities, and services that club has to offer. However, if your copy is focused purely on the product (the fitness club) and little else, then you will not have answered the number one question customers ask when reading a promotional piece: "What's in it for me?"

Customers don't just want to know about the product and all its wonderful features. They want to learn how your product will help them to achieve their goals, solve a problem, meet their needs, ease their workload, increase their income, alleviate their fears, or make their dreams come true.

**ALERT!**

Your target audience must take center stage in your copy. If they don't, you risk creating nothing more than a "brag and boast" piece. And you know what happens to those. (Wastebasket basketball, anyone?)

Consider these two copywriting examples:

**Example 1:**

Speed-Med Courier offers one-hour delivery of confidential patient documents.

**Example 2:**

As an oncologist, you understand the importance of getting test results returned to your office quickly. That's why you'll be glad to learn that Speed-Med Courier offers one-hour delivery service—exclusively for confidential patient documents.

Which do you think has the greater chance of being read and acted upon? The answer is obvious. The first example is product focused and seems dull and ordinary. It's a yawner. The second example is customer focused and therefore much more engaging and relevant to the reader. Quite a difference in impact, isn't there?

As you can see, you'll need to walk a mile in the moccasins of your customers—at least figuratively—before you can write effective copy that persuades them.

How do you do that? The key is research.

Salespeople can be a valuable source of information on your target audience. After all, they deal with customers every day! So when you're asked to write copy for a product or service, ask to speak to someone involved in selling it. You'll gain insights that are difficult to find anywhere else.

If you are writing to plumbing contractors, learn more about these people! Attend a plumbing contractor trade show, read a few issues of the trade publications they subscribe to, and speak to some plumbers in person or over the phone. Then, when you're writing a promotion for a new kind of flexible hot water piping, you'll be able to speak their language.

If you're writing to working moms, read some of the excellent Web sites dedicated to these hard-working people, or hang around a daycare center and watch as they drop off their kids in the morning. You'll soon see just how busy these moms really are. This will give you the perspective you need to explain how "The New Stay-Hot Commuter Coffee Mug" will make their lives easier.

Of course, it's not always possible to do extensive research on your target audience, especially when deadlines are tight. Do the best you can. Take full advantage of any market research reports available and the Internet. The more you understand your customers, the more effective your copy will be.

**ALERT!**

When writing about benefits, it's very easy to get carried way. Before you know it you're making claims that border on exaggeration. That's dangerous territory. Go ahead and be enthusiastic, but also be candid and realistic when describing product benefits. Honesty is always more persuasive than hype.

## Bring the Benefits to Life

If you're shopping for bed sheets, 300 threads per inch may not mean a whole lot to you. Until you discover how much that density adds to the comfort, warmth, and longevity of the linen.

Similarly, when you subscribe to a Saturday morning newspaper, you're not just buying the five pounds of paper inked with news stories. You're buying the enjoyment of reading that information, perhaps while sipping a morning coffee on the back deck. You may also be buying the convenience of having that paper delivered to your home so you don't have to get dressed and march over to the corner store to get it.

When you decide to purchase a product, it's often the perceived benefits that motivated you much more than the product features.

When bringing the benefits to life, be sure you're actually describing a benefit, not a feature. Features describe the product—how it's made, how it works, what it does, how well it does it. Benefits describe the effect those features will have on you, the customer.

The benefits of a product might be that it saves you time, makes you money, solves a problem, advances your career, improves your relationships, entertains you, or makes you healthier.

If a product is one that is sold mainly to businesses, accounting software for example, the benefits might be improved cash flow, greater productivity, less risk of tax penalties, higher employee moral, a competitive advantage, and lower operating costs.

Writing about features is fairly easy. All you need is the detailed product information. Your real challenge as a copywriter is to bring the benefits derived from the features to life.

## Differentiate from the Competition

Imagine two identical looking oranges for sale. Your job is to write copy that convinces people to buy the one on the left.

How would you do this? You would have to find some way to differentiate the left orange from its competitor on the right. Otherwise, there is no reason for the customer to choose one over the other. She might as well flip a coin!

You could write about how the left orange is juicer and therefore better tasting, or is seedless and easier to eat, or is locally grown, or is a Sunkist and therefore a trusted brand, or can be delivered free to your home, or that old standby, costs less. But until you explain why your orange is different—and better—than the competition, you'll have difficulty persuading a customer to buy it.

**FACT**

According to advertising research, on average, most business products have five direct competitors, and most consumer products have seventeen direct competitors. So, chances are your target customers will have plenty of alternatives to your product to choose from.

Most products, even close competitors, do not look as similar as two pieces of fruit. A Dell laptop computer doesn't look exactly the same as a Toshiba notebook. But as a copywriter, you still have to provide a good reason, ideally many good reasons, why a customer should choose the Dell over the Toshiba (or vice versa).

## Standing Out in a Crowd of Look-alikes

There are many ways to differentiate the product or service you're writing about from all the other options available. Here are a few examples:

- *Differentiation technique:* A unique approach to serving customers. Copy example: "Do you feel pressured meeting with prospective wedding planners? Our stress-free services let you plan the wedding of your dreams right from your computer."
- *Differentiation technique:* A better guarantee. Copy example: "Try it 60-days risk free. If you're not satisfied, your money will be cheerfully refunded."
- *Differentiation technique:* A known and trusted brand. Copy example: "Replacement windows backed by the most trusted name in the business."
- *Differentiation technique:* A long track record of success. Copy example: "Montreal's favorite smoked meat sandwiches for 39 years."
- *Differentiation technique:* More endorsements by customers. Copy example: "Read what customers are saying about the new Turbo Plus Rug Cleaning System."
- *Differentiation technique:* Better payment terms. Copy example: "Don't pay a cent for twelve months!"
- *Differentiation technique:* Longer lasting. Copy example: "The ACME 12B Forklift Truck has a 5-year operating life even under the most extreme warehouse conditions."
- *Differentiation technique:* More glamorous. Copy example: "Get Hollywood's dirty little secret. Volcanic Facial Mud that makes you look up to 5 years younger, overnight."
- *Differentiation technique:* Costs less. Copy example: "You'll pay less at Outrageous Ed's! If you find a better deal on featured electronics anywhere else, we'll beat that price by 10%."
- *Differentiation technique:* Easier to learn and use. Copy example: "The average training time on our contact capture system is less than five minutes per user!"
- *Differentiation technique:* Extras are included. Copy example: "While others may charge extra for training, we include a half-day seminar free with every program license sold."

A great way to brainstorm how to differentiate your product or service is to ask this question: "Why would a customer buy this product and not some other product with similar features?"

## When Products Are the Same

It's easy to write copy when a product has distinct advantages over the competition. But what if you're writing a brochure for a local print shop and, well, color printing is color printing? The solution is to focus your copy on the services provided along with the product. That could be free delivery, twenty-four-hour service, or a thirty-day free trial.

Avis had this problem in the 1970s. The cars they rented, and the prices they charged, were similar to other major car rental companies. The only obvious difference was that they were number two in the industry. So they took that difference and positioned it as a benefit. Their famous ad campaign featured the line, "We're number two. We try harder." No other car rental company could claim the same thing. Now that's differentiation!

## Build Belief

The brochure says: "The ACME 32A brews espressos and cappuccinos on your kitchen countertop that taste so good, the local French café will be jealous."

Oh really? Says who?

Unfortunately, customers are skeptical of the marketing materials they read these days. And who can blame them? They are constantly being bombarded with spam, hype, inflated claims, and broken promises.

Avoid rounding up when making a claim with a percentage or statistic. Saying that customer satisfaction is 95 percent sounds like the writer made it up. Instead, be specific. If customer satisfaction is actually 92.3 percent, say so in the copy. Customers are more likely to believe it's true.

As you write your copy, you're going to have to explore ways to overcome this hurdle. Otherwise, few people will believe all the benefits that you so carefully flushed out and presented. There are three ways to do this: prove your claims, offer a guarantee, or make a personal pledge. Following is a look at each technique in detail.

## Prove Your Claims

Solid proof is the surest way to get customers to believe what you're saying in your copy.

Imagine you're writing a Web site for a kitchen remodeling firm. Just saying that the company is qualified and does great work is probably not going to convince a homeowner to part with $15,000, especially when there are so many stories circulating about people getting burned by disreputable contractors. You're going to have to prove your case.

How do you do that? For the kitchen remodeling company, you could point out that their installers are certified by the National Kitchen and Bath Association. You could show before-and-after pictures of successful renovations, along with testimonials from satisfied customers. If available, you could also feature any news articles and other press on the company. Perhaps they had a renovation profiled in a home improvement magazine?

As a rule, try to back up every claim you make with a proof of some kind. Here are a few examples.

- *Claim:* "The best software for personal time management'" Proof: "Says *PC Plus Magazine*."
- *Claim:* "Fast, overnight delivery of your envelopes and packages throughout the United States." Proof: "99.2% of our deliveries arrive by 10:30 A.M. the next business day."
- *Claim:* "The safest minivan in its class." Proof: "According to collision tests conducted by the American Automotive Safety Association."
- *Claim:* "The toothpaste dentists recommend most." Proof: "We surveyed hundreds of dental professionals from across the country."
- *Claim:* "The freshest vegetables in town." Proof: "Our produce is delivered fresh every morning."

## Offer a Guarantee

Another way to build belief is to put your money where your mouth is. In other words, offer a guarantee. A training firm could say in their proposal to a prospective client, "Your sales team will increase the number of appointments they generate from cold calling by 25% within three months, or your investment in this training program will be refunded."

The problem with this technique is that just about every product or service comes with a guarantee of some kind these days. (A product is conspicuous if it doesn't have one.) So this technique has lost much of its bite. Still, it does help to build belief because at least some customers will think "If they offer a guarantee, then their product must be good."

## Make a Personal Pledge

Sometimes a public promise by the company owner or other senior executive can go a long way in building belief. Who can forget those famous Hair Club for Men infomercials when Sy Sperling shows us his full head of hair and says, "I'm not only the Hair Club president, I'm also a client."

**FACT**

A personal pledge doesn't necessarily have to come from someone in the company. A well-known celebrity endorsement can work very well, too.

A company offering printing services that could be ordered on the Internet was new and unknown. They had great service, but that claim was difficult to prove. So the company president posted a letter on the front page of the Web site offering his personal guarantee that customers would be treated well and satisfied with the quality. The technique worked.

## Put Price in Perspective

You're in a store specializing in travel clothing. You notice a beautiful cotton shirt on display. It looks great. You touch the material; it feels great. Then you look at the price tag: $90. Ouch! More than twice what you're used to paying for a shirt.

Will you buy it?

That depends on how well the store put the price in perspective for you. If the signage, display materials, and information tag clipped to the garment persuades you that the shirt will not wrinkle, even when stuffed in a suitcase; is extremely comfortable, even on the longest trips; and can be rinsed and hang-dried overnight in a hotel room, then $90 might seem like a bargain.

Putting the price in perspective is a key ingredient of successful copywriting, especially when you're dealing with a product that costs more than most other options available.

Now it's time to take a look at the various ways to accomplish this in your copy.

## Show a Little TCO

The price isn't the only cost of owning some products. Often there are other costs as well, such as maintenance, support, repairs, operation, and, when something breaks down or wears out, replacement. Think of a laser printer. The initial price may be $350, but the cost of replacement cartridges over time could easily exceed that amount.

In the business world, this issue is commonly referred to as total cost of ownership (TCO). It's an effective way to show how a big-ticket item may actually be quite affordable.

If a company is purchasing a new forklift truck for the warehouse, they know that the $35,000 price tag is just the beginning. It takes fuel to run this piece of equipment. The rubber wheels may wear out and need replacing every few months. There may also be training costs associated with learning how to operate the truck. So if another forklift manufacturer can demonstrate that their $40,000 vehicle has longer lasting wheels, better fuel economy, and is easy to learn and operate, then they might get the sale—even though the price tag is $5,000 higher.

## Highlight the Payoffs

The benefits derived from using a product can often far outweigh the price.

For example, a sales manager may balk at the $12,000 price tag for a two-day sales training seminar. "That works out to $6,000 per day! An outrageous fee," she might say. However, when she realizes that the payoff is a significant boost in sales, and possibly a nice bonus for her for achieving quota, then the price suddenly seems like a drop in the bucket.

**QUESTION?**

**What if I'm writing copy for a cheap product?**
If you're promoting a product that is cheaper than most of its competitors, you still need to put the price in perspective but in a different way. You have to demonstrate that the low price does not mean low quality.

The payoffs of purchasing a product don't necessarily have to be tangible. They can be emotional as well. For example, a brochure for a weight-loss clinic explains that the basic price of the program is $900, a hefty price tag for most people. However, the copy goes on to explain that more than 94 percent of clients lose at least fifteen pounds in the first six weeks. "Imagine how great you'll feel," the copy might read, "as you shop for new thinner clothes for the healthier great-looking you."

## Break It Down

Houses often cost hundreds of thousands of dollars. However, most people don't get alarmed by the price because they break it down. They focus on the $750 per month mortgage payment rather than the $300,000 list price.

If your product has a high price tag, consider breaking it down into more digestible chunks for the customer. It's a great antidote to sticker shock.

A direct-mail piece for a business magazine offered a special annual subscription price of $370 per year. Even for business people, that's a significant chunk of change. The copywriter was smart, however. He put the price in perspective, explaining that, "This executive subscriber program works out to just $1.43 per day. Hey, that's less than the price of a café latte!"

The magazine is more expensive than its rivals. But by comparing it to the cost of a daily cup of java, any price comparison seems trivial.

## *Inspire Action*

You've written a terrific advertisement, Web page, or brochure. Now what is it you want the reader to do? Visit a Web page and fill out a form to get more information? Call a toll-free number and place an order at a special one-day-only price? Visit the local hardware store and purchase the product before supplies run out?

Copywriting, in virtually all its forms, is about getting the customer to take action. Whether it's an obvious "Call Now!" or conveyed more subtlety in the subtext, you must communicate what it is you want the reader to do. If you don't, your promotion will be like a cruise ship without a rudder. It may look good, but it's going nowhere.

**FACT**

In advertising and marketing the call to action is the section of the promotion that encourages the reader, listener, or viewer to take some specific step toward buying the product.

It's amazing how many advertising and marketing pieces contain no clear instruction on how to buy the product or learn more about it. If you write such compelling copy that the customer becomes interested, why leave any doubt as to what he or she needs to do next?

Here are a few examples of calls to action used in advertising, marketing, and public relations.

- "Click here for a free White Paper on…"
- "Call today for a no-obligation free consultation…"
- "Visit our Web site for a free online demo…"
- "Order now and get free delivery…"
- "Order today and save 15% …"
- "Download this free report: 9 Ways to Recognize a Disreputable Renovation Contractor…"

- "To learn more about how our State Tax Savings Program works, click here to request a case study featuring a company in your industry..."
- "Reply today and we'll extend the 30-day free trial to 60 days. That's two full months of benefits at no cost..."
- "Subscribe today and save $27 off the cover price..."
- "Ask your local pet products retailer for a free sample of Cat Yummies..."

You might think that the piece you're writing makes it obvious what the reader needs to do next. If you're creating a glossy brochure for a new car, it may seem like a no-brainer that the reader should go to the dealership and ask for a test drive. But according to research in the automotive advertising industry, this isn't necessarily so. Studies shows that a brochure that includes the line "Visit your local dealership for a test drive" or something similar motivates more readers to do so.

Inspiring action is the most important goal of any sales, marketing, or public relations communications. In your copy there should be no doubt what it is you want customers to do.

Chapter 6

# The Copywriter's Bag of Tricks

Just about every profession—from law to dentistry to ceramic tile installation—has its own unique knowledge base of insider tips, tricks, and techniques. The copywriting trade is no different. There are dozens of proven best practices you can rely on to get the results you need from your sales, marketing, and publicity materials. This chapter features the very best of these tricks and shows you how to apply them.

## *Create a Multisensory Experience*

If you're writing a direct-mail letter promoting a new series of cookbooks, one of the first things you will do is put yourself in the prospect's shoes. To get into the mindset of your target customer, you will imagine that you're a cooking enthusiast in a well-stocked kitchen whipping up a gourmet meal.

You want your copy to be so enticing that the prospect will practically be salivating to get those books in her hands so she can indulge her passion for cooking. And the way you do that is by engaging her imagination using every sensation possible: seeing, touching, feeling, hearing, and tasting.

That's what creating a multisensory experience is all about. To maximize the effectiveness of your promotion, you must get all the senses firing—or at least most of them—so that the prospect can really "feel" the benefits.

**E ALERT!**

A big mistake that copywriters make is to utilize only one or two senses to describe product benefits. For example, a car might be touted by how great it looks. But what you see isn't the only allure of owning a great automobile. What about how it *feels* when you sit in the comfortable leather seats? Or the *sound* of the engine quietly accelerating? Or the commanding *touch* of the solid steel gear shift?

Even seemingly uninspiring products can engage many, if not all, of the senses. Consider the following list matching the senses to the features and benefits of an electric toothbrush.

### Creating a Multisensory Experience for an Electric Toothbrush

Sound: The quiet hum of the oscillating brushes

Taste: The clean, fresh sensation in your mouth after you brush

Touch: The firm comfortable grip of the handle

Sight: The slim design that fits easily into even the most crowded toiletry bag

Smell: Clean, fresh breath that lasts for hours

You can't always engage every sense for every product or service you promote. But create as broad a multisensory experience as you can for the reader. It helps to make the features and benefits seem more real and affecting. After all, it's not just the coffee that wakes a prospect up, it's the smell of it.

## Tell a Story

Consider this lead paragraph from a direct-mail sales letter:

"On a beautiful late spring afternoon, twenty-five years ago, two young men graduated from the same college. They were very much alike, these two young men. Both had been better than average students, both were personable and both—as young college graduates are—were filled with ambitious dreams for the future."

This piece, written by copywriting legend Martin Conroy, is one of the most famous direct-mail letters of all time. Used to promote the *Wall Street Journal*, this simple two-page letter was mailed in various formats for more than twenty-five years and, by some estimates, was directly responsible for generating nearly one billion dollars in subscriptions.

In the two young men sales letter, both men go to work for the same company. Twenty-five years later one man is the manager of a small department within the company and the other is the president of the company. The difference between them, the letter implies, is simply that the president had read the *Journal* throughout his career. Talk about a convincing story!

The "two young men" letter is now a classic. It clearly demonstrates the power of storytelling and how it can significantly boost results in just about any marketing and publicity campaign. The strange thing is, storytelling is not used nearly as often as it could be in copywriting. In fact, it may be the most underutilized copywriting best practice of them all.

Why is storytelling so effective? People remember stories much more than they do facts and figures. Think of the last time you were at a social or business gathering. Weren't the main topics of discussion centered around stories? Weren't those discussions the ones that lingered in your mind, the ones you perhaps remembered most and retold to others?

Storytelling can be used in just about any type of copywriting. In fact, whenever you have to describe how a product works, bring a benefit to life, explain a feature, tout an advantage, highlight a prospect problem, bring in a solution, or just about any other persuasive writing task, you should try to do so using a story.

Consider these two examples of brochure copy for a lawnmower.

### Example 1:

The XBX Lawnmower doesn't just cut your lawn, it also gathers and mulches the grass, effectively cutting any lawn care job down to less than half the time. So you can spend more time with your family.

### Example 2:

You pivot to the left, turn, and then take the shot. But your ten-year-old son intercepts, jumps, and scores a basket. Saturday morning b-ball with the kids has never been so enjoyable. That's because you've been able to get the lawn cut, raked, and mulched in less than half the time it used to take you. Thanks to the all-in-one XBX Lawnmower."

The second example obviously has a lot more impact. What's the difference? The first merely explains the benefit: "...you can spend more time with your family." The second example, by contrast, creates an appealing story of a dad who finally has time to play some "b-ball with the kids."

Notice that a story doesn't have to be a long narrative. You don't have to write a Hollywood movie! It can simply be a slice of life that illustrates the benefit in a way that appeals to the prospect.

Some types of copywriting projects lend themselves naturally to storytelling, such as television and radio commercials, press releases, and case studies. However, stories can be equally powerful in brochures, Web sites, presentations, and other sales, marketing, and publicity materials.

And using stories in your copy is not only effective, it's fun, too. Pretend you're a fiction writer. Paint a scene or tell a story that makes the product benefits jump off the page or screen. For example:

- Don't just say that a coffee machine makes a great cup of coffee. Describe the brightening look in a woman's eyes as she takes a satisfying sip before beginning her busy day.
- Don't just describe how a golf club can help to correct a bad slice. Tell the compelling story of a man having a great game with his friends as he hits every shot straight toward the greens.
- Don't explain that a seminar can help to create effective presentations. Feature a woman actually giving a winning presentation, hearing the applause, and even getting promoted!

Don't underestimate the power of storytelling. It makes your copy more compelling than any adjective or expressive phrase you could ever think of using.

## Flash Facts and Stats

A fact is a powerful thing. While a prospect can be justifiably suspicious about a product claim or understandably skeptical about an overhyped description of the benefits ("Great tasting chicken. Crisp, tender, and juicy. Cooked to perfection!"), a fact is immutable. It doesn't require belief. Prospects accept it as truth. That's why flashing facts, stats, and other evidence throughout your copy is so important.

**ESSENTIAL**

Strangely, a fact doesn't necessarily need to relate directly to a product benefit to add power to your copy. "The Gizmo 9000 is produced at our 14,000 sq. ft. state-of-the-art manufacturing plant in Chicago." The size and location has little to do with the product benefits. Yet the very mention of these extraneous details makes the copy more convincing.

Facts in your copy are like nails that hold a house together. If you don't have enough in place, your entire structure will fail to stand up to scrutiny. Like a house of cards, even the slightest wind of skepticism will blow the whole thing down.

Consider the following example:

Our friendly customer service staff is here to help you.

Do you believe that claim? Or have you heard that one, or something like it, so many times before that it no longer has any impact? Now read the revised version of this copy below.

Our full-time customer service staff of 15 is here to help you, 8 A.M. to 4 P.M. Monday to Friday. We're working hard to earn a CSA award this year for customer service excellence. And we'll keep working hard until we win Gold.

Isn't it amazing how adding a few simple facts makes the copy more convincing? Notice that there still isn't any hard evidence that the customer service staff is friendly or helpful. But just by adding facts—even the fact that this customer service department hasn't earned a CSA award!—makes the copy more persuasive.

Here are the types of facts that can add substance and credibility to your copy:

- Sizes, colors, shapes, styles, dimensions, and quantities
- Testimonials
- Product reviews
- Test results
- Research reports
- Studies
- Surveys
- Press
- Explaining how the product is made
- Explaining how the product works
- Compliance standards met ("The Acme ZXL is ASA tested and certified for use in construction raised platform applications.")

Beware of facts that seem too good to be true. Can the new time-management system really cut two hours off a manager's busy day or is that just the hopeful thinking of the marketing manager (or copywriter) promoting the product? If you have a fact that will likely ignite the skepticism of a prospect, be sure to back up that fact with other facts and outside endorsements. For example: "An independent survey concluded that 82% of managers who used this time-management system were able to cut two hours off their day."

## *Tout the Advantages*

A car has a very useful benefit. If you turn on the engine, shift the gear into drive, and step on the gas pedal, the car will move forward—taking you, hopefully, where you want to go. But is this a benefit you should highlight in your copy? Probably not. The reason is that all cars do this. It is of no particular advantage when compared to the competition. (Unless the competition is bicycles!)

When you research a product or service, you'll soon discover that not all features and benefits are equal. There is going to be at least one feature— hopefully more than one—that is a distinct advantage over anything else available on the market. And if that's the case, you should tout that advantage in your copy. Bring it up front and shout it from the roof tops. It's your best foot. Put it forward!

So what exactly is an advantage? It is simply a feature that the competition either does not offer or does not do as well.

A stapler, for example, might have the ability to make 2,000 staples before reloading is required. If every other stapler on the market only takes 500 staple cartridges, that's quite an advantage. Everyone who has ever worked in an office knows the hassle of having to fumble through a desk drawer looking for staple cartridges. So a stapler that lasts five times longer is a real convenience.

**ALERT!**

Highlight the advantage of a product or service, but don't ignore the other features and benefits. They're important, too! While the main advantage should take center stage, be sure to cast the other features and benefits in strong supporting roles.

You can determine the advantage of a product or service by filling in the blanks of the following statement:

"The [product or service] is the ONLY one that has [this] or does [that], which is meaningful to the prospect because [the reason]."

So for our stapler we can say: "The OfficeMate Stapler is the only one that features 2000-staple cartridges, which is meaningful to the prospect because refilling an empty stapler is a time-consuming hassle."

## *Pile on the Reasons Why*

This technique is particularly useful when there isn't one big reason to buy the product, just a lot of little ones. What if you're tasked with writing a Web site to promote a new therapeutic massage clinic. Simply saying that a massage is relaxing and makes you feel good may not be enough to attract a lot of customers to the clinic. However, if you list a lot of reasons why—better immune system, better circulation, lower blood pressure, improved flexibility, less aches and pains, younger looking complexion, insurance benefits, and a discount for first timers—then a customer may be more persuaded to book an appointment.

**ALERT!**

Don't overdo it. When piling on the reasons why, make sure each reason can stand on its own as a distinct benefit. Saying that the roof of a car will keep rain off a driver's head—just so you can add another reason why to the list—is getting a little ridiculous.

Here is an example of a Web page promoting a teleseminar for freelance writers. The topic of the class is working with designers. Although there is no single big benefit to attending the class, there are a lot of little reasons for signing up.

During this TeleClass, Michael and I will explain exactly how to set up business-building partnerships with freelance designers and design firms.

You'll learn such insights as:

- How to approach a freelance designer or design firm about forming a partnership
- What to say, and how to say it. (Also, what NOT to say!)
- 5 painful mistakes when partnering with a designer that can seriously hurt your business. (We'll show you how to avoid these.)
- How to create an agreement to share clients, leads, and opportunities so you can attract more clients, faster.
- How to do a joint promotional program that generates twice the business for you at half the cost.
- How to get better, higher paying clients to work with you—because of your strategic relationship with a great designer.
- How to save thousands of dollars on your Web site, stationery, and other marketing materials.
- How to coordinate and work effectively with a designer on the same client project. (Who takes the lead? You'll find out.)
- How to become known to twice as many potential clients, virtually overnight.
- How to get freelance designers and design firms to recommend you to their clients—even if you DON'T have a partnership with them!
- And much, much more.

In addition, they'll be plenty of time to ask questions and get all the answers you need. In fact, you might want to prepare your questions in advance.

In my opinion, partnering with freelance designers and design firms is the best way to rapidly grow your copywriting business. You'll learn faster. Get more clients faster. Reach your business goals faster. It's an unbeatable business-building strategy.

The "reasons why" approach works well because it creates a critical mass. The prospect is presented with so many little reasons to take action or buy the product that it becomes one big reason to say yes.

## Push the "Ouch" Button

What do you do when something hurts? You look for relief. You try to find a Band-Aid or pill that will stop the pain. This is the idea behind the "push the ouch button" technique. By reminding the reader of his problem or pain, you motivate him to look for a solution—which, of course, is your product or service.

For example, imagine you're a small-business owner who has been struggling to do his own bookkeeping. You fall behind frequently. You make mistakes. You miss things. It's a real pain. Then one day you receive a direct-mail letter with the headline: "No More Bookkeeping Blues! Here's a Fast and Simple Way to Manage Your Small Business Accounting." That gets your attention. Suddenly you're open to investing in an easy-to-use software that makes bookkeeping fast and easy.

The "push the ouch button" technique is very effective when your product or service solves a specific problem. It reminds the prospect of her pain. And motivates her to do something about it. Of course, the solution is right there in front of her—in the promotional piece you wrote.

You have to be careful with this technique. If you push the ouch button too hard for too long, you might come across as opportunistic. No one likes to be reminded of their problems, frustrations, pains, or misery. So push the button just enough to gain attention and remind prospects of their pain, then quickly bring in your product or service as the solution.

## Make It Urgent—Even When It Isn't

Sometimes the toughest part of writing a promotion isn't getting the prospect to buy the product. It's getting him or her to buy *now*. After all, can't it wait? Where's the fire?

There are a lot of products and services that don't have a built-in urgency. These include magazines, newsletters, electronic gadgets, entertainment, collectibles, travel, and many others. As a potential customer, you may want one of these products or services, even need it. But you can probably delay your purchasing decision for a few days, weeks, or even months without suffering any serious consequences.

That's a real challenge for you as a copywriter. Your promotion needs to inspire immediate action. Otherwise, it fails. Yet how do you motivate the prospect to act when there is no immediate necessity to do so?

The trick is to create that necessity. And there are many ways you can accomplish this in your copy.

## Have a Sale

A sale is the most common means of creating urgency. That's why so many flyers, direct-mail pieces, letters, and other promotions you receive are often centered around a sale.

Although it's a good idea to put a deadline on a sale, it's not absolutely necessary. Offering a special price implies that there is a time limit, even when one is not mentioned in the copy.

On sale now—a one-year subscription to *Forbes* magazine at 62% off the cover price!

## Give Something Away for Free

Sweetening the deal with a free giveaway (which is explained in more detail later in this chapter) is an excellent way to get the prospect to act now, especially if there is a firm deadline.

Purchase your Acme Laptop before July 15 and get three years of next-day, on-site support at no extra cost!

## Highlight the Consequences of Not Buying Now

After you have presented all the compelling benefits, an effective technique for inspiring action is to remind the prospect of what he stands to lose if he doesn't buy.

Why play one more game with an embarrassingly bad golf swing when you can correct even the most severe hooking problem in just one day?

## Stand Up to the Competition

There are some types of products and services where the competition is so strong and dominant that the only way to gain attention is via a direct attack. That doesn't mean you write a lot of nasty things about the competitor! That may actually create sympathy for them and often comes across as being mean-spirited or desperate. However, you can present the reader with a side-by-side comparison, essentially asking: "Hey, Mr. Prospect. Before you buy from them, take a closer look at us."

In order for this technique to work, you really have to know what specific advantages (as explained earlier in this chapter) your product or service has over the competition. Then you have to:

1. Highlight the specific advantage you have over the competition.
2. Show that prospects can get the same or similar benefits from you that they would expect to receive from the competition.

As an example, you're writing copy to promote a contact management software product, and the main competition is ACT, a well-known and respected brand in this market. How can your unknown software compete?

Take a look at this example of a direct-mail letter:

Dear Professional Contractor:

Stop! Before you consider spending hundreds of dollars on ACT, there are three important things you need to know about XYZ Contact Manager.

- It has all the features and functions you need to manage your contacts quickly and effectively.
- It is tailored specifically to professional building contractors like you. In fact, no special customization is required. Just install the software and it works!
- It costs 25% less!

XYZ Contact Manager is a mythical product created for the purposes of the above example. But if it were real, can you imagine trying to sell this unknown product with a fierce competitor like ACT dominating the market? It would be an uphill battle to say the least! People would reasonably say, "XYZ Contact Manager? Never heard of it. I'll just get the product I know best, ACT, the one everyone else uses and trusts."

But by challenging the competition head-on, you get the prospect thinking in a new way: "Why not take a look at XYZ Contact Manager? It looks like they have some special features that ACT doesn't have. And it costs less, too."

Use this technique with care. Once you've established that you may be a better choice than the market leader, you need to do all the heavy lifting required of any promotion: build belief, bring the benefits to life, and inspire action. Throwing stones at the competition isn't enough. Your product or service has to stand on its own two feet with its own set of compelling features and benefits.

## Sweeten the Deal

"But wait! There's more." says the announcer on the late night infomercial. "If you order now, you also receive this premium set of steak knives at no extra cost!"

Your product may be tantalizing, but that may not be enough to get prospects to take action or place an order. At least not right away.

For example, you receive a direct-mail piece promoting a new wine magazine. The promotional piece is full of enticing facts. You learn that the publishers attracted a first-rate list of wine writers and columnists, and there is even a special section on cooking. Just what you were looking for! However, there is no urgency. You can always subscribe some other time, or even pick up a copy at your local newsstand.

If you were the copywriter, how would you make the offer so compelling that prospects will subscribe right away? One of the most popular means of doing this is sweetening the deal. This involves throwing in something extra to make the offer even more enticing.

For our wine magazine subscription promotion, you could say something like this: "Subscribe today and receive a FREE Wine Guide. Don't wait! Supplies are limited."

There are many ways you can sweeten the deal. You can:

- Offer a special price
- Throw in the extras
- Extend the service plan
- Give away something for free
- Offer a no-charge upgrade
- Extend the payment terms
- Add on free accessories

The "sweeten the deal" technique accomplishes two things: It motivates the prospect to accept the offer, and it motivates him to do so—now.

## Put It in Quotes

Don't take it personally, but prospects don't automatically believe what you write. They assume, perhaps rightfully so, that the words you put in the marketing and publicity materials you create are biased. After all, you're a paid advocate for the product or service. You are supposed to say nice things about it. That's why building belief and credibility can be such a challenge for a copywriter.

The "put it in quotes" technique can help. You simply find an opportunity in your copy to use quotations to describe or dramatize a particular feature or benefit of the product. Consider the following examples.

**Example 1:**
The XM-50 Turbo-Mower cuts your lawn up to 30% faster than other lawnmowers in its class.

**Example 2:**
"I love my XM-50," says John Smith of Denver, Colorado. "I've tried other models. And this one cuts my lawn at least 30% faster."

Prospects may be skeptical about what you, the copywriter, say in the promotion. But they will believe, almost unconditionally, what a fellow customer tells them. The assumption is that customers will tell it like it is about the product or service, with no bias. You can argue whether that assumption is correct or not, but it does exist.

What if you don't have a customer testimonial to use? The next best alternative is to use a representative testimonial. If you know for a fact that many of the customers are raving about the product and saying great things about it, you can legitimately write in your copy something like this: "Customers tell us frequently how much faster the XM-50 cuts their lawn."

Even quotes from someone inside the company can add weight. For example, you could have the company president quoted in your promotion as saying, "The XM-50 will cut your lawn faster. Guaranteed." That's much more persuasive than simply making that statement without quotations.

## Lay on the Kudos

Who would you hire to remodel your kitchen: a qualified contractor or an award-winning contractor?

The answer is obvious. When a product or service is given awards, praise, great reviews, and other kudos, people take notice. It is a signal to potential customers that the product or service is something special. "This electric frying pan must be good quality," they think. "It won a Cuisine Cooking Award!"

If your product or service has won an award or some other accolade, put this fact front and center in your copy. It is a very persuasive marketing message.

Here are some examples of this technique in action:

- *Award.* "Hire this ACE Award-winning copywriter for your next subscription promotion…"
- *Consensus.* "Voted the #1 new car in its class by Automotive Magazine…"
- *Endorsement.* "Recommended by the American Society of Automotive Engineers…"

- *Testimonial.* "9 out of 10 customers agree, End-All Migraine Tablets make migraines disappear in half the time..."
- *Exclusivity.* "The only tax consultancy invited to speak three years in a row at the Tax Managers Symposium..."
- *Longevity.* "Celebrating 25 years of helping dentists build more profitable and personally rewarding professional practices..."

The assumption is that an award is a good indication of product or service quality. And it usually is. However, there are some industries—advertising is a prime example—that hand out awards all the time. If an ad agency enters enough competitions, it's bound to win something!

Still, an award implies that a high-level, unbiased endorsement has been given. It's a credibility booster that just can't be beat. So lay on the kudos where you can. All things being equal, people will tend to choose the award winner.

# Chapter 7
# Headlines, Body Copy, and More

Now you've reached the nitty-gritty. This chapter explains how to write all the individual text elements of your promotional piece: the headlines, paragraphs, sentences, sidebars, callouts, body copy, and more. Each element plays an important role in convincing the prospect to take action. Just one lazy headline or uninspiring starburst can torpedo your entire promotion. And you don't want that to happen!

## *Headlines*

In his legendary 1932 book, *Tested Advertising Methods*, author John Caples says, "If the headline of an advertisement is poor, the best copywriters in the world can't write copy that will sell the goods. They haven't a chance. Because if the headline is poor, the copy will not be read."

Studies in print and online advertising confirm that readers respond to an advertisement more because of the headline than any other element in the ad, including the design. No matter how flashy the images or compelling the body copy, headlines are the real workhorse of marketing and publicity. Some copywriters have been able to increase response by up to 400 percent simply by tinkering with a headline. Rarely can this be accomplished by rewriting the body copy or altering the visual.

And headlines are not just found in advertisements. These powerful devices are used in just about every type of promotional piece, including press releases, Web pages, e-mails, sales letters, postcards, brochures, and many others.

**ALERT!**

Your ability to write an effective headline, one that stops the reader in her tracks and gets her to read or at least scan the promotion, will have a lot to do with defining your success as a copywriter. So when you sit down to write a headline, make it a good one!

What is a headline? That may sound like a no-brainer of a question. A headline is that big block of text you see in an advertisement or on a Web page. However, headlines can also include:

- *Secondary headlines*. Smaller headlines placed above, below, or beside the main headline
- *Subheads*. Used to break up or organize the body copy
- *Subject lines*. In e-mail campaigns
- *Section headers*. In longer promotional pieces, such as catalogs or Web sites

- *Stoppers.* Headlines positioned in unexpected places on the page to gain attention

## Headline Writing Basics

How do you craft a winning headline? Fortunately, there are tried and true approaches to writing highly effective headlines that you can follow. You don't have to just sit there and wait for inspiration to strike.

There are two general types of headlines used most often in promotional pieces.

- Teaser headlines
- Benefit-oriented headlines

A teaser headline tries to do what its name suggests: tease you into reading the piece. A teaser headline can be a fun play on words, a joke, a puzzle, a curious statement, a witty remark, a riddle, or some other bit of creative inspiration.

An ad for an exotic and very expensive luxury car had this teaser headline:

No, we don't offer mortgages

The idea behind the ad was that the company was offering 1 percent financing on their luxury automobiles, which are priced at over $150,000. You don't discover this benefit until you read the body copy. The writer of this ad was hoping that you, the reader, would become so intrigued and curious to decipher the meaning of the headline that you just wouldn't be able to help yourself.

Do teaser headlines work? They do—sometimes. But it's a gamble. If the headline doesn't captivate the reader sufficiently, she won't bother to read the rest of the ad; therefore, she won't get even a gist of what the benefit of the product or service being promoted is all about. Teaser headlines often do not contain even a hint of the key benefit or information concerning the offer.

That's why a benefit-oriented headline is a lot less risky. It implies or expresses a benefit to the reader. In just a few choice words, it says loud and clear what the main benefit or offer is. So if you were to rewrite the above luxury car ad using the benefit-oriented headline approach, you might try this:

Now You Can Stop Just Dreaming About It!
1% Financing On All Models Until The End Of The Month

The headline in the second example may not seem as clever as the first. However, it certainly is more strategic. Benefit-oriented headlines stand a much greater chance of gaining reader attention. And even if the body copy of the ad is not read, the reader can still get the gist of the main sales message.

## Headline Idea Generator

Here is a list of effective headline writing techniques.

Technique: Use the words *how to*
Example: How to save a bundle on your UPS imports. And save YOU a lot of work!

Technique: Use a customer testimonial
Example: "After over half a million hours of air using AVBLEND, we've had no premature camshaft failures."

Technique: Put the offer in the headline
Example: Try Rogers Digital TV—One month free

Technique: List the reasons why
Example: Three good reasons why you should order the NEW 2007 Thomas Register today…

Technique: Offer a free gift
Example: Let's trade. Send us your business card and we will send you a sleeve of PRECEPT extra distance golf balls

Technique: Provide helpful advice
Example: 5 Proven Ways to Prevent the Onset of a Migraine

Technique: Give away free information
Example: FREE report: What other ASPs don't want you to know

Technique: Make an invitation
Example: You're invited to spend the evening with the most influential decision-makers in the software industry today

Technique: Use the word *discover*
Example: Discover a powerful and affordable desktop surfacing solution that works entirely within AutoCAD

Technique: Use the words *last chance*
Example: Last chance to introduce PaperPort to your OmniPage Pro OCE Software at reduced pricing

Technique: Make a seemingly outrageous claim
Example: Holds wood together better than wood does

Technique: Paint a picture of the benefit
Example: Can you picture your employee's faces when they see how smoothly their move went?

Technique: Simply state what the product or service is
Example: Surgical tables rebuilt. Free loaners available.

Technique: Mention an award
Example: Awarded the best lens by OptiMed Magazine

Technique: Quote a glowing review
Example: Voted #1 Family Minivan of the Year by Family Travels Magazine

Technique: Quote an expert endorsement
Example: "I recommend Silk Skin MDM to all my patients with problem rosacia."

Technique: Put a great price or discount in the headline
Example: Subscribe to CB Business today and save 76% off the cover price. That's less than the cost of a café latte!

Technique: Use the word *announcing*
Example: Announcing a new way to deliver flowers without water

Technique: Turn a perceived negative into a positive
Example: Buckley's Mixture tastes awful. But it works.

Technique: Ask a thought-provoking question
Example: If your e-commerce orders double, could your infrastructure handle it?

Technique: Differentiate from the competition
Example: You've never seen an 80kA surge protector this small

Technique: Agitate the problem
Example: So, you have to pick up the kids, make dinner, help with homework, and get your presentation done by tomorrow…

Technique: Say you're number one
Example: Presenter's #1 free-space mouse

Technique: Make a big promise
Example: Double your folding carton production uptime with Velocity

Technique: Ask if they need it
Example: Need a simple way to handle product returns?

Technique: Tell them what you're looking for
Example: We're looking for a few good distributors

Technique: Promise to turn a dream into reality
Example: We turn good writers into published authors!

When brainstorming headlines, create a list of as many candidates as possible. Don't worry if some are obviously not good. You'd be surprised how often a seemingly bad headline idea can be tweaked into something great. Once you have your list, circle those that have the greatest potential. Then whittle that shortlist to the top three. When you finally pick the winner, don't discard the rest of the list! You might need it again to revise the ad or create a new one, or put it in your swipe file of headline ideas.

## *Lead the Way with Great Leads*

The lead is the opening few sentences or paragraphs in a magazine article or news story. Its purpose is to hold the reader's attention so that he or she keeps on reading right to the end.

Leads in promotional pieces—such as an ad or a sales letter—play the same role. Despite how effectively the headline gains attention, if the lead does not hold that initial reader interest, the body copy won't get scanned or read. And if that doesn't happen, the key message will not have any impact because the prospect will not have read it.

**FACT**

In direct-mail marketing, a lead test is when one version of a letter is tested against another that has a different lead. All the other text in the direct-mail piece is exactly the same. The purpose of a lead test is to discover which version generates the most orders. A new lead can dramatically lift response rates.

Here's an example of a sales letter lead.

Dear Entrepreneur,

In ancient Greece, business owners would attempt to collect on overdue accounts by throwing stones at the customers. This forced the debtor to either pay up or face a daily bruising.

Today, things are more civilized. But debt collection is no less frustrating. Collection agencies tend to be overly aggressive, destroying relationships. Lawyers can be outrageously expensive, and many won't touch accounts worth less than $10,000.

So what's the solution?

Does this lead motivate you to read on, at least until you find out what the solution is? If you are an entrepreneur who has had difficulties in collecting on overdue accounts, then, yes, you would probably be eager to read on.

There are many ways you can open your promotional piece with a great lead. You can:

- Tell a compelling story
- State an interesting fact
- Ask a provocative question
- Highlight the great offer
- Quote a satisfied customer
- Feature the key benefit
- Make a big promise
- Focus on the main problem

Leads are challenging yet fun to write. Like a headline, you should develop two or three lead ideas (you don't have to write them out fully) and then pick one you judge will be the most effective given the target audience and the theme of the promotion.

## The 3 Cs of Effective Body Copy

The body copy is sometimes neglected in a promotional piece. In the effort to get the headline and lead right, as well as a strong close and call-to-action (described later in this chapter), the body copy can get short shrifted. This is unfortunate because the body copy typically contains most of your sales messages. If these are poorly presented, the success of your entire promotion is at risk.

So what makes effective body copy? It has the following ingredients, which are referred to as the 3 Cs:

- Make it clear
- Make it complete
- Make it conversational

## Make It Clear

Many copywriters struggle to write copy that is lyrical or creative. They rack their brains trying to come up with intriguing metaphors or a clever turn of phrase. But what the prospect wants most is solid information presented in a clear, accurate manner. Sure, he wants great writing, but it doesn't have to read like Hemingway. It's simply good writing that communicates effectively. So write to express, not to impress.

If it comes down to it, always choose clarity over creativity. Explain product features simply and in detail. Use your words to help the reader feel the benefits, and be liberal in your use of facts, stats, quotes, and specs.

Does all this mean your copy shouldn't be creatively written? No. On the contrary, your words should be interesting, even entertaining, to read. However, never forget that your primary objective is to communicate the sales messages in a way that is understandable and meaningful to your target audience. Don't let your need to be creative override clear communications. Does this mean your copy has to be dull? No. It simply means that crisp, clear explanations beat the poetic rhythm of a clever phrase any day.

## *Make It Complete*

Readers expect the body copy of an ad or brochure to provide them with all the information they need to make a decision regarding the next steps. Don't let them down.

**ALERT!**

To the reader, there is no worse sin than that of omission. There are countless marketing materials—especially letters and brochures—that are so lacking in information that it's surprising that anyone could expect the reader to make an intelligent decision based on what's written. So always be complete.

Try to anticipate the questions a prospect may ask, and make sure you address these in your copy. For example, when a prospect sees your promotion, she might wonder:

- Who is this for?
- What does this mean?
- Is it really for me?
- What's in it for me?
- What is the product?
- What problem does it solve?
- Do I have this problem?
- Who is the company?
- Why should I trust what they say?
- Where's the proof?
- Why should I buy this product?
- What should I buy now?
- Why should I buy at this price?
- Why buy from this company and not from the competition?
- What guarantee do I have?

- How much time will this take?
- How much does it cost?
- How do I order?

Be sure your body copy tells the whole story. Vanquish all doubt. Answer all questions. Give the prospect every possible reason to say yes to your offer.

## Make It Conversational

Think about the last really good nonfiction book or article you read. Wasn't one of the things that made it great the writer's voice? You could almost hear him or her speaking from each page. It was as if you weren't reading at all, just listening.

Why should marketing or publicity materials be any different? Remember, you are having a conversation with the reader. In some ways it's very intimate. You are asking the reader to make a buying decision that will affect—in a modest or even major way—his life, career, or business. Doesn't he or she deserve a friendly conversational tone?

A conversational tone in copywriting doesn't necessarily mean casual or lazy. Two engineers discussing a new propulsion valve system would talk very differently than two surfers debating the merits of a new board wax. Conversational writing is about connecting with the target audience by copying the style, tone, and language those prospects use when talking about a particular class of products or services.

It's no surprise that the most successful promotional pieces ever written have a conversational tone. In many of these, you get a real sense of the writer's voice, and what a helpful, informative, and persuasive voice it is. That voice may be more obvious in a sales letter and less so in a brochure or press release, but it's there.

## *Sentences That Sell*

The persuasive case you're trying to make to the prospect is built with sentences. So it makes sense that you pay particular attention to how you craft them.

The mechanics of writing effective sentences is covered extensively in *The Everything Writing Well Book*. However, there are several guidelines that are particularly applicable to copywriting. The objective is to make the sentences as clear and easy to read as possible. Remember, no one is forced to read your promotional piece, nor will anyone read it for enjoyment as they might a novel or magazine article. So keep these guidelines in mind as you craft your copy:

- *Vary the length.* Reading one full sentence after another is tiresome. Mix short and long sentences.
- *Don't be afraid to use sentence fragments.* Like this one. This may not be grammatically correct. But it is the way people talk.
- *People also begin sentences with and, but, and for when they speak.* And doing so in copywriting is okay, too. Just don't overdo it.
- *Be sure to spell out acronyms and explain buzzwords at least once in the body copy.* For example, say LTL (Less Than Truckload) the first time you use the term and then LTL later. Sure, transportation professionals already know what LTL stands for. But does the new accounting manager who needs to approve the purchase order?
- *Don't try to impress the reader with your voluminous vocabulary.* Use the simplest, best word possible. There's no advantage in saying "enables" when "helps" will do just fine.
- *Emphasize key words and phrases with bolds, underlines, italics, text boxes, arrows, and other devices.* Just don't overdo it. As famed copywriter Herschell Gordon Lewis often says, "If you emphasize everything, you emphasize nothing."
- *Avoid word repetition at close range.* You don't need to say "proven" as an adjective sixteen times in your body copy. The English language has more than enough synonyms to go around.

- *Use an active voice.* Don't say: "Weight loss was achieved for 92% of patients through the use of the StaySlim program." Do say: "StaySlim helps 92% of patients lose weight."
- *Create mental pictures with your words.* Provide examples, stories, scenarios. Bring the benefits to life. Give the reader a snapshot of what her life, work, or business will be like once she buys your product or service. Every prospect has an imagination. Engage it!
- *Avoid trying to impress the reader with your witty prose and agile wordplay.* Instead, impress them with the content of what you're saying.
- *Don't try to cram too much into a single sentence.* A good rule of thumb to follow is one idea, fact, statement, thought, or key message per sentence. Once you've expressed it clearly, push the period key and move on.

## Powerful Paragraphs

Paragraphs are the building blocks of a successful promotion, especially in longer pieces, such as Web sites, brochures, and sales letters.

Paragraphs can be as short as a single sentence or even a single word, or as long as several sentences taking up a large chunk of the page or screen. However, it's a good idea to mix things up in your body copy. A combination of short and long paragraphs makes the text look less intimidating and is easier to read.

**ALERT!**

There is a myth that short paragraphs are the rule in copywriting. Not true! Your paragraphs should be as long as they need to be to make and support your point. However, as in all good writing, your paragraphs should be as tight as possible. So once you've made your point—clearly and persuasively—hit that return key.

That being said, you should avoid overly long paragraphs if possible. These can look intimidating to a prospect when he sees them on the page or screen and may dissuade him from reading the promotion. Ideally, each paragraph in your body copy should be no more than seven lines on a standard 8½" × 11" page. That's about one hundred words. If your paragraph creeps over that limit, take a second look. You may be trying to express two or more ideas that would be more effectively stated as separate paragraphs. Or you might be too wordy. Of course, your paragraph could be just right as it is despite its length. If that's the case, don't change a word.

## Transitions

There is a special kind of paragraph called a transition. This is typically a sentence that connects one idea to another so that the reader has a smooth ride through your copy.

A transition acts like a bridge, showing the reader the way to the next point in your promotion. If you don't have this bridge, or if your transition is ineffective, then everything comes to a stop. Indeed, the prospect may not continue reading.

The last thing you want is to disturb the flow of your copy. Effective transitions keep things moving smoothly.

Stuck for a transition? Here's a technique that almost always works. Start your next topic, point, or idea in your copy with a question. Just like this paragraph did. It's the simplest way to guide the reader from one point to the next.

And if you really get stuck—if the break between two sections of your copy just has no logical connection—then try using a subhead. It says to the reader, "There's more you need to know."

## Other Useful Text Devices

In addition to headlines, paragraphs, and sentences, there are numerous other text elements that you can employ to build your case and persuade the prospects to act. Following are some of the most commonly used text elements in promotional pieces.

## Bullet Lists

A bullet list is simply a list, whether actual bullets are used or not. This is a useful device in copywriting for two reasons:

- It makes the promotional piece more readable. Like subheads and other text elements, a bullet list helps make the copy less intimidating than a page filled with weighty paragraphs.
- It's a better way to present a lot of details. If you have a long list of features and benefits, a list will help them stand out more.

Use a bullet list when you need to present a lot of facts or other details that lend themselves to itemization.

Consider using checkmarks in place of bullets, especially when creating a list of key features or benefits. Checklists, with the checkmarks already in place, communicate value and completion. The prospect gets a sense that he is getting everything he needs—and then some.

## Callouts

A callout explains key sections of an illustration or diagram, usually with text accompanied by a line drawn to the particular area.

Callouts are extremely useful in explaining the key components of a product or how a product works. For example, explaining how a time-management system works, with all its forms, fields, and sections, would be difficult without a detailed illustration and callouts. If you attempted to do so with paragraphs you would come across as long-winded, and perhaps make the product seem even more intimidating.

## Captions

A caption is the copy that is associated with or explains a photo or illustration. It usually runs along the bottom, top, or side of the visual.

The great thing about captions is that just about everyone reads them. So these are very handy devices for getting key messages across to prospects that may or may not read all the body copy.

A caption doesn't necessarily have to relate directly to the photo or illustration it's associated with. For example, a picture of a hotel suite at a holiday resort could say: "The local nightlife in Aruba is perfect for couples who enjoy music and dancing." This may not have anything to do with the hotel room, but the caption is a great way to get the nightlife message across.

## Sidebars

A sidebar contains information that is associated in some way to the main body copy. In a brochure describing a luxury car, for example, a sidebar may feature color and style options.

Sidebars are handy for breaking up the text to make it more scannable and inviting to read. In addition, they are also very useful for emphasizing key information that might otherwise be lost in the main body of the text.

## Pull quotes

A pull quote is a quotation from the main body of the text that is literally pulled out and emphasized. This is very common in brochures, case studies, and other longer promotional pieces. It is a very effective way to emphasize an impressive fact or customer testimonial. Most pull quotes are quotes from satisfied customers.

## Starbursts

You've seen these before in flyers, catalogs, direct-mail pieces, and other promotions. A starburst is a big star with text in the middle that seems to literally jump from the page. Because starbursts scream at the reader, it's an ideal place to feature a compelling offer, such as a special discount or free giveaway. Starbursts are also used to add a sense of urgency to the promotion: "Don't Wait! This Sales Ends Saturday."

# The Call to Action

As any salesperson will tell you, you are not going to make the sale unless you ask for the order. That's why in copywriting the call to action is so important. It is the very objective of your promotional piece!

The call to action can involve a number of things, depending on what is being sold and at what stage in the selling process the promotional piece represents:

- Request more information
- Download a brochure
- Agree to see a salesperson
- View an online demonstration
- Accept a free trial
- Ask for a free estimate or quotation
- Place an order

**ALERT!**

A call to action is more than just telling the prospect what to do next. As the copywriter—and de facto salesperson—your job is to motivate the prospect to take action. You need to inspire him or her to make the decision to fill out the form or make the call to respond to the offer.

## Start with the Objective

The way you write an effective call to action is by starting with the objective. What is it, exactly, that you want the reader to do next?

For example, if you are writing a direct-mail letter promoting a new business directory, the objective of your call to action might be to get the prospect to fill out the enclosed order form and mail or fax it back. So your call to action might be the following:

Complete and return the enclosed order form.

That's not bad. In fact, it's actually more than many promotional pieces do, some of which have no call to action at all. However, the above example isn't very motivating. What's missing? An effective call to action has these characteristics.

- It explains clearly what the reader must do to respond to the offer
- Tells the reader exactly what he or she is going to get
- It expresses, or at least implies, a major benefit
- It asks the reader to do it now, and provides a good reason why
- It says "Please"

Based on the above points, it's time to take another look at the business directory call to action:

Need a fresh crop of qualified sales leads for your business? Please complete and return the enclosed form today to activate your subscription to *Endless Leads Monthly.* Don't delay. The special price is due to expire Jan. 15th.

Does the above example meet the five conditions above?

- It clearly tells the reader how to respond: "...complete and return the enclosed form..."
- It describes what the reader is going to get: "...your subscription to *Endless Leads Monthly*..."
- What about the benefit? That's in the very first sentence: "...qualified sales leads..."
- It tells the reader to do it now ("today"), and backs this up with a good reason why: "The special price is due to expire..."
- And, of course, this call to action says "Please"

Where do you put your call to action statement? That depends on the promotion. In short pieces, like advertisements, put it at the end. In a longer promotion, such as a sales letter, it's effective to repeat the call to action more than once. However, always have one at the end.

Chapter 8

# Copywriting Mechanics

When you have a good draft of your copy written, it's a great feeling. You've done all the strategic and creative work—the heavy lifting. Now you're on the home stretch! However, sometimes that final mile can be the toughest, requiring you to deal with a myriad of nitty-gritty details that are all too easy to miss. These are the copywriting mechanics. It's tedious stuff but critical to the success of your promotional piece.

## The Last Mile

In the graphic design field there is a stage called the mechanicals. This is sometimes also referred to as prepress, although these days this word isn't particularly suitable to Web design, so the term preflight is growing in popularity. The mechanicals is that part of the design process that is all about fine-tuning the layout and images, and making sure everything will appear correctly in print or online.

What does all this have to do with copywriting? Writing copy also has its mechanicals stage. They are simply all the little things you need to do to get your draft copy from almost there to done.

Copywriting mechanicals involves proofreading, getting the facts straight, presenting your copy, getting approvals, making sure the copy fits, and numerous other little details. Most writers hate this part of the process because all the fun stuff is behind them—the creative thinking, the carefully wrought out words and phrases, the great ideas, the masterful selling job. It's like painting a room your favorite color, then having to do the tedious job of touching up the trim, cleaning the brushes, and putting everything away. Yet the job isn't complete until you do so.

## Proof Your Copy

It may seem like a no-brainer that your copy needs to be proofread. Yet it's amazing how many promotional pieces are published that are riddled with errors. (The polite term is *typos*, but there's no doubt about it that these are blunders.) Like everything else in your copy, an error communicates a message, but certainly not a very persuasive one. Rather than promoting the product or service, a misspelled word or grammatical goof up says to the reader that the company is careless.

Proofing your copy is more than just reading it over to make sure all the words are spelled correctly. (Although this is a very good start!) Proofing is a strategic exercise to make sure that the spelling, punctuation, and grammar are consistent with the overall sales message you want to convey. Think of it as similar to writing a resume. Do you really stand a chance of getting the job if you put down that you have a *bacheler's degree* when you meant *bachelor's degree?*

Never be the sole proofreader of your copy. Always have someone else check for errors as well. Why? Because you are so familiar with the text that your eyes will skip over even the most obvious mistakes. You'll swear you read "You're", only to find out later on—perhaps after the piece is published—that "Your" is a typo.

You might think that with so many people reviewing and proofing the copy it's almost impossible for an error to sneak past. Think again. An advertisement for a major restaurant once had the headline: "Whose Hungry?" That little ditty managed to get past the marketing department, ad agency, and the folks at the magazine who published the ad!

Before this book covers the specifics of proofing your copy's spelling, punctuation, and grammar, here are some important overall tips.

## Don't Proofread on the Computer Screen

Not only is it difficult to see your mistakes, but you're so used to seeing your copy in this way that you won't notice even the most obvious errors. Instead, print the copy and proofread it on paper. This will give you a fresh perspective. You'll be surprised how many typos seemingly jump off the page.

## Proofread Everything, Not Just the Main Points

Start with the headline and check all the text right to the end of the document, including contact information and phone numbers. Surprisingly, many writers neglect to proofread headlines. Not surprisingly, this is a common area where typos occur.

### *Pay Close Attention to Numbers*

Just about anything with a number in it is not only prone to errors, but it is also often overlooked during proofreading. Imagine getting a phone number wrong. That would torpedo your whole campaign. Even a decimal point in the wrong place can be catastrophic. Is the filter on the home water purifier you're writing about rated 2.10 microns or 21.0 microns? The first will get you the sale. The second will have people going thirsty rather than drink water filtered by your product.

## *Getting Down to the Nitty-Gritty*

Once you've done an overall proof, it's time to look at the three main elements of your text more closely.

### *Spelling*

Is it school busing? Or school bussing? There's quite a difference. The first is about getting your kids to school. The second is about what goes on in a high school hallway between periods!

Pay particular attention to regional variations in the spelling of certain words. If you're writing an ad that will appear in a British newspaper, then you need to know that they spell "jail" very differently. (It's gaol.) In Canada, you write someone a cheque, not a check.

The number one mistake that copywriters make is putting too much trust in their computer's spell-checker. In fact, some people rely on this feature so explicitly that they don't bother to do any further proofing. Not a good idea. Although computer spell-checkers are a wonderful tool, they are just that, a tool. They do not do all the work for you any more than accounting software will do your books. Proofing always requires a human set of eyes.

The most common typos that get missed are the homonyms (words that sound alike but mean different things). Many of these words also look alike, which makes catching these errors that much harder. Watch out for:

- its, it's
- who's, whose
- their, there, they're
- you, your, you're

Also be careful when you use the contraction *there's*. For example, "There's rules to writing great copy" is not correct. "There *are* rules to writing great copy." *There's* is not a contraction for *there are*.

Double-check personal names and product names. Early in her career, pop singer Avril Lavigne was often called April because reporters assumed that the "v" was a typo. Also pay close attention to gender. Well-known copywriter Chris Marlow is a woman. But some articles about her use *him* and *he*. Product names, too, can be easily misspelled and go unnoticed.

## *Grammar*

You're trying to win the hearts (and wallets) of customers, not the approval of your sixth-grade English teacher. However, grammar does play an important role in persuasive communications.

There is a mistaken belief among some copywriters that grammar gets in the way of crafting effective copy. "Adhering to strict grammar guidelines results in copy that is too formal and even a bit unfriendly," they say. That's not necessarily true. Understanding the rules of grammar can often help get your sales message across more effectively. The majority of grammar goofs are often those that create a lack of clarity and even confusion for the reader—hardly the ingredients of good copy.

An overview of grammar is beyond the scope of this chapter. If you'd like to learn more, pick up a copy of *The Everything Grammar and Style Book*.

### The Copywriter's Grammar Guide

Copywriters don't break the rules of grammar, though the rules are often bent a little. That's because much of copywriting is about connecting with the reader on a personal, conversational level. This is especially true in e-mails and sales letters where the copy style and tone is very much like someone talking. And people don't always follow the strict rules of grammar when they talk.

So what are the style and grammar rules that a copywriter can bend if required?

- *Using clichés.* Many people think, speak, and write in clichés. And they'll keep on doing it until the cows come home. Now that doesn't mean your copy should be riddled with them. There are times when a cliché is useful for making a particular point.
- *Sentence fragments.* It's a myth that copywriters always write in short, staccato sentences. Not true. Absolutely not. It's a lie! However, in order to maintain a conversational style and tone, sentence fragments are common. Like this one.
- *Contractions.* Copywriters use these a lot, especially in sales letters, e-mails, and other direct one-to-one communications. "You're" sounds more informal and friendly than "you are." Just don't overdo it and contract everything. Rule of thumb: Try not to use more than one contraction in a sentence.
- *Repetition.* Repetition is one of the keys to persuasion. In copywriting, the benefits, advantages, offers, call to actions, and other key messages are repeated over and over again. Just don't be tiresome. Explore new ways to say the same thing.
- *Redundancies.* How many times have you seen the phrase "free gift" in a direct-mail piece or other promotion? Isn't a gift supposed to be free? Yep. But adding the word free helps to quell the skepticism in the reader. So free gift it is.
- *Personal pronouns.* Copywriters frequently use "I," "we," and "you" to connect with prospects and customers on a more personal level. This is appropriate in direct communications, such as sales letters, telemarketing scripts, and e-mails. For brochures and Web pages, however, the tone may need to be slightly more formal.

## *Punctuation*

Punctuation is more than just periods. There are at least a dozen other punctuation marks used in the English language: commas, colons, dashes, ellipses, exclamation marks, and more.

This is another area that is not taken seriously by copywriters during the proofing process. But it should be. Here are some common punctuation mistakes and issues:

- When should you use a colon or semicolon?
- Should you put a period at the end of every bullet or just on the last one?
- Do you need a period at the end of a headline or subhead?
- Should you use an en dash or an em dash?
- Are commas used correctly?
- Is there excessive use of exclamation marks? (This is a common ailment in many promotional pieces!)

**ALERT!**

Punctuation typos are particularly difficult to miss. These little guys are small! It's easy to miss an unintentional comma in place of a period at the end of a sentence. So don't just check for typos in the words you use, look closely at your punctuation marks as well.

The most important thing is consistency. A period used to end one subhead but not the others looks like carelessness, and it is. It's for this reason alone that you should proof your document for correct use of punctuation marks as diligently as you would spelling and grammar.

## *Formatting*

Correct formatting is important. Why? Because errors and inconsistencies can easily creep into the final layout without anyone noticing. For example, one subhead in a brochure may have all the words capitalized, while the other just below it is in small caps. You don't want an oddity like that to compete with your sales message for reader attention.

Here's what Dianna Huff, author of *12 Tips To Avoiding Embarrassing And Expensive Typos*, suggests you pay particular attention to when proofing your document for formatting.

- *Subheads*: Is each word capitalized? Are there periods at the end of each? Should the subheads be numbered? Are the numbers in order?
- *Bullets*: Are all the bullets visible? Are they all the same color and size?
- *Photo captions*: Are captions italicized or roman? Are there periods at the end of the caption?
- *Pagination*: Are page numbers in order? If an article is continued on another page, is the "continued on page x" showing the correct page number?
- *Columns and margins*: Are columns and margins the same width throughout the document?
- *Font*: Does the font change or look funny anywhere in the document?
- *Extra spaces*: Look for extra spaces between words and after periods. The standard is now one space after a period, not two. (The use of two spaces creates rivers of white that are clearly visible once the document is designed.)

**FACT**

Some project types have their own formatting requirements. Press releases, as you'll discover in Chapter 13, have some very rigid rules as to how certain text elements should be placed on the page. Articles, case studies, sales letters, and other promotional pieces also have their own quirky formatting conventions.

Formatting may also be a strategic decision. You may want to indent the second paragraph of a sales letter for effect—to draw the reader's attention to it. So make sure the draft of the sales letter you send to your boss or client for review is clearly formatted in this way.

## Brand Guides and Style Guides

The company you're writing for may have a brand guide or style guide that you'll be expected to adhere to while crafting copy for their products or services. This will usually come from the marketing or public relations department, but an ad agency or major design firm may also create one of these documents for its client.

**ESSENTIAL**

Most computer programs, such as Microsoft Word, will allow you to add special words with unique formats to the dictionary database to prevent these words from being flagged as typos. This can save you a lot of time and help you to avoid errors when dealing with branded names and phrases.

A brand or style guide contains a list of rules or guidelines concerning the style and tone of the copy, as well as specific words, phrases, blurbs, and other sales messages to be used. These documents also contain information for graphic designers, including color palettes, layout templates and guidelines, and instructions on how to treat logos and other visual elements.

Here's an example of what you might find in a corporate style guide affecting copywriting:

In informal documents, such as customer letters and e-mails, the company can be referred to as "we." For more formal documents, such as press releases and corporate materials, use "the Company."

Pay particular attention to any instructions on how certain brand names need to be formatted in the text. For example, Morris Real Estate Marketing uses the term AGENT*access*. It's spelled the same way every time, with the capitalized AGENT and the italicized *access*. The two words are also grouped together as a single compound word. This is important to know because computer spell-checkers may want to pull these two words apart. And that error could easily find its way into the final layout.

If you need to follow a brand or style guide, keep it handy on your desk as you work on a project. It's easier to follow the guidelines the first time than it is to make corrections and alterations to your copy later on.

## Fact Checking

It's easy for project teams—copywriters, designers, strategists, and clients—to get enthusiastic about the features and benefits of a product, so much so that the promises and benefits can grow larger and larger without anyone noticing. Before you know it, "a leading company" becomes "the leading company." It's just a one-word difference, but it turns a factual statement into a lie.

Service companies are particularly guilty of exaggeration, as the benefits of a service can be subject to interpretation. Just how clean can a carpet cleaning company get your rugs? If the brochure says they "eliminate 95% of dust mites," is that really true? Is it just someone's estimation?

That's why you should always do a fact check before submitting your copy for review. Be the skeptic. Question every claim, promise, benefit, or statistic used in the copy. Make sure quotations from product reviews are not taken out of context. Don't use "loaded with some great features" when the reviewer actually wrote "loaded with some great features, but lacking in the most important functions."

Pay particular attention to any promises made, especially concerning the performance of the product or service. There is a legal term called "expressed warranty." It basically says that a warranty is created when you make a claim that is more than the product or service can deliver. So you may have to refund unhappy customers, regardless of what it may say in your published warranty.

# Presenting Your Copy

Now that you've checked and rechecked your copy, how do you submit it to your boss or client for review? What font type and style do you use? How do you format the headlines, subheads, and sidebars? How do you indicate your ideas for visuals?

The brand or style guide explained earlier in this chapter may have guidelines on how your text should be submitted. The company or client you're writing for may also have a preferred way that copy should be formatted. Be sure to ask. Advertising agencies usually have a set format for submitting copy to their clients for review. And they expect their employees and freelancers to follow it.

Beyond that there are really no industry standards for presenting your copy. The most important thing is clarity.

Example of copy submitted to a client:

Advertisement—Copy Draft
Headline:
Double Your Up-Time With Velocity

*Visual:*
Before and after pictures of folding carton production line: the first using the competitor's adhesive, the second with the product.

*Body copy:*
The pressure is on to ramp up production speeds while maintaining performance. This means turning downtime into uptime and making certain all process components are operating efficiently—especially the adhesive you use.

So don't get unglued with adhesives that cause rejects, gun misfires, tip buildup, throwing, and other performance-related problems. Velocity is specially designed for fast machining at line speeds up to 1,650ft/min. with clean cut off, developing a precise bead line with aggressive tack. It maintains consistent viscosity and clean machining so folding carton equipment can be run longer between clean-ups.

When it's time to open the throttle on your production line, Velocity will deliver the goods.

*Reply Form Tear-away:*
FREE Digital Demonstration:
Use this form, or call us at 1-905-XXX-XXXX, for a free video demonstration of Velocity in action.

Make sure your copy clearly indicates headlines, subheads, text boxes, pull quotes, and other key elements of the promotion. You don't want your client to be confused as to which page of a brochure or Web site a particular passage of text is intended for, or whether something is a headline or a callout.

## Permissions and Approvals

Permission means just that—a permission to use something in your promotional piece. If you interview a customer for a product success story, you should get a special permission or release form signed by that person before you use the information.

You may also need permissions to quote substantial sections of product reviews, research reports, studies, white papers, and other sources that you have used to support your product claims.

**ALERT!**

As your copy is going through the approvals process, be sure to date each new draft you prepare. Otherwise, you may not know which one is the most recent. When the final draft is finally approved, label it as *Final*. This will indicate to everyone involved that this draft is good to go.

In addition to obtaining permissions, your copy is likely going to have to get a number of approvals—and not just from your immediate boss or client. There may be approvals required from senior management and the legal department. The copy has to be signed off by all concerned before it can go into production.

# Chapter 9

# Writing Advertising Copy

Advertising copy may be relatively short when compared to other forms of marketing and publicity, but—*wow*—is it powerful. Using just a few choice words, advertising has been generating interest, changing minds, motivating buyers, and making sales for more than 150 years. Writing a successful ad requires all the skill and talent a copywriter can muster. This chapter explains what you need to make it happen.

## *Ad Writing Basics*

Advertising is expensive. It can cost you, your company, or your client hundreds or even thousands of dollars just to place a single one-time ad in a newspaper or magazine. Radio and television commercials can be even more expensive. And this is in addition to the costs of creating the ad. So the stakes are high. If the ad you write is ineffective, all that money goes down the drain. (No pressure!)

So to make sure you start off on the right foot, you need to know the basics of writing an effective advertisement.

The first thing you need to know is that there are two basic types of ads:

- Awareness or brand advertising
- Direct-response advertising

Awareness or brand advertising—also referred to as image advertising—is all about getting potential customers to remember and prefer the product. These tend to be the most clever and creative forms of advertising because they often employ humor, controversy, interesting concepts and wordplay, and other tactics to get people to think about the product in a positive way. Often there is no direct attempt to get the prospect to buy the product. This type of advertising just wants you to be aware. It's all about gaining mindshare.

**FACT**

Brand advertising often tries to associate a product or service with specific thoughts or feelings. When you see the Volvo logo, what is the first thing that comes to your mind? Probably safety. What do you think of when you hear the word *Jaguar* or see that wild cat lunging from the dashboard? Prestige.

## Brand Advertising

Brand advertising is usually created by advertising agencies and major design firms. That's because it is often a part of a major mass-advertising campaign with a huge budget. Brand advertising can also be developed for smaller businesses targeting local markets, such as pizzerias and retail stores.

## Direct-Response Advertising

The other form of advertising, direct response, works very differently. It is not concerned with lofty ideas of awareness and mindshare. The primary concern of direct-response advertising is to generate a response of some kind. This type of ad wants you to call a toll-free number, visit a store, go to a Web site, use a coupon, or clip and mail back a reply form.

So while a brand advertisement wants to *impress* you, a direct-response ad wants to *sell* you.

## Focus on the One Thing

In the Billy Crystal movie *City Slickers*, crusty old cowboy Curly says, "Want to know what life is really about? It's about one thing. That's it. Focus on that and the rest don't mean ___ ." (If you can't fill in that blank yourself, watch the movie!)

Despite the differences between a brand ad and a direct-response ad, the ultimate writing rule is always the same. You need to take Curly's advice and decide: What is the one thing that you want the reader to think or do when they see the ad? Is it to:

- Visit a store and buy the product?
- Choose your product rather than the competition's?
- Associate fun and excitement with the product name?
- Visit a Web site and register?
- Remember the product name?
- Clip the coupon integrated with the ad to take advantage of a discount?
- Form a positive impression of the product so that when a salesperson calls he'll be interested in learning more?

That's the real key to successful advertising. Focus relentlessly, exclusively, and without distraction on the one thing you want the reader to think or do, and then write the ad to accomplish that specific objective.

## Print Ads

Print ads are the oldest form of marketing. In the 1800s, copywriters would spend their entire careers writing print advertising and little else.

These days, print ads are still everywhere, in newspapers, newsletters, magazines, conference materials—virtually anything that is published in print or online. Like it or not, it's advertising that makes a lot of the materials that we read and enjoy possible.

**ESSENTIAL**

Many trade magazines—those that target professionals like plumbers and lawyers—feature a special reply card that readers can send in to receive more information on advertised products or services. So your call to action might be worded as "Call us for a free product brochure, or circle 37 on the reader services card."

The format for a print advertisement is relatively straightforward and hasn't changed much in over a century. The typical components are as follows:

- Headline
- Visual
- Body copy
- Call to action

### Ad Writing Secrets

Composing an ad is like writing a song. You want to make sure it's a hit! Too long, too soft, too boring, or too whatever and your ad won't get any airplay. People won't listen. That's what makes writing a successful ad such a challenge. Even though you may only have to come up with a headline and fifty or so words of text, it can take hours to get those words just right. You can't afford to have even one awkward sentence, uninspiring metaphor, or impotent adjective.

Here are the top tips for writing a successful print advertisement:

- *Put a benefit in your headline.* Sometimes a clever or humorous headline can be effective, but it's a gamble. For every humorous headline that does work well, there are hundreds that do not. Clever headlines often make the copywriter or agency look good—"Aren't we smart!"—but do little to sell the product. A more surefire approach to creating a winning ad is to put a benefit in the headline.
- *Make your ads easy to skim.* These days, everyone is busy, especially business people. So make it easy for readers to skim the ads and still get the message. Use bullets, subheads, bold and underlined text, and descriptive visuals to quickly communicate the key points.
- *Use customer testimonials.* These are extremely effective in ads, yet rarely used. Think about it. Your customers expect you to be biased. But they will trust their fellow customers to be impartial.
- *Focus on the customer.* As with any promotional piece, answer the reader's question: "What's in it for me?"
- *Use Y words.* An ad is no place to sound self-absorbed. Use words like "you" and "your" to describe the benefits rather than "we" or "our." For example, "You will write 50% faster" is much stronger than "Our training program improves writing productivity by 50%."
- *Spend time on the headline.* This is by far the most important component of an ad. Spend the time necessary to get it right. Brainstorm. Develop a list of possibilities. Scrutinize each one until you come up with a potential winner. The body copy and visuals may be important, but it's the headline that will often make or break your ad.
- *Be your own worse critic.* Imagine your ad on a page cluttered with other ads and articles. As the reader, ask yourself: "Would I notice and read this ad?"
- *Put a coupon in your ad.* That's what copywriting legend Bob Bly advises in his book, *Business-to-Business Direct Marketing.* "Coupons visually identify your ad as a direct response ad, causing more

people to stop and read it or at least look at the coupon to see what they can get for free."

- *Hit a home run with the body copy.* If the prospect notices the headline and starts to read your body copy, this is your chance to convince him or her to act. Give it your best shot with the most persuasive body copy you can write.

As you write the ad, try to think of a visual that will support the key messages and help make the ad better and more effective. Don't leave this up to the designer—he or she may not be knowledgeable in print advertising and may mistakenly use a visual that competes with rather than complements your key messages. The best visuals illustrate the benefit in some way.

## *Advertorials*

Have you ever read an article in a magazine or newspaper only to discover that you are actually reading an advertisement in disguise? Welcome to the world of advertorials! An advertorial is an advertisement written and designed to mimic the editorial in a magazine or newspaper. It's a combination of *adver*tisement and edi*torial*, hence adver-torial.

**FACT**

Most reputable publications clearly identify advertorials as such. Often you'll see the words "advertisement," "advertising supplement," or "sponsored section" on the top of the page or section. In addition, some publications also insist that advertorials be set in a different typeface and layout style to further distinguish it from the main editorial.

Because it appears to be an article, readers assume it contains useful information—and the best usually do—which is why advertorials tend to have a much higher readership than traditional advertising.

That doesn't mean that advertorials are any less sales oriented. They do need to get results in terms of leads and sales. But advertorials tend to explain rather than pitch, which makes this approach seem softer and less "hard sell" than traditional ads.

## Writing Strategies

An advertorial can be any size, from a fraction of a page to several pages (as part of a special advertising supplement). Here are some useful advertorial writing tips:

- *Write it in article format.* Don't make it sound like an ad or a sales letter. An advertorial should be interesting and informative; just what you'd expect from any other article.
- *Read the publication.* Unless the guidelines forbid this, write the advertorial in the same style, tone, and format as the publication it will be published in.
- *Use success stories.* Case studies and product success stories work extremely well as advertorials.
- *"How to" tips work well.* Any practical strategies that the reader can use to solve problems, make decisions, do his or her job better, make more money, or achieve specific objectives are very effective.
- *Use quotes.* Instead of just explaining problems and the products and services that solve them, convey this information in quotes from key people in the company or from customers. For example: "'Upgrade burnout is a serious issue among software users,' says John Smith, Director of User Documentation. 'That's why we now include six training DVDs that make it easy to…'"
- *Don't forget the "ad" in advertorial.* It may look like an article, but it isn't. So close with a strong call to action—ideally a compelling offer—that motivates the reader to take the next step.

The toughest part of writing an advertorial is striking the right balance between providing useful information—the editorial part—and carefully weaving in the sales messages—the advertising part. Too far on the editorial side and the advertorial won't do its selling job. Too far toward the advertising side and readers will be turned off and won't read it at all.

# Classifieds

Writing a classified ad is tricky because you have so few words available to you. Most publications severely restrict the space allowed for classified ads, or charge extra fees if your copy requires an additional line. So writing concisely is the rule.

You may wonder why classified ads even work. After all, they are usually buried at the back of a magazine or in the special section of a newspaper. Often there aren't even any interesting articles placed near them, as with larger display ads. So who reads the classifieds?

The answer is why classifieds can be so darn effective. The people who read them are either looking for something (which makes them great prospects) or love to shop (which also makes them great prospects!). Although not as many readers will see a particular classified compared to regular ads in the same publication, those who do are in buying mode.

## Ready to Buy

Most people who read the classifieds are looking for something—a used car, computer network components, home business opportunities, copywriting services! So your headline should make it easy for them to find you. That's why a classified ad headline isn't the place to be cryptic or clever. If the reader is looking for something specific, you want your headline to be like a person jumping up and down waving "Here I am!"

The proven headline writing formula for classifieds? State what you sell and one key benefit.

That's why simple headlines often work best in classifieds. If someone is looking for used filing cabinets, an ad that says "Used Filing Cabinets. Free Delivery" is going to get attention.

## The Coffee Shop Technique

Perhaps the best way to write a winning classified ad is by using the coffee shop technique. Here's how it works: Imagine you're at a coffee shop, and you happen to overhear a conversion from the table next to you. Judging by what is being said, someone is looking for your particular type of product. You have just once chance to go up to that person and make your pitch—in twenty-five words or less. What would you say? Your answer could possibly make a great classified ad.

To keep the copy tight, copywriters often use words, sentence fragments, short forms, and acronyms to keep the word count down. For example: "Have a great nite's sleep w/porta-pillow. Fits into purse/pocket. Grt for travel." This is fine, so long as it can still be interpreted and make sense. You don't want your ad to seem nonsensical.

## Billboards

Drive in any major city in America, or even along some less populated side roads, and you're bound to encounter several billboard advertisements. These are often produced on large rectangle boards. The most common sizes are 14" × 48", 12" × 24", and 5" × 11". However, there are many variations.

In addition, advertising that you see at bus shelters, subway stops, shopping malls, and other places frequented by the general public can also be considered billboards.

Billboard advertising is most suited to businesses that have a broad customer base, such as car dealerships, pharmacies, and major retail stores. This type of advertising is used to reach as many potential customers as possible. And what better way than to catch them while driving or walking somewhere!

The most important thing to consider when writing a billboard ad is that people are usually moving past it—trying to get somewhere. So you only have time to persuade them with a few words at most. That's why a captivating headline and strong supporting visual is so important. Body copy is rarely used.

The objective of a billboard ad is to get people to remember the product or service. You want to make a lasting impression, typically with a strong enticing benefit. For example: "Kids Eat Free At Danny's Pizzeria!"

**FACT**

In the industry, billboards are grouped under the category of outdoor advertising. The reason is obvious. Most (but not all) billboards are located outdoors, usually along busy highways and pedestrian walkways. You can also find billboards inside airports, in sports stadiums, and at other large indoor facilities where people gather and become a captive audience for the advertiser.

## Radio Spots

What do more than 80 percent of commuters do when they travel to work each day? They listen to the radio! It's an ideal target audience. No wonder such a wide range of businesses advertise using this medium—pitching everything from investment advice, gardening products, software upgrades, the latest movies, business consulting services, and even industrial fittings!

Radio advertising is often written by freelancers who specialize in this area, as well as staff writers at ad agencies and at the radio stations themselves.

The average ad is usually ten to thirty seconds long. So you have to make every word count. Even in a thirty-second spot with a fast-talking announcer, the maximum is only about one hundred words.

### Types of Radio Spots

The simplest radio commercial to write is the announcer spot. This is essentially a person reading from a script, with little if any sound effects or interaction with anyone else. The announcer can be:

- An actor, actress, or professional voice
- An on-air personality at the radio station who agrees to do the commercial, usually for a fee
- A spokesperson from the company placing the ad, such as the company president

At the other end of the spectrum is the multicharacter radio ad. This is a lot like a television commercial in its complexity in that it involves actors, dialogue, and scenes. For example, a radio commercial for a holiday resort might feature a husband asking a wife where to book their summer vacation. "Let's drive to Delawana Resort. It's just two hours away. And I just found out that if we book before May 15th, we get 25% off!"

## Writing for the Ear

If you're used to print communications—brochures, Web pages, sales letters—then writing a radio advertising script can be a challenge. Although the basic elements of persuasive writing covered in Chapter 5 still apply, the format is very different. For example, there's no headline!

Unlike a printed piece, the listener can't go back and read something he didn't understand the first time. So you have to clearly and memorably convey your sales message. Here are some tips for doing just that:

- *Use an easy-to-remember phone number or Web address.* A radio listener may not be able to write anything down, especially if he or she is in a car. So instead of saying 1-800-742-5877 say 1-800-PICK-UPS.
- *Use directions instead of street addresses.* If your radio ad is for a local business, people will remember the intersection or other milestone location more so than the actual street address. Don't say "1254 Jamieson Street West." Say "on the corner of Jamieson and Oak."
- *Don't give too much information.* Provide one or two bite-size nuggets at most. People are probably working or driving when they hear your spot; they don't need to be too distracted.
- *Mention your most important message,* such as the business name, phone number, Web address, or special offer at least twice during the commercial—in the middle and at the end.

Be sure to read your script out loud. Make sure it sounds natural and does not run over the allotted time. If possible, also read it to other people. Ask them if they understand it the first time. If they don't, rewrite it.

# Audio-Visual Advertisements

Audio-visual advertisements include television commercials, Web page video ads, ads featured at the beginning of a video or DVD, video billboards, and any other type of advertising that uses sounds and images.

There's a lot of glamour that surrounds television commercials. Most copywriters who begin as junior scribes at advertising agencies dream of the day when they will be writing and producing commercials for the Super Bowl. In fact, a television commercial is considered the most prestigious assignment in all of advertising. It is the top of the ad agency mountain.

Commercials are almost always written by advertising agencies and other creative firms that specialize in broadcast media. However, sometimes freelance copywriters and staff writers at companies also get involved.

**FACT**

A *super* is a title or caption superimposed over a picture. It's used to strengthen the sales message by displaying additional information not spoken in the narration or dialogue. For example, "Order now. Operators are standing by."

Commercials and other audio-visual advertisements can range from simple and straightforward, such as an announcer holding up a product while explaining why you should buy it, to fast-paced stories with all the flash and pizzazz of a major Hollywood feature film!

Writing audio-visual scripts can be challenging but a lot of fun too. It is enormously satisfying to watch actors or spokespeople speaking words that you wrote—in scenes that originated in your own imagination.

## Getting the Format Right

The three basic television commercial lengths are ten, thirty, and sixty seconds. Lengths for other audio-visual media vary. An Internet banner video, for example, can be as short as five seconds.

What does a television commercial script look like? The format is a page with two columns: VIDEO (what you see) described on the left, and AUDIO (what you hear) on the right. Usually each scene is numbered. So there could be one, five, or even twenty scenes for a single commercial. (The more scenes that need to be shot, the higher the productions costs tend to be.)

## Scripting Tips

Audio-visual ads give you a lot of elbowroom for creativity. You're not restricted to just words. You can write sounds, images, scenes, and even a character's facial expressions. But don't forget that your primary objective is to sell something! Here are techniques you can use to create a compelling script:

- *Take advantage of the visuals to help deliver your sales message.* Don't use adjectives and expressive prose to describe how great the chicken tastes. Instead, show a family at dinnertime enjoying the food.
- *Viewers can only take so much audio and visual at one time.* So if your commercial depends on a lot of strong visuals, keep the words to a minimum. Conversely, if you need a lot of words to convey your selling message, keep the pictures simple.
- *What happens when a commercial comes on TV?* It's break time! Someone runs to the bathroom or goes to the kitchen to get a snack. So make sure your commercial is interesting and important enough to gain and hold your customer's attention.
- *If you're writing a video for a Web page banner ad, keep in mind that the customer may not be able to hear it.* He might have his computer sound turned down or off. So be sure the key messages can be conveyed solely with the pictures or captions.
- *Use all the elements at your disposal*—sound, visuals, words, dialogue. If you show pancakes simmering on the grill, make sure the viewer can also hear them crackle.

- *As with radio spots, repeat the product name, company, or offer at least twice*—once in the middle and again at the end.
- *Audio-visual commercials have an advantage over print communications.* They allow you to show and sometimes even demonstrate the benefits of the product. So don't just say how well a contracting company builds a deck. Show a deck being built, with professional tradespeople in nice, clean uniforms!

The budget plays a huge role in how you write a commercial. If the budget is just a few thousand dollars, it's doubtful you'll be able to have multiple characters in exotic locales driving prestigious cars in a spy scenario. So your James Bond theme will have to be downsized a little!

# Chapter 10
# **Writing Direct Marketing Copy**

Direct marketing is one of the highest-paid specialties in the copywriting field. And for good reason! If you write a sales letter, catalog item, or telemarketing script that actually generates sales, you're making money for your company or client. It's like being a salesperson at the keyboard. However, convincing customers to buy using just your words isn't easy. This chapter gives you all the basics, plus many inside secrets too.

## Sales Letters That Sizzle

You've probably heard the expression "Don't sell the steak, sell the sizzle." It was first coined by Elmer Wheeler, one of the greatest sales professionals of the 1940s. In the 1970s, another great steak salesman, Hershchell Gordon Lewis (he wrote direct-mail promotions for Omaha Steak Company), rejiggered the phrase to "Sales letters that sizzle."

A sales letter doesn't have to be about steaks for this adage to be appropriate. Selling the sizzle—or the benefits—is one of the fundamental principles of any successful promotion.

**FACT**

The sales letter is the cornerstone of many direct-mail campaigns. Even postcards, self-mailers, catalogs, and elaborate 3-D packages often incorporate a letter or personal message of some kind. That's why mastering letter writing is a requirement for anyone writing in the direct marketing field.

## A Timeless Format

The enduring power of the sales letter is astonishing. It has been used in advertising and sales since the early 1800s. And today, despite the proliferation of electronic communications, the old-fashioned sales letter is used more than ever, with hardly a change in its basic format. We may not receive that many personal letters from friends and family anymore, but people who want our business certainly haven't stopped writing to us!

In addition to what you would expect to see in a personal correspondence—a salutation ("Dear Jane"), body copy, a signature ("Sincerely yours")—a sales letter can also utilize elements used in other marketing materials, such as headlines, reply forms, text boxes, starbursts, picture captions, and more. But be careful. A big mistake that some marketers make is getting carried away and creating a sales letter that looks more like a brochure than a personal communication.

## *How to Write It*

Sales letters are the most personal and direct form of copywriting. Remember, it starts by calling the prospect or customer "Dear"! For your letter to be effective, the style and tone must be that of one person writing to another.

Always use a postscript (P.S.) in your sales letters. A P.S. stands out in a letter; it almost always gets read. So use a P.S. to highlight an additional benefit, sweeten the deal with a free gift or other give away, create urgency with a deadline, or reinforce a guarantee.

That's the best way to craft a letter: Create a picture of your ideal prospect in your mind, and then write directly to that person. Here is an example of a sales letter written by master copywriter Ivan Levison for one of his clients, a freelance graphic designer.

**Profit-building art direction and design are just a stone's throw away**

Dear <name>:
Who should design your next direct mail piece, advertisement, HTML, e-mail, or brochure?

You could choose a top-of-the-line, full-service graphics design firm. Sure they do nice work, but they also charge outrageous prices. (Hey. Someone has to pay for the espresso machine and the Creative Director's cool sunglasses!)

Let me suggest a far better alternative.

Me.

I'm a freelance graphic designer who's been producing direct mail, ads, brochures, and lots more for over twenty-five years. For clients like Lucent, Fujitsu, and Symbol Technologies.

My home office is located extremely close to your office and I have a knockout portfolio that I'd love to show you.

Give me a call at <phone number> and let's set up a meeting to discuss your next marketing piece. Or pick up the phone and just say hello. If I don't hear from you, I'll take the liberty of giving you a call on Thursday.

Isn't it time you discovered what Adobe, Intel, Hewlett-Packard, and Sybase have already learned?

That high-impact art direction and graphics design are just a stone's throw away.

Sincerely,

Notice how the opening grabs your attention? This is one of the toughest parts of a letter: the beginning. It's also the most crucial. After all, if you don't capture the reader's interest within the first few sentences, then your letter will quickly be thrown in the trash with all the other junk mail.

Here are some great ideas that will help:

### Ten Ways to Start a Sales Letter

- *State the free offer upfront.* "Free Investment Calculator when you renew your subscription today."
- *Make an announcement.* "Our going out of business sale ends this Saturday."
- *Tell a captivating story.* "When she hung up the phone she knew she could never make a humiliating cold call again."
- *Cite a fascinating fact or statistic.* "Life expectancy in America is predicted to increase 15 years within the next decade. Are your retirement savings going to be enough?"
- *Flatter the reader.* "Our research tells us you're one of the top teaching professors in the country."
- *Write to the reader as a peer.* "If you're like me, golfing is more than just a passion."
- *A personal message from the president.* "This is my personal invitation to join me for a breakthrough training program."
- *Ask a question.* "Are you struggling to attract enough clients?"
- *Identify with the reader.* "If you're like me, you don't trust anything that even remotely smells like a get-rich-quite scheme."
- *Solve a problem.* "Here are 6 sure-fire ways to reach your sales quota this quarter."

- *Highlight the benefit.* "How to reduce your shipping costs by 22% or more."
- *Make an invitation.* "You're invited to attend a free teleclass."

If you decide to use a headline at the top of your sales letter—and in most cases you should—it may work well as an attention grabber. However, you still need to make the opening sentences just as captivating.

## Letter Writing Tips from the Masters

There are hundreds of tips for writing effective sales letters. Here are the ones that professional copywriters rely on most to get results.

- Write to one person, not to a group.
- Make it personal. Use the word "you," even in business-to-business letters.
- Put your strongest selling points up front within the first two or three paragraphs.
- Use bullets when there are lots of key benefits to convey.
- Avoid technical jargon unless you're sure the reader will understand it.
- Don't try to warm up or tease the reader in the opening paragraphs. Get to the key points of your sales message right away.
- Keep paragraphs short. It's okay to use single-line or even single-word paragraphs. (As in the example sales letter from the graphic designer.)
- Don't ask questions that require the reader to respond with a no.
- You can't change a reader's mind with a sales letter. For example, you can't persuade someone to like golf. Instead, assume the reader is a golfing enthusiast when you pitch your "Swing Doctor" training video.
- Keep the copy tight and easy–to-read. One rambling or convoluted paragraph can act like a roadblock that stops the reader from going any further.
- Keep your letter focused on one overall sales message. Don't introduce other products, services, or even accessories.

These tips are in addition to the lessons you learned elsewhere in this book on effective copywriting, especially those strategies featured in Chapters 5 and 6.

How do you end a letter? That's the easiest part. Always close a letter in the same way: with a strong, motivating call to action. If the sales letter is promoting a new car, you might say, "Call your local dealership within 7 days to reserve your test drive, and you'll receive a $500 discount certificate." If your letter is trying to get magazine subscribers to renew, you might close with, "Renew today. This 65% discount offer won't last long."

## The Classic Direct-Mail Package

An envelope arrives for you in the mail. You open it. Inside is a letter asking you to take advantage of a new credit card (Hey, you're pre-approved!) and a reply form. Welcome to the classic direct-mail package!

It's called classic because this format has been the workhorse of direct-mail for more than a century. The majority of direct-mail packages consist simply of a sales letter inside of an envelope, sometimes with other elements added to the mix, such as an order form and brochure.

In the direct-marketing industry, this classic direct-mail format is also referred to as an envelope mailing to distinguish it from postcards and other self-mailers.

Following is a tour of a simple direct-mail package featuring an envelope, letter, and reply element.

### The Envelope Please

In North America, envelopes used in direct mail come in a variety of standard and nonstandard sizes. Everything from the #10 (4 ⅛" × 9½") envelope that most bills are mailed to you in to large #13 (10" × 13") envelopes that you can fit a large brochure into, plus dozens of more sizes. There is also an endless array of envelope options, including windows, flaps, and even special effects like peel-away stickers that reveal a hidden message underneath.

### To Tease or Not to Tease?

Your most important decision as a direct-mail copywriter is whether to put promotional copy on the envelope. Envelope copy—referred to in the industry as the teaser—is used to motivate the prospect to open the envelope. The advantage of using a teaser is that it gives you the opportunity to pique the reader's interest as to what's inside. You can tell him that "Your discount certificate is enclosed," or "Inside: The truth about dust mites and your vacuum cleaner." The disadvantage is that you tip your hand. Once you put a teaser on the envelope, the prospect knows full well that it's a promotional piece of some kind. So your mailing might end up in the trash unopened, no matter how compelling your envelope message is. That's why the teaser has to be very effective.

The purpose of a teaser is not just to get the envelope opened. It must also set the stage for what's inside. Ideally, you want the prospect to open the envelope eager to read or at least scan through the contents. If the teaser is not logically connected to what's inside, the envelope might get opened, but the contents may not get read.

You don't have to have a teaser on the envelope. Direct-mail marketers will often test a plain envelope against one with teaser copy to find out which works better for their particular promotion.

A plain envelope is also referred to in the industry as a white envelope mailing. It works because it looks like any other personal or business correspondence.

### Envelope Copy Tips

If you're going to use a teaser on the envelope, here are some proven strategies:

- Remind the reader he or she is a customer. "Important for *IT Insights* subscribers."
- Ask a provocative question. "Do you close the bathroom door even when you're the only one home?" This is a famous teaser written by legendary copywriter Bill Jaymie.
- State your free offer. "Get two months of *Psychology Today* free."
- Start a story. "I was literally one day from declaring bankruptcy until I learned this incredibly fast and simple way to make money on the Internet."
- Sometimes an odd shape, custom-cut window, or nonstandard size can also get the envelope opened. However, this can drive up the cost of a mailing considerably.

## The Reply Element

A reply element is that part of the mailing that the reader uses to reply to the offer. It can be as elaborate as a detailed order form with a postage-paid envelope attached or as simple as a telephone number.

When writing a reply element for a direct-mail piece, follow these tips:

- *Eliminate guesswork.* Explain completely and clearly what the prospect has to do to reply to the offer.
- *Make it easy.* If you're using a reply card or envelope, make sure that the postage is prepaid. Provide a 1-800 number for faster service. If possible, have the reply card already filled in with the prospect's name and address.
- *Provide multiple ways to respond.* Not everyone will be comfortable filling out an order form on the Internet. If possible, include other options, such as a toll-free number or paper order form that can be mailed or faxed.
- *If there's room, summarize the most important benefits on the reply form.* "Here's your chance to save 50% on your next vacation at the Delawana Resort, if you book today."

- *Make it urgent.* Give the prospect a compelling reason to act now. "Please return this order form by July 16 to take advantage of the early bird discount."
- *Put a benefit in the confirmation line.* That's the line in the copy next to the checkbox. "Yes! I want to learn how to make $1,000 per day writing for the case study market. Please send me the handbook right away."

A reply form doesn't have to be a separate piece in the mailing. It can also be integrated with the sales letter as a perfed tear-away at the bottom or top. This is often a very effective technique as it allows the prospect to read the letter and respond to the offer without any interruption in the sales message.

## Dimensional Mailers

Remember when you were a kid and you received a parcel in the mail? You couldn't wait to find out what was inside. With your eyes wide with anticipation, you eagerly peeled away the wrapping paper and opened the box.

That feeling of anticipation never leaves us as grownups. We still get excited when we receive a box in the mail. Even when we're fairly certain it's a promotion of some kind, we open it up anyway. It's irresistible.

And that's the reason why dimensional mailers—boxes, tubes, and even tin cans!—work so well in direct-mail marketing. Unlike an envelope, a dimensional mailing can achieve nearly a 100 percent open rate. And that's not all. According to a 1993 study by Baylor University, dimensional mailers can significantly improve direct-mail response rates.

Dimensional mailers can certainly generate a lot of buzz and excitement. If you open a box and a cutout picture of a hammer jumps out like a jack-in-the-box with the message, "Let's hammer out a better deal for your corporate cell phones!" it gets your attention.

## *The Same Rules Apply*

Just because a dimensional mailer may have a lot of pop-ups, gimmicks, and other bells and whistles doesn't mean that the established rules of copywriting go out the window. A box may indeed gain attention, but the message you craft for the inside components still must sell the prospect. Most dimensional mailers include standard elements found in most envelope mailings: a sales letter and a reply form.

**QUESTION?**

**If they work so well, why aren't dimensional mailers used more often?**
In a word: costs. A direct-mail package sent in a box or other 3-D carrier is very expensive to create and mail. Imagine the costs of putting together a box that pops up when it is opened! That's why dimensional mailers are used only for very small lists, or when the value of the sales generated is large enough to justify the cost of the mailing.

## *Postcards and Other Self-Mailers*

As the name implies, self-mailers mail themselves. No envelope is required. They come in a variety of standard formats:

- *Postcard.*
- *Double postcard.* Contains a second card, usually acting as the reply form, which can be perfed off and mailed back.
- *Card deck.* This is a stack of postcards bundled together in a single mailing.
- *Self-mailer.* This is often a single page, folded twice and sealed at one end. However, there are many variations.
- *Snap-pak.* This is a mailing with the outer component sealed at the edges, doing double-duty as the envelope. The customer perfs off the edges to open the package and get at the inside components.

Unlike an envelope mailing, there is no chance of fooling the prospect into thinking your correspondence is personal or general business mail. The instant he sees a self-mailer he knows it's promotional. So it is more important than ever to make sure your copy tantalizes and persuades.

**ALERT!**

Space is limited when writing copy for a self-mailer. A postcard can only hold the equivalent of a half page of copy at the very most. So every word has to count. That's why the best self-mailers start strong and stay strong. As songwriter and singer Sting says about writing rock music, "You have to burn from the very first bar."

## How to Write It

When crafting a self-mailer, one of the most effective techniques is the problem-solution model. You simply state the problem that the prospect might be having, and then quickly follow that up with the solution. Then you immediately instruct the reader how to respond. Here are a few examples:

Got the winter blahs? Win a free holiday vacation in the sun!
Struggling to get clients? Enroll now in the marketing coaching program.
Want to save on your spring wardrobe? Get 50% off this weekend.

Here are some other proven tips for crafting a winning self-mailer.

- Don't cram in too much information. Stay focused on one clear sales message.
- In a folded self-mailer, consider writing the inside panels like a sales letter.
- If appropriate, use photos or other visuals to illustrate or dramatize your message.
- Take the time to create a powerful headline. It's your best means of gaining attention.
- Make the copy scannable. Use plenty of headers, bolds, underlines, and text boxes.

One of the most challenging aspects of writing a self-mailer is keeping the copy short enough to fit the requirements of the piece yet still convey enough information to persuade the prospect to act. In this respect a self-mailer is a lot like a print advertisement. You have to make optimum use of limited space.

## Catalogs

Catalogs have been around a lot longer than most people suspect. In her book *Write On Target*, author and famed copywriter Donna Baier Stein claims that an English gardener named William Lucas issued one as early at 1667. And gardening catalogs are still all the rage today.

Thousands of catalogs are published each year targeting both consumers and business people. They also flourish on the Internet, as the success of Amazon.com proves.

**FACT**

A catalog can be as short as a two-page flyer or as thick as a five-pound volume with hundreds of pages. It traditionally features a collection of products that can be ordered through the mail, by fax, by phone, or on the Internet.

Although there are a few general-purpose catalogs that promote personal and household items to a mass market, most catalogs these days are created for specialty audiences, such as business people, tradespeople, and hobbyists.

### The Copywriter's Role

The cornerstone of great catalog copy is the item description. This is what sells the product. If the description is weak and uninspiring, readers may not place an order.

The challenge is you don't have much room. A typical catalog page can feature five to ten products, even more. So you only have a paragraph or two at most to persuade the reader to purchase the item. That's in addition to explaining the necessary product features, such as sizes, colors available, pricing, and other characteristics.

Here are the top tips for crafting effective catalog copy:

- Tell the reader exactly what they are going to get. Pictures don't necessarily tell the whole story. Be exact with product descriptions. What's the size? What are the technical specifications? Which components are included? How is it shipped? Is assembly required? What colors does it come in? Can it be customized?
- Make the information easy to find. Use large headlines for major sections, smaller headers for categories.
- Consider including a president's letter at the opening of the catalog. This builds credibility, which is especially important when the catalog is from an unfamiliar company.
- State the guarantee loud and clear. Show how sending back the order form or ordering online is virtually risk free.
- Make the copy interesting to read. Most catalog copy is dull.
- Include lots of product details. Consumers, and especially business people, will often use a catalog as a reference.

Here's an example of typical catalog item copy:

**Father's Day Special!**
Magellan Meridian Platinum Portable GPS
Whether he boats, sails, or paddles, dad will never get lost with this rugged handheld GPS system. Using advanced satellite technology, the Meridian Platinum displays your exact position—on water or on land—on a built-in background map. The large, bright viewing screen is squint-free in just about any weather condition. And if dad accidentally drops it in the water, this GPS is waterproof and floats!

## Don't Forget to Be Persuasive

It's easy to settle for merely describing the product and letting the reader draw his own conclusions about the benefits. That's a mistake made in many catalogs. Don't settle for bland copy, even if you're confident that the picture will do the selling for you. It might not. In the space you have available, craft the most persuasive copy you can.

# *Telemarketing Scripts*

Just as you sit down for dinner the phone rings. Yep. It's one of those annoying telemarketing calls! Someone wants you to switch phone companies, donate to a charity, or buy insurance. Usually you can't wait to get the salesperson off the phone. But sometimes the offer interests you, and you buy.

Business people get these calls, too. Telemarketers (in business-to-business marketing, the industry prefers the term *teleselling*) are continually trying to persuade them to schedule a sales presentation, buy a directory, agree to visit a trade show booth, sign up for a seminar, or respond to any number of campaign objectives.

Teleselling is one of the most effective ways to reach prospects. It may be annoying to some people, but the technique works.

Unfortunately, one of the reasons that telemarketing has gotten such a bad rap is that the telemarketing scripts—sometimes called *guides*—are often poorly written. That's where you, the copywriter, come in.

The good news is there are proven techniques to putting together an effective telemarketing script that:

- Minimizes the number of people who get annoyed when they receive the call
- Gets the desired results

**ESSENTIAL**

In business-to-business telemarketing, a gatekeeper is a person, often a receptionist or assistant, who attempts to screen a call. He or she may ask questions like: "Which company are you from? What is the purpose of your call? May I take a message?" Telemarketers will try to get past the gatekeeper and talk to the prospect directly.

## *Be Ready for Anything*

You normally have to write more than one version of a telemarketing script. That's because you never know who's going to answer the phone. What if the telemarketing campaign is to make people aware of a sale at a ladies' fashion boutique—and a husband answers the phone? Your script will need to include a section on how to handle this situation.

Forget everything you learned from those dinner-hour telemarketing calls. A successful telemarketing script has the following characteristics:

- Friendly, courteous, and conversational
- Never pushy and aggressive
- Short and to the point
- Clearly identifies who is calling and why
- Leaves the prospect with a good impression, even if he or she doesn't buy
- Conveys an enticing offer
- Clearly tells the prospect what do to next

Here is an example of a very simple telephone script. This one invites prospects to a Web seminar (Webinar) as part of an overall lead-generation campaign:

"Hi [contact name], this is Jane Doe calling on behalf of ABC Company.

"The reason for my call is to inform you of a 20-minute Webinar we're sponsoring called The Future of Loss Payee Notification. It features how companies like Permanent General Insurance and Tower Hill Insurance Group are reducing costs by 50% while virtually eliminating risks. The Webinar is hosted by Dr. John Smith, a recognized expert in the field.

"[contact name], I'd like to e-mail you an invitation to this FREE Webinar. Would that be okay with you?"

If Yes:
    "Thank you. What is your e-mail address?"
If No:
    "Is there someone else in your company we should be talking to?"

## *Scripting Techniques*

When writing a telemarketing script, follow these guidelines:

- *Write for the ear, not the eye.* Your script must sound natural and spontaneous. Have a friend read it back to you, preferably over the phone. If it seems like a canned sales pitch, rewrite it.
- *Soften your tone.* "Mr. Prospect. I'm calling to ask if you want to double your department's productivity in just 60 days. Guaranteed." This may work in a sales letter, but on the phone you'll quickly hear the dial tone. A better opening: "Mr. Prospect. I'm calling because we've recently helped ABC Company double the productivity of their accounting department. May I ask you three quick questions to help determine if we can do the same for you too?"
- *Suggest, don't ask.* Use the word "suggest" when wording your call to action. For example, "If you're interested in learning more, may I suggest that you go to our Web site and download our latest free White Paper."
- *Use the words "I'm just curious."* For example, "John, I'm just curious. How many employees do you have in your accounting department?" For some reason putting "I'm just curious" in front of what otherwise might be considered an impertinent question tends to get a friendly answer.
- *If possible, make reference to other known companies.* This builds credibility. "John, we recently implemented this solution at XYZ Company here in Chicago. And their productivity soared 24% within three months."
- *Keep it short.* Write in chunks. Prospects get frustrated and tune out when a telemarketing call is a long-winded sales pitch. Most people will just hang up.

One final note. Make your script easy to read and deliver. Remove any hard-to-pronounce words or difficult passages. You never know the level of experience a telemarketer who is using your script will have. It's your job to craft words that work effectively, no matter who may be speaking them.

Chapter 11
# Writing Internet Copy

Less than two decades ago, few marketing or publicity professionals knew the Internet even existed. Today, the Web plays a huge role in the communications of just about every kind of organization. Many companies, like Amazon.com, wouldn't even exist outside the online world. As a copywriter, you'll be writing many Internet-specific projects, such as Web pages, banner ads, e-zines, blogs, and more. This chapter shows you how.

# Web Sites

Web sites are so commonplace today that they require very little, if any, explanation. Most people will know what you mean when if you say you're copywriting for a dot-com. This is incredible given the fact that Web sites were completely unknown to most people just a couple of decades ago. Yet, at any given time today, millions of people are visiting Web sites to buy things, book vacations, download information, request information, read, research, and even watch videos.

A company without an effective Web site is at a serious competitive disadvantage. In fact, the first thing that business buyers often do when they want to learn more about a product or service is look on the Internet. Consumers do the same thing. Need some knitting supplies? Just type in what you're looking for into a search engine. In all likelihood there is a Web site, perhaps several, that will cater to your needs.

## Writing for the Computer Screen

Capturing and holding reader attention on a Web page or site is much more difficult than it is in print communications. That's because it's so easy to click away from a Web page. So your toughest job is to make the copy current, relevant, informative, and interesting.

There are many types of pages you may be asked to write for a commercial Web site. These include:

- *Front page.* This is the first page a visitor sees when he or she visits the site.
- *Product or service page.* This is the page or section that describes the products or services in detail.
- *Transaction page.* This is the page or section where a visitor can place an order or request more information.
- *Company page.* This is the page or section that provides information on the company. It often includes historical information, management biographies, company news, and more. This is the online equivalent of a corporate brochure. (See Chapter 15.)

- *Other pages.* There may be several other pages and sections of a commercial Web site used to convey needed information, such as technical specifications, store locations, customer service information, and FAQs.
- *Contact us.* As the name implies, this is the page visitors' click to when they need phone numbers, addresses, and other contact information on the company.

## Rolling Out the Welcome Mat

The front page is by far the most important on a commercial Web site. If it doesn't gain attention and motivate visitors to click around, explore, shop, download—whatever the objective is—then the whole site fails.

Perhaps the biggest mistake that writers make on a home page is focusing too much on the company and its products and not enough on the customer. Here is an example of the front page of a commercial Web site that is very effective, simply because it is so customer focused.

Imagine a future of certainty and success
Working exclusively with past clients and referrals!
Welcome to Morris Real Estate Marketing Group
Specialists in Referral & Repeat Marketing
We understand the challenges you face:

- Mass advertising costs are increasing, while their effectiveness is decreasing.
- Geographic farming is unpredictable, competitive, and also very expensive.
- Cold calling is tough to do, and does little to elevate your professional stature.
- New privacy guidelines and Do-Not-Call legislation are making things even more difficult.
- Trying to beat the stampede to potential new listings is humiliating and unproductive.
- Too many of the leads you're getting end up being a complete waste of time.

- You want more referrals and repeat business, but don't know exactly what to do to make that happen.
- Producing and distributing your own marketing materials is a time-consuming hassle.
- You want to do the "little things" to build client loyalty and referrals, but you just don't have the time.
- You feel guilty about losing contact with past clients and you don't know how to rekindle the relationship.
- Marketing-related activities are robbing you of valuable time.
- You have to work hard to get sales—too hard—and wonder if that will ever change.

There must be a better way. And there is.

At Morris Real Estate Marketing Group, we help build your business in the same way lawyers, accountants, doctors, and other successful professionals build theirs—through referrals and repeat clients.

Want to substantially increase your referral and repeat business?

Explore this site to learn more. And, if you have any questions, contact us anytime.

Another often neglected section of a commercial Web site is the Contact Us page. When a prospect clicks to the contact page, that's the online equivalent of someone in a retail store trying to find a salesperson. She has a question, needs information, or wants to buy. So make your copy more motivating than simply displaying a phone number and address.

Here's an example of an effective contact page:

Let's Talk!

Now that you're interested in making the commitment to growing your referral and repeat business, contact us for a no-cost, no-obligation initial phone meeting:

- Call us at 1-905-XXX-XXXX, or
- Submit the online form below and we will call you.

Our aim in the initial phone meeting is to learn more about your business development goals and assess how we may be able to help.

Ready to get started? Contact us today!

## Web Site Writing Essentials

Here are some additional tips for writing an effective commercial Web site.

- *Focus on the objectives.* What is the Web page trying to do? Generate leads? Handle customer service? Provide information? Sell a product? Whatever the objective is, focus your copy on achieving it.
- *Use lots of headers.* Great headlines and subheads are the real secret to success in writing for the Web.
- *Use short paragraphs.* No more than five or six lines each. It's difficult to read large chunks of copy on screen.

It's also important to keep things current on a Web page. Information ages fast on the Net. If you're using a 1997 statistic to prove a product claim, even if that statistic is still relevant, try to replace it with something more up-to-date. The Internet is evolving so quickly that users tend not to trust information that is even just a couple of years old.

## Microsites

A microsite is a special Web site built around a specific marketing campaign. It is usually completely separate from a company's main site.

Here's an example: A travel company is promoting a new holiday resort in the south of France. On the back of the postcard sent to potential customers is a special Web address to a microsite that contains detailed information on the resort, along with a virtual tour online. On the site, prospects can also fill out a form for a chance to win a free trip.

## A Web Site That Sells

Unlike a typical company Web site, a microsite doesn't include pages that are meant to just convey information. Every page—every word—is constructed for one reason only: to get a response. Microsites are designed specifically to motivate you to click or call to request more information, enter a contest, sign up for a newsletter, download a special report, request a demonstration, make a reservation, subscribe to a publication, or order the product.

Because they are so focused, microsites are rarely more than ten pages, and often a lot less. Usually there is a home page, two or three descriptive pages on the product or service being promoted, and a transaction page.

## Making Every Word Count

Most people will go to a microsite only once and never return. So your words must do the job right—the first time! Here are some tips that will help:

- On the front page, make sure there is a logical link between the main headline and the promotion that brought the visitor to that screen. The headlines and copy style—along with the design elements—should all be similar. You want the reader to sense that the microsite is a continuation of the postcard, e-mail, advertisement, or letter that brought him there.
- Provide all the information that the reader needs to make a decision. For example, if the microsite is promoting a new magazine, include all the details needed for that person to make a decision to subscribe.
- Include a link to the final transaction page on every page. Some readers may decide that they want to respond early and will get impatient by having to click through more Web pages.
- Summarize the benefits on the final transaction page. This will increase response by motivating some of those who are still hesitant to respond to the offer.
- Be informative. Prospects are quickly annoyed when they go to a microsite only to find puffed up sales talk with little substance. A tip:

Make it a true information center for the product or service you're promoting.

In many ways a microsite is like an online sales presentation. And, as the copywriter, you are the salesperson. You must accomplish a lot of things very quickly in the few minutes—or even seconds—you have with the reader. So make every word count!

# Sell Pages

A sell page is a Web page that is designed to persuade you to place an order—usually online. It often includes an online order form or link to a shopping cart checkout page.

Writing sell pages can be a challenge because your words have to do all the work in getting the prospect to take the next step in the buying process. That could be to request a quotation, subscribe to a publication, download a free report, or buy the product.

Sell pages go by many other names:

- *Landing page.* This is the Web page that is associated with an e-mail, advertisement, direct-mail package, e-zine article, or even another Web page as part of a two-part marketing campaign. The initial promotion motivates you to visit the Web page. The Web page persuades you to respond to the offer.
- *Order page.* This is the page on a Web site that contains a summary of the benefits and an order form.
- *Subscription page.* This is the same as any other sell page, but the product is a subscription to a publication, database, or other content.
- *Offer page.* This is a page where prospects can respond to a specific offer, usually for some kind of free information, trial, or demo.

Here is an example of an offer page. This one pitches a free trial for a software product.

Here's your opportunity to try

QuickFile™ 4Outlook – Lawyers Edition

FREE for three weeks

(If you decide to keep it, please take 35% off the purchase price!).

Simply complete and submit the form below. You'll automatically be sent an e-mail with your download link. That means you can plug in and start using QuickFile™ right away.

This is a full-version plug-in, not a lightweight trial version. You get to enjoy ALL the benefits of QuickFile™ for one full week. You'll save time, gain more billable hours, and deal with your e-mails faster and more effectively than you may have thought possible.

You do not have to send a payment now. At the end of the trial period we'll contact you by e-mail offering a special price of just $97. That's 35% off the regular price.

Ready to eliminate the risks associated with e-mail management?

Submit this form for your free one-week trial today.

> Name: _____
> E-mail: _____
> [Button]Download now

A sell page must be easy to follow, restate the offer, spell out exactly what the reader is getting or buying, and summarize the main benefits so that buyer momentum is maintained.

## Banner Advertising

It's almost impossible to surf the Internet for even a few minutes without coming across dozens of banner ads. They're everywhere. Banner advertising has become one of the main ways that many commercial Web sites generate revenues, just as magazines and newspapers are supported by print advertising.

A banner ad is simply an advertisement that appears on a Web page. It works like this: You click the ad and are taken to another Web page, which can be a sell page (which we covered in the previous section), a microsite, or the company's main Web site. Regardless of where the campaign leads you, the overriding purpose of a banner ad is to get clicked.

**FACT**

In print advertising, space is usually sold by inches. On the Internet, however, the size of an ad is sold by pixel dimensions. A pixel is a unit of measurement on a computer screen. 486 x 60 is the most common banner ad size, which is a long, thin rectangle.

## Plain and Fancy

The most basic banner advertisement is the static image. Like most print ads, there are no special effects. Usually just a headline followed by one or two lines of copy.

However, some advertisers are taking advantage of the multimedia capabilities of the Internet by using GIF-animated banners. These are ads that display several different images in quick succession. The effect is like animated motion—similar to that old trick of making a stickman walk by flipping through several pages of drawings.

Then there's a thing called rich media, which adds sound and video to a banner ad. Some of these rival even the best television commercials.

## Writing a Better Banner

Writing an effective banner ad can be a challenge simply because of the size restrictions. You don't have much space. Most banners have less than ten words, which doesn't give you much elbowroom to get the reader—perhaps already captivated by other elements on the Web page—to notice and click it. Here are some writing tips that will help:

- Focus on what the readers will get when they click the banner. That could be a free report, free shipping, an online demonstration, or a virtual tour.
- Edit the copy to its bare essentials. Get rid of any extraneous words (often these are the adjectives) that don't add much oomph to the sales message.
- Don't assume that the reader will know they have to click the ad. Make sure you clearly say, "Click here," "Go there now," "Visit today," or some other call to action.
- If possible, work closely with the graphic designer. Make sure the layout and the images are as motivating as the text. The graphics should help the reader see the benefits. For example, a banner ad for a travel destination might show a family throwing a Frisbee on the beach.
- For animated banners, make sure each image is effective on its own. For any number of technical reasons, the prospect may not see all the images.
- For banners that contain audio and video, make sure the ad works well without sound. The prospect may have his or her computer speakers turned down or off.

In a traditional print advertisement, you can sometimes get away with a headline that is cute or clever—an interesting play on words perhaps, or some other headline that requires the reader to decipher its meaning. Not so in banner advertising. Your ad must contain a clear benefit to the reader, and a good reason why he or she should click now. The curiosity headline "Sales Should Always Be This Easy!" won't work as well as the benefit-oriented headline "7 Secrets of Rejection-Free Cold Calling."

## E-zine Advertisements

If you subscribe to e-zines (e-mail newsletters) you probably have noticed the advertising that appears in many of these publications.

E-zine ads work the same way as banner ads. There is usually a "click here" or similar call-to-action link that takes the prospect to a sell page, microsite, or Web site. The only drawback to an e-zine ad is the lack of visuals. The vast majority of e-zine advertising is entirely text based. Your words have to do all the work. There is no fancy graphic design to help you.

E-zines are often targeted to very specific niche markets, much more so than their print counterparts. For example, a travel e-zine might cater specifically to those who enjoy kayaking adventures. Rather than write an advertisement targeting the general travel market, tailor your copy to the characteristics, problems, needs, and desires of this specific group.

E-zine ads are similar to print advertising in that they often feature a strong attention-grabbing headline, motivating body copy, and a call to action. Take a look at this example:

How To Tap The Largest Writer's Market In The World

There are more than 70,000 ad agencies, design firms, PR firms, and similar marketing consultancies throughout North America.

Virtually all use freelance copywriters and business writers.

Are you getting your share of this lucrative market?

In a new teleclass, "Secrets of Writing for Ad Agencies & Design Firms," Steve Slaunwhite explains exactly how to approach agencies for freelance work, who to talk to, how much to charge, and what to expect when you get the job.

Just one major ad agency or design firm can fill your schedule with freelance work for weeks or even months. So it's worthwhile taking a closer look at this market.

Space is limited. For information on how to register today, click on this link:

Click here for teleclass information

E-zine ads are often placed within the flow of the other news and articles in the publication. Make sure your copy has a similar style and tone. The more your ad blends with the editorial, the more effective it will be.

## Search Engine Advertising

You're looking for used office furniture. Where do you start? If you're like many people these days, your first stop is at one of the popular Internet search engines—Google, Yahoo, MSN, or AOL Search.

When you type "used office furniture" into the search field, you'll see a relevant list of Web sites. You'll also see something else: a number of advertisements located to the right and top of the screen. Depending on the search engine, these ads are referred to as sponsored sites, sponsored links, or sponsored results. *Sponsored* means the advertiser pays a fee every time someone clicks on the link.

The elements of a search engine ad are fairly standard across most of the major Internet search engines. Typically, there is:

- A headline
- Two short lines of body copy
- A link to a Web page

Here is an example:

Become a Copywriter
Earn great money working from home.
Free workbook shows you how
www.ForCopywritersOnly.com

When writing a search engine ad, be sure to include the search term in the headline or body. This will be boldfaced on most search engines when the results are displayed. It's common for advertisers to prepare several versions of a search engine ad to target all the various search terms the target audience might type in.

Search engine ads often contain less than twenty words. How do you deliver a strong selling punch when you have so little room to maneuver? Begin by writing a complete ad, with a compelling headline and motivating body copy. Then go back and take out every word that does not absolutely need to be there. Strip your copy down to its essentials. When you do, a great search engine ad will often emerge.

**ALERT!**

Each search engine has strict limits regarding word count. Typically, you only have 25–35 characters to work with per line. That's about seven words at most, which is what makes writing an effective search ad so challenging. There are often other restrictions regarding word usage and content. Be sure to read the advertising guidelines before you begin writing.

## SEO Copywriting

If you type "wedding planner" into your favorite search engine, thousands of results will be generated, with links to everything from wedding consultants and e-books to gift registries and bridal boutiques. Only ten or so of these Web sites will be listed on the first screen. If you want more options, you have to click to the next screen.

How did those few lucky Web sites, competing with thousands of others, make it so high in the search results?

A major influence on search engine rankings is what is called SEO (search engine optimization) copywriting. This is simply a technique of finding and placing certain words and phrases in your copy that will help push the Web site to the top of the heap whenever someone types in a particular search phrase.

SEO techniques also include strategically placed text within the HTML code (the underlining code used to create most Web sites).

## The Words Are the Key

One of the most effective techniques in SEO copywriting is integrating certain words and phrases into the text. This is called keyword placement. This sounds technical, but it's really quite simple. For example, when writing a Web site to promote your freelance copywriting services, it's a no-brainer that you'll have to use the term "copywriter" somewhere in the copy. Otherwise, people looking for that kind of service will never find you!

**FACT**

Search engine companies use software programs called spiders to regularly crawl the Internet and analyze Web sites. Spiders glean information from each site visited, making judgments about the content and determining how best to categorize and describe the Web site in search engine results. This is the data that search engines use to rank a Web site.

SEO copywriters take this idea a lot further. They make sure that the most popular words and phrases typed into search engines by people who are looking for copywriters—or whatever product or service that is being promoted—are mentioned in the copy. To optimize a copywriter's Web site, you would have to integrate the following words into the text:

- Copywriter
- Copywriting
- Copywriting services
- Marketing communications
- Marcom
- Freelance copywriter
- Copy
- Marketing writing

Take a look at this example for DH Communications, the Web site of B2B copywriting and SEO expert Dianna Huff. The words are italicized only to show you the keywords. These are not italicized in the original published copy.

Let's face it—hiring an "unknown" B2B *marketing communications copywriter* can be tough.

Especially when your important projects and reputation are on the line.

I'm Dianna Huff and my job is also my passion—making you look good. And I do that by helping you achieve results with your B2B *marketing communications (marcom)* projects.

If you've been let down in the past by *freelance copywriters* who produced shoddy *copy*, missed your deadline, or simply didn't understand your B2B marketing objectives, you can rest assured that won't happen when you work with me. (Check out my client testimonials for proof.)

You want to look good—to your boss, to your audience, and maybe even (a little) to your competitors. And that's my job, to make you look good, and to help you achieve B2B *marketing communications* results like:

- *Copy* that drives sales leads—Online and off
- Proven B2B marketing strategies that work—From e-mail to Web to print
- Less wasted time—You won't be sending my *copy* back for endless rewrites (or doing it yourself because it isn't up to snuff)
- Worry-free "vendor" relationship—Project work delivered on time, every time

Take a look at my B2B *marketing communications* Copywriting Services and Success Stories pages to see how you can put my award-winning B2B *marketing writing* expertise to work for you.

**QUESTION?**

**How do you determine which keywords to use?**

There are a number of free and paid services available that will give you insights into which words and phrases people are using to search for information on search engines. SEO copywriters typically pick the most popular words and phrases to integrate into the copy.

## Avoid Keyword Stuffing

Notice how the writer in the DH Communications example was able to integrate all the keywords, in some cases more than once, without making the copy sound convoluted or nonsensical. This is a real challenge in SEO copywriting. The text has to read smoothly and persuasively, without seeming like it's obviously stuffed with specific words and phrases.

Keywords alone can never replace the principles of persuasive copywriting. The keywords may help your prospects find the Web site, but it's your compelling messages that will make the sale.

# E-mail Campaigns

Checked your e-mail today? Chances are someone has sent you a promotion of some kind, especially if you're active on the Internet and subscribe to e-zines, alerts, and other forms of e-mail communications.

An e-mail campaign or promotion is like a direct-mail sales letter. It is an attempt to persuade you to click somewhere to get more information, take advantage of a special deal, download a free report, renew your subscription to a magazine, sign up for a Webinar, buy a product at a special price, or any number of other campaign objectives.

Structurally, an e-mail campaign is relatively simple. It is typically made up of a motivating subject line, compelling message, and a call to action of some kind. The campaign is often linked to a sell page, microsite, or Web site.

## The Subject Line

Subject lines are extremely important. In just a few well-chosen words you have to convince the reader that your message is intended for them, is important, and is not spam. By some accounts, business people receive upward of fifty e-mails per day. The number one way they manage their inboxes—deciding which messages require attention now, which can wait until later, and which can just be deleted—is via the subject lines.

One of the challenges of writing a great subject line is that they're short. You only have about sixty characters at most, about five to ten words. That's not much considering what you have to accomplish. You don't have even a single word to waste.

### What is an Autoresponder?

An autoresponder is an automated series of e-mails that is timed to be delivered at specific intervals. For example, if you download a thirty-day free trial of a new software product, you might receive an e-mail on day one, another on day fifteen, and then another on day thirty—that one probably containing a tempting discount if you decide to buy now.

Here are some examples of effective subject lines.

From: Trader's Library
Subject: 2 FREE books of your choice: This week only

From: The Hoover's Online Team
Subject: Your free pass to Hoover's. Today only.

From: Selling Magazine
Subject: Six ways to detect "buy" signals

From: IT Monthly
Subject: Your subscription has expired. But here's the good news…

A winning subject line has one or both of these characteristics:

- It creates a sense of urgency, effectively saying to the prospect: "You need to read this now."
- It implies that there is an enticing benefit contained within the e-mail message itself.

## *The Message*

Once the prospect has clicked open the e-mail (due to your highly effective subject line, of course!), you then have to do in the e-mail what all sales copy must do—gain the reader's attention, hold it, and get him or her to respond to the offer.

E-mail promotions that are written like a good sales letter tend to do much better than those that are formatted like advertising. After all, e-mail is a personal communications channel. Relatives, friends, colleagues, vendors, and customers are writing each other—via e-mail—all the time. It makes sense to align your sales message with this format.

That's why the tips to writing an effective sales letter (see Chapter 10) are applicable to most e-mail campaigns as well. However, there are a few notable differences you need to be aware of.

In sales letters you can get away with stating your offer (or call to action) at the end. Not so with e-mail promotions. You must state the offer early, either in the headline or within the first two paragraphs. You don't want to force readers to scroll down to find out what your e-mail is all about. Most won't.

Spam is a huge issue these days. So the less your e-mail marketing piece looks like spam, the more successful it will tend to be. And never participate in a spam e-mail campaign. It's illegal in most jurisdictions and you'll get yourself into a lot of trouble. Besides, there are plenty of legitimate e-mail campaigns that need talented copywriters.

Be very clear within your e-mail how the reader should respond to the offer. Don't assume that just because a word or phrase is blue and underlined—"Renew at 58% off the cover price"—that the reader will know he has to click on it to get to the renewal page. You must say something to the effect of, "Click here to renew at 58% off the cover price."

Chapter 12

# Writing Sales Communications Copy

Each day, thousands of salespeople across the country pound the pavement to sell their company's products and services. In addition to the gift of the gab, these professionals also need a range of written communications—brochures, model letters, proposals, and scripts—to help them get appointments, make persuasive presentations, and close sales. These materials are referred to as sales communications.

## Helping Salespeople Sell More

Imagine you're a photocopier salesperson. Your income, not to mention job security, depends on you persuading local business owners that your product is the best one to buy. It's not easy. There are many other salespeople in the same market, competing for the same customers. You need all the help you can get!

That's where great copywriting comes in. Copy is critical to the effectiveness of the brochures, sell sheets, presentations, and other materials that salespeople rely on to help them sell their company's products and services. These materials become an essential part of the salesperson's toolkit, helping them to persuade more successfully.

**FACT**

Salespeople aren't the only group who need good sales communications. If you own your own small business, chances are you wear the sales hat from time to time. Because you don't do the job full time, solidly written sales materials are probably even more important to you.

When you're crafting sales communications copy, you're taking on the role of assistant salesperson. Your job is to make that person's job easier by presenting the information about the product or service in an informative, compelling manner.

## Product Brochures

Brochures are so common in sales communications that it's hard to imagine a salesperson without one! And for good reason. Brochures are remarkably versatile. You can use this timeless format to effectively convey just about any kind of sales message, from information on how a product works to its features and benefits to how to place an order.

Even the growing use of the Internet hasn't replaced the conventional print brochure. These still are produced by the truckload by hundreds of thousands of companies across the country.

Brochures certainly are not going the way of the dodo. Whether you're a copywriter, corporate manager, or small business owner, if you're involved in creating sales communications, brochures are going to be an important part of the mix. And that's good news! Because brochures often are fun and fascinating to write.

**ALERT!**

If you get an assignment to write sales communications copy, be sure to talk to at least one of the salespeople who will be using the materials. This will give you insight into what the sales team is trying to accomplish, so you can structure your copy to help them achieve those goals.

## A Salesperson's Best Friend

Salespeople rely on brochures to help them accomplish a variety of objectives:

- To distribute during a trade show, seminar, or similar event
- As a visual aid to help make a sales presentation more persuasive
- As a leave-behind after a sales presentation so the prospect or customer can review the information later on and share it with colleagues
- As something to send to prospects and customers who request more information on a product (sometimes referred to as fulfillment)
- To enclose in an introductory letter to a prospective customer ("I have attached a brochure explaining the new BX-927 Scrubber System in detail.")
- To clip to a price quote or proposal as a reminder of the great features of the product

There is hardly a selling situation when a brochure would not make things easier for the salesperson, and increase the likelihood of getting the order.

## *Shapes and Sizes*

Brochures can be produced in every imaginable shape, size, and configuration. The possibilities are virtually endless.

**FACT**

Brochures that have odd sizes, weird folds, or other nonstandard elements can be very effective. Why? They stand out. A brochure that unfolds into the shape of a jigsaw puzzle piece will get your attention. However, due to the fact that they are nonstandard, these types of brochures can be very expensive to produce.

Most brochures begin life as a flat sheet of paper in one of three sizes:

- 8.5" × 11" (letter)
- 8.5" × 14" (legal)
- 11" × 17"

From these dimensions, the paper can be folded in a variety of ways to create the brochures we most often see today.

These are just the standard sizes and folds. Brochures can be customized into an astonishing variety of shapes, cuts, and dimensions to suit just about any requirement or creative fancy.

## *How to Write Brochures*

People often read brochures because they are looking for specific information about a product or service. So don't disappointment them! Your writing style should be as informative and educational as it is compelling and persuasive. Make sure you include all the product details required for the reader to make a buying decision. Remember: The salesperson may not always be there with the brochure to answer questions.

Take a look at this excerpt from a sales brochure written by copywriter Ed Gandia.

### Web-to-Print Services

Our Web-to-Print services enable you to efficiently create short-run and personalized marketing materials customized for your specific needs. Through a secure, Web interface you can access your own image database, choose the appropriate images, enter your text, pick a mailing list, and proof your document in real time. Jobs are then automatically routed for production to our digital press and are ready for you in hours—not days or weeks.

Notice how the copy lists a lot of features yet still focuses on the benefits. That's the challenge in writing most brochures. They are often fact filled, yet you have to convey what those facts mean to the prospect ("ready for you in hours—not days or weeks").

**E ALERT!**

Don't just put the title on the cover of a brochure, such as "The X18B Photocopier." Yawn. The cover copy should motivate the reader to open the brochure and get involved in the piece. Example: "The X18B Photocopier. So easy to use, it even loads its own paper. So fast, you could print a Tolstoy novel in less than 2 minutes…"

Most people scan brochures rather than read them word for word. They flip back and forth between the pages and dart their eyes this way and that throughout the text. So make good use of bullets, sidebars, captions, lists, and other text highlights. You want the copy to be highly scannable.

The main challenge of writing a brochure is keeping the content focused. Most brochures are either too lightweight and don't contain enough useful information, or too weighed down with extraneous facts and long-winded puffery. Decide exactly what the brochure is meant to accomplish, and then write all the copy needed—and not one word more—to achieve that goal.

## *Sell Sheets*

Sell sheets are really a specialized type of brochure, but they are so unique and useful that they deserve their own section in this chapter.

Typically, a sell sheet is 8.5" × 11" unfolded with printing on one or both sides.

These little guys have been around for decades, but they have become increasingly popular in recent years. A sales professional is more likely to have her briefcase stuffed with sell sheets than traditional brochures.

While a conventional brochure usually contains broad product information, a sell sheet is more narrowly focused. It often is used to explain only a specific aspect or application of a product or service. That's why only one or two pages is needed.

Why are sell sheets so popular? Versatility. When a salesperson is selling a product, she can customize her approach and presentation using those sell sheets that relate to the customer's specific needs. This increases her chances of success.

Here's an example: You're tasked with writing copy for a new software product targeting human resource managers. You probably would need to craft a general-purpose brochure to promote the product. You might also need to develop two sell sheets: one targeting human resource managers, and the other aimed at IT managers. Each sell sheet would provide unique information applicable to its particular audience.

## Rule of Thumb

Sell sheets are easy to read simply because they are so short. They fit neatly into file folders or can be attached easily to proposals and purchasing recommendations.

The rule of thumb for writing a sell sheet is "benefits on the front, features on the back." The front usually has an attention-grabbing headline and one or two paragraphs of benefits-focused copy. The back goes into the product details deeper, usually spanning several paragraphs, and often includes technical specifications.

However, this rule is often broken. The structure of a sell sheet should reflect the objective of the piece. If it needs lots of copy on the front to accomplish that goal, so be it.

# Case Studies

Case studies are another type of sales communications that have become increasingly popular in recent years. This is especially true among those companies that sell complex products, such as enterprise software applications, or consulting services, such as sales training programs. Customers want to know how well these products and services have performed at other companies before they invest in it themselves.

**FACT**

Case studies also are known as success stories, application briefs, user stories, and case histories. They often are used in business-to-business sales and marketing communications. See Chapter 17 for more information on how to write copy for businesses that sell products and services to other businesses.

If you're not familiar with case studies, don't let the name fool you. We're not talking about a dry, technical, or scientific document here. Cases studies—at least the ones used in sales, marketing, and public relations—are essentially product success stories. They're often written in an editorial style similar to what you'd find in a business or trade magazine. A case study tells the tale of "customer meets product" and how everyone lived happily ever after.

## What Case Studies Look Like

There are numerous formats for a case study. Some are just half-page summaries. Others are full-blown feature articles. Typically, they are published on one or two pages and run about 500 to 1,000 words.

Case studies are popular not just as a selling tool, but also in public relations (which is covered in Chapter 13). In fact, the best case studies often get referenced, or sometimes even reprinted verbatim, in industry publications. That's free publicity! No wonder everyone in sales, marketing, and PR loves them.

**ALERT!**

An effective case study should reflect the realities of purchasing, implementing, and using a product. If you paint too rosy a picture of the experience a customer has with a product, readers won't believe it. So go ahead and write about delays, setbacks, and glitches and how these issues were eventually resolved. It will make your case study more credible.

Before you write a case study, read a few. Many company Web sites have case studies available that you can download. It's a great way to learn more about this fascinating hybrid of brochure, testimonial, and article.

## Points to Cover

Here is the recommended format for writing an effective case study:

- *The challenge.* Begin by introducing the key issue. What problem or condition was the customer trying to change or improve? If possible, use the customer's own words in the form of a quotation.
- *The customer.* Introduce the customer to be featured in the case study. Who are they? Where are they located? What products or services do they offer? What is their most interesting characteristic?
- *The journey.* What steps did the customer take to solve the problem? What other products or services were investigated? Why didn't these work out? Many case study writers skip this section. Don't you skip it. This is the place in the story where the reader begins to identify and empathize.

- *The discovery.* How did the customer find out about the product or service? In an ad? At a trade show? Through a media interview? This section often acts as a bridge to the remainder of the case study.
- *The solution.* This is where you have unbridled freedom to pitch the product or service without fear of sounding too promotional. The earlier sections have earned you this right.
- *The implementation.* How was the product or service installed or implemented? Did everything go smoothly? Be honest about any problems that arose and how these were resolved. Highlight instances where your company or client went the extra mile to satisfy the customer.
- *The results.* How well did the product or service solve the customer's problem? Be as specific as you can here. Use hard numbers such as cost savings, revenue gains, sales growth, and return on investment. This is another good spot to include a customer quotation. And it's a great place to summarize and close your story.

Take a look at this excerpt from a case study:

**Savvy Sales Literature Positions Company as the Industry Leader**
Effective sales literature—whether it's a series of brochures or a comprehensive corporate folder—can be tough to produce. That's because it often must succeed on multiple fronts. For example, the same brochure may be used as a visual aid during sales presentations, handed out to visitors at trade shows, and used in mailings to prospective clients. In addition, brochures are everywhere. So how do you create one that doesn't get lost in the clutter?

Those are just some of the problems faced by Robert Brakel & Associates, a sales tax consulting firm. "As the leader in our industry, the competition is constantly nipping at our heels," says company president Jim Brakel. "We needed a sales literature package that would immediately set us apart and position us as the best."

To tackle the problem, he gave Michael Huggins of Mindwalk Design Group a call…

Notice how this case study is written like a compelling story. You want to find out how it ends! It also follows the case study format closely, starting with the challenge and the customer. It's not until the third paragraph that the product—the services of Mindwalk Design Group—is introduced. A case study is most effective when the writer focuses on telling the success story rather than selling the product.

## Get the Story

Where do you get the quotations from happy customers to use in the case study? Somebody has to interview the customer to get the story. Review the interviewing tips and best practices provided in Chapter 3. Following are some of the more common questions that copywriters ask during case study interviews.

Be sure to prepare a list of questions before you interview the customer. Don't just try to wing it! You should also visit the customer's Web site, if they have one, and familiarize yourself with that company's history and products.

- What does your company do? What is it most known for?
- Before you started using [*product name*], describe the challenges that you were facing.
- What were these challenges costing you, in terms of money, productivity, downtime, competitiveness, sales growth?
- Before choosing [*product name*], what other products or solutions did you consider? How did these alternatives compare to what [*product name*] offered?
- How did you come to discover [*product name*]? Did you see it at a trade show? In an ad? Did a salesperson contact you?
- What specific problems were you hoping that [*product name*] would solve? What expectations did you have?
- What made you finally decide to purchase [*product name*]? What factors played a role in your decision making?
- What concerns did you have about implementing or installing [*product name*]?

- How did the implementation or installation go? Was it smooth? Was it difficult? If there were problems, were they dealt with to your satisfaction?
- How has [*product name*] performed since it was implemented? Has it met your original expectations? Did [*product name*] solve most or all of the original challenges you were facing?
- Specifically, using numbers if you can, how has [*product name*] impacted your sales, customer service, productivity, competitiveness?
- Describe instances when [*company name*] (the makers of [*product name*]) went above and beyond the call of duty to resolve an issue?
- Would you recommend [*product name*] to colleagues and other companies?

## *Presentations*

When a salesperson makes a presentation, it's often make-or-break time. Either she wins over the prospect or customer, or she goes back to the office empty-handed. That's why presentation slides are so important. They are the visual aids that can mean the difference between a successful pitch and a flop.

Gone are the days of cumbersome transparencies and unwieldy slide-show carousels. Virtually all presentation slides these days are composed using PowerPoint or similar presentation software, which makes it easy for just about anyone to put together and present a slide show.

**FACT**

Microsoft PowerPoint and other presentation software programs allow you to create slides, organize a presentation, and deliver that presentation to an audience. If you want to write presentation slides, learn how to use PowerPoint or some other popular presentation program, such as Lotus Freelance Graphics, Corel Presentations, or Harvard Graphics.

Presentation slides can be shown on a laptop computer during a one-to-one presentation or on a big screen before a group using an LED projector. The salesperson guides the presentation along from one slide to the next by punching a computer keyboard key or using a handheld remote.

Sales professionals use presentation slides in much the same way they do brochures. It's an organized, interesting, highly visual way to present product information, features, and benefits.

## Write the Show

How do you write a PowerPoint or similar slide-oriented presentation? Here are the top tips:

- A typical slide has a main headline and then three or four bullets.
- Write in bullets, not in full sentences.
- Keep the text light. Don't crowd a slide with copy.
- If you need more copy to make your point, create a new slide.
- Incorporate visuals to support your points. Charts, graphs, and illustrations work very well in slides.

Remember, there's usually a person presenting the slides. So your copy doesn't need to explain everything in detail. Hit the main points in each section. The speaker will take care of the rest.

## Model Letters

Most salespeople would rather talk than write. Sitting down in front of a computer, struggling to dream up the right words for a letter or e-mail, is unproductive. It takes time away from meeting with customers and pursuing new sales opportunities.

That's why model letters and e-mails are so important to salespeople. It saves them time, which translates into more face time with prospects and customers.

Some salespeople can write well. Others cannot. Well-written model letters and e-mails help a company maintain a professional image in its written communications. Imagine a customer receiving an e-mail from a sales rep riddled with muddled messages and spelling errors. Ouch!

**QUESTION?**

**What's the difference between a model letter and a real letter?**
A model letter, or a template as it is sometimes called, is basic text that can be customized by the salesperson. Often there are just a few blanks to fill in. So instead of taking an hour to compose a letter or e-mail from scratch, the salesperson can knock one off in just a few minutes.

## The Salesperson's Ghostwriter

Copywriters can write several different kinds of model letters for salespeople. Here are the most common:

- The *Thank You for Your Time* letter or card that is sent after a sales presentation.
- The *Appointment Confirmation* e-mail to confirm a date and time of a scheduled meeting.
- The *Request a Meeting* e-mail or letter. This is often used in tandem with a phone call or voice mail in an effort to secure a meeting with a new prospect. "I'll be in your area on Tuesday. May I drop by to quickly introduce you to our latest solution for reducing international shipping costs?"
- The *Invitation* letter, e-mail, or card. This is used to persuade a prospect or customer to visit a trade show booth, product demonstration, or similar event. "Please drop by our booth during the Annual GIZMO Conference. We'll be giving away chances to win."
- The *Special Offer* letter or e-mail. "Until the end of this month, we're offering a 35% discount to our best customers. I'll call you this week with more details."
- The *Service Reassurance* e-mail. "Sorry to hear you're having trouble with the Gizmo BX4. I've notified Rich in our technical department and he will be scheduling a service call with you for early next week."

The most important thing to remember about writing model letters and e-mails is to keep it conversational. Remember, it's from a real person. If the copy screams form letter, this will turn off both the customer and the salesperson.

# Sales Proposals

If you're selling a product to a consumer, there is usually just one person who makes the decision. Often you just quote the price, haggle a little, and, hopefully, get the sale. However, when you're selling a product to a business—especially a big-ticket item like an industrial machine or a management consulting contract—then many people may have to approve the purchase.

That's where sales proposals come in. A sales proposal is a combination sales presentation and price quotation. It can run anywhere from just a few pages to more than a dozen. The purpose of these documents is to make a solid business case for buying the product. It's a pitch on paper.

Usually the salesperson initiates the sales proposal. She might say something like, "Mr. Smith, I think we've established that your manufacturing plant could benefit from this chemical safety program. May we submit a proposal for your consideration?" If Mr. Smith says yes, that's a strong indication that he is interested in the program and is ready to make a buying decision.

## Anatomy of a Proposal

A sales proposal often begins life as a template that the copywriter creates. It includes all the basic information on the product, features, benefits, and pricing. The salesperson then customizes the document accordingly.

In many ways, a proposal is like a sales presentation. It usually contains the following elements:

- A cover letter
- A highlight of the problem or issue
- Details on the proposed product or service
- Support information

- A compelling statement as to why the product or service should be purchased
- Background information on the company offering the product
- Delivery, installation, and implementation details
- Any other important information that is required
- The price, including payment terms and schedules
- The next step (what the prospect needs to do next if he or she wants to purchase the product or service)

Sales proposals are not always initiated by a salesperson. Sometimes it's the other way around. For example, a company might send out a request to a list of manufacturers for proposals to replace its fleet of warehouse forklift trucks. This is commonly called a request for proposal, or RFP.

The writing style for a proposal should be persuasive yet highly informative. Resist the urge to hype. Instead, present your business case clearly and concisely. Companies use proposals to make important buying decisions. They will be swayed much more by facts than platitudes.

## Chapter 13
# Writing PR Copy

Ink. Publicity. Buzz. Whatever you want to call it, there are a lot of advantages to getting your products or services featured in the press. People are naturally more trusting of articles in a magazine than ads in that same publication. That's why companies work so hard—using effective copywriting strategies—to communicate the latest news about their offerings to editors and journalists.

## Romancing the Press

Imagine you're flipping through a magazine and notice an article on your favorite topic: coffee. As you read the piece, you come across a paragraph that describes a new portable cappuccino maker—so portable, in fact, that it can sit unobtrusively on your desk at work. The article even features a picture of the machine. You think, "Wow, that company was sure lucky. They just got free publicity for their product!"

Free publicity is just a myth. Although most publications will not accept payment to mention products and services in their editorial (it's obviously unethical), companies invest a significant amount of time and money communicating with the press. These activities are often referred to as public relations, press relations, media relations, or PR for short.

Copywriters play an important role in gaining good publicity for products and services. There are a variety of written materials that need to be developed to inform editors and journalists about a company's offerings and capabilities.

When writing PR copy, the key word is newsworthy. Editors and journalists are sensitive to sales pitches and marketing hype. What they respond to best is communications that describe the real news concerning products and services and why that information is important to their readers, listeners, or viewers. The best PR copy is fact filled, with an unbiased tone. The media loves great stories, so the more of these you can weave into your copy the better.

## Traditional Press Releases

The classic press release has been around for decades. It's still the workhorse of virtually all public relations campaigns, helping companies get the word out about their products and services.

When a journalist receives a press release from a company, she may use it in a variety of ways—or not at all. For example, she may decide to do a feature article based on the release, or use some of the information in another story she is developing. She may also contact the company and request additional information or an interview with a key contact.

In some cases, an editor might choose to publish the press release in its entirety—especially if it is a good story. This hardly ever happens in consumer magazines, but it does occur more frequently in trade and professional publications.

**FACT**

There are only minor distinctions between a press release, a media release, and a news release. For all practical purposes, they are interchangeable terms.

A press release is typically one to two pages in length, although there are exceptions. It's usually written just like a news story, with a headline on top followed by several supporting paragraphs and a sprinkling of subheads as needed. This is intentional. A company wants the release to look like the news and get "picked up" by a publication.

## The Expected Format

Unlike most other projects that copywriters handle—where there is a lot of elbowroom for creativity—press releases have an established format. You have to follow the rules. Reporters expect to see a press release that looks like one, and if it doesn't it will probably be ignored. Here are the general formatting guidelines:

In the section above the headline, the company name and address should go on the left side with the date on the right. The words "FOR IMMEDIATE RELEASE" should also appear in this section. In some cases, however, a company may not want the news released to the public until some future date and is trusting the editor to keep the secret. So something like "EMBARGO FOR RELEASE UNTIL NOV. 16, 2007" might be written in this section instead.

The location of where the story is originating—called the dateline—should appear below the headline at the start of the first sentence of the first paragraph. This is a throwback to an age when press releases were distributed via teletype machines. These days there is no good reason why this formatting rule still exists. Call it a time-honored tradition!

Next comes the main guts of the press release, the body copy. Journalism 101 teaches that a good news story or feature article addresses the 5 Ws: who, what, where, when, and why. Your press release should convey the same thing. Present the facts in a compelling manner, or tell a great story. Make sure the content is relevant and important to the audiences of your target publications.

**E ALERT!**

Press releases often are distributed electronically by media distribution companies that may have their own preferred formatting guidelines. Make sure you know what these are so your release complies.

A final paragraph usually contains a boilerplate description of the company. In some press releases this may be separate from the main body copy but still located at the end of the release.

Many press releases end with "###," "END," or "-30-." Again, another quirky press release thing.

Here is an example of a typical press release:

DH Communications Wins Gold MarCom Creative Award for Web Site/e-Zine Copywriting

Dianna Huff, President of Boston-area B2B marketing communications copywriting firm DH Communications, has received a Gold Award from the MarCom Creative Awards for her work with a client's e-newsletter.

*November 28, 2005* - Dianna Huff, President of DH Communications, Inc. has been awarded a "Gold Award" from the MarCom Creative Awards in the category of Web Site/e-Zine copywriting.

Huff's winning entry was for the e-newsletter, "Particle Matters," which she writes for her client, Boston-based Cabot Corporation. The semi-monthly e-newsletter features articles and news about Cabot's fine particles. (Fine particles are found in many products, including tires, cell phones, glass roof enclosures, and cosmetics.)

"My client, Cathy Beckman, eBusiness Manager for Cabot, and I are very pleased with 'Particle Matters,'" states Huff. "When she first approached me last year about doing an e-newsletter, she wasn't sure how we would cover the company's many business units and hundreds of product lines. We also knew we wanted fresh, original content, versus content derived from press releases, something we've been able to achieve with each issue. Cathy gets over 100 new subscribers a month and has a very low opt-out rate. She considers it a great success and is as thrilled by this award as I."

The MarCom Creative Awards is an international competition that recognizes outstanding achievement by marketing and communications practitioners. There were 4,613 entries from throughout the U.S. and several countries. Entries receive the prestigious Platinum Award, a Gold Award, or an Honorable Mention. The Gold Award is presented to those entries judged to exceed the high standards of the industry. Approximately 16 percent of the entries received the Gold Award.

DH Communications, Inc. is a full-service marketing communications firm offering B2B marketing communications copywriting and consulting. Dianna Huff, who has won three other awards for her work, is also a MarketingSherpa Contributing Editor.

What if the editor has questions? Contact information for the release is located at the very bottom. For example: "For more information, please contact Jane Smith, public relations manager, at _____ ." Other information can also be located here, such as the availability of pictures, background information, and access to experts for interviews.

## PR Writing Primer

Here are some tips to help get your press release noticed by the media:

- *Promote the news value.* While you may believe a new product should be front-page news, an editor might have a very different opinion. When assessing whether a topic is really news, ask yourself: Will readers be interested in this story? Is it timely? Relevant? Unusual? Does the topic affect many people? Does it have a lasting importance? Is it truly new, better, or different? How will it affect someone's life, career, or business?

- *Include quotes.* Always quote key personnel and others involved in the story to make it more credible and interesting. Quotes not only makes the piece more interesting to read, but they also may help editors decide to use the statements in a related story.
- *Write in the third person.* Never use "we" or "I" unless it is part of a quotation.
- *Think like an editor.* Would you reprint the press release in your magazine or trade journal? Will the information captivate your readers?
- *Prove all claims.* If possible, quote third-party experts, research reports, surveys, and other supporting evidence. Editors love this kind of information, and it will make your press release seem more unbiased.

The most successful press releases are written with a style and content that is similar to the publications they are targeting. For your writing to be more effective, do some research beforehand.

## Media Advisories

A media advisory is a one-page description of a future event. It is meant to give reporters the heads up so they will, hopefully, mark their calendars accordingly. For example, a company is coming out with a new product and is planning a major launch event at a swank hotel. Local politicians and other industry dignitaries are invited. Getting the press to be there too would help generate some much need publicity.

Media advisories can be used to invite the press to product demonstrations, major company announcements, grand openings, in-store events, VIP visits, ribbon-cutting ceremonies, speeches, seminars, community sponsorship activities, and, of course, general press conferences.

A media advisory is rarely more than one page. It typically features such details as:

- The name of the event
- The names of speakers, moderators, special guests, hosts
- The date and time

- The location, along with instructions on how to get there
- Basic background information about the event, answering that all-important question for reporters: "Why is this important?"
- Contact information

**QUESTION?**

**What is the difference between a media advisory and a press release?**

A press release contains all the information a reporter needs to write the story. By contrast, a media advisory functions more like a teaser, containing just enough information to motivate the journalist to attend the upcoming event.

The format for a media advisory is similar to that of a press release. Of course, you need to put MEDIA ADVISORY at the top of the page, *not* FOR IMMEDIATE RELEASE. Be sure the headline is tantalizing, and that the contact information includes phone numbers and e-mail addresses. If a photo opportunity exists, highlight this in the advisory. It will help to attract photojournalists in addition to reporters.

## Media Kits

A media kit is a package of information about a product, service, or company that is made available to the media. Companies create these kits for the same reason they do press releases—to help them generate publicity.

A media kit, also known as a press kit, can be distributed in a variety of ways. It can be mailed, handed out at trade shows and similar events, distributed at press conferences and product launches, or even downloaded from a company Web site.

What's inside a media kit? This can vary dramatically, but you'll usually find press releases and promotional materials such as product brochures, case studies, testimonials, and copies of ads. Even product samples, demos, photos, or artist renderings are sometimes thrown in on a CD. Below are two other information pieces that you are likely to find in a media kit.

## Fact Sheets

In *Dragnet*, the popular detective television show of the 1950s, Sgt. Joe Friday famously says, "The facts, ma'am. Just the facts." That's what a fact sheet is all about. It provides editors and journalists with a summary of the most important facts about the product, service, or company. It is often in the form of a bullet list or Q&A. Rarely is it longer than two pages.

Companies include fact sheets in media kits for two reasons. First, they want to make sure the publications get the facts accurate. Second, by suggesting which facts are the most important, a company gains some influence over what the media might say in a news item or article. At least that's the theory.

**ESSENTIAL**

Customize your fact sheet to specific media audiences. For example, produce two versions of a fact sheet about a new sales training program: one for editors of sales-oriented publications, the other for human resources and training publications.

When writing a fact sheet, stick to the facts. If the copy seems too promotional, editors and journalists won't take it seriously.

## Backgrounders

While a fact sheet is a quick summary of a product, a backgrounder goes into much more detail. It often tells a broader story of the product— what prompted its development, what problems or issues it solves, or what new technology, research, or ideas were part of the development. A backgrounder may also include biographies of the product development team, sales forecasts, and even lofty predictions on how it may change the way people think or behave.

If you were a reporter writing about Apple's iPod—a device that really did change the way people listened to and purchased music—you would want details about its development. Who came up with the idea? How long did it take to develop? Did the company predict it was going to be such a hit? That's what a backgrounder is for.

These documents are usually five to seven pages long. In the case of technical products, they may be longer as they are appealing to engineering and scientific publications that prefer a lot more detail.

# Articles

Each year, companies produce thousands of articles for their own newsletters and e-zines, as well as for publication in the business and trade press. And for good reason. Articles enjoy a higher readership than most other marketing-oriented pieces that a copywriter might produce. Think about it. You probably read articles all the time. But how often do you cozy up on a Sunday afternoon with a good brochure?

Articles also are very effective in spreading the word about a new product or service. Imagine a salesperson making a cold call and the prospect saying, "Yes, I read about your new Gizmo XL6 in last month's *Semiconductor Monthly*." Suddenly, a foot is in the door.

## The Copywriter's Role

A company will create and submit an article to a publication in the hopes that:

- The article will be published as is, or with just a few changes.
- Portions of the article will be used by the editor in a related article.
- The article will persuade the editor to plan a new article or feature on the topic.

Articles usually run between 500 and 1,500 words, with 750 words being about average. This can vary depending on the target publication.

**QUESTION?**

**Do publications really publish articles submitted by companies?**
It does happen quite frequently with trade magazines and regional business publications. That's because they don't have the budget for staff writers and freelancers, so they depend on such contributions. National consumer magazines, however, will rarely run such an article.

Here is an excerpt from a typical article published in a trade journal. This one originates from Thordon Bearings, a manufacturer of marine bearings.

Thordon helping to catch marlins in sportfishing yachts

In Ernest Hemingway's classic novel, *The Old Man And The Sea,* an aging fisherman ventures far beyond the coastal waters in search of a great marlin. For weeks he sails his noisy skiff, exhausted, unable to get close enough to hook his elusive prey. If only Thordon Bearings were available back then. He might have been able to stalk the big fish more quietly.

Noise has always been the Achilles' Heel in sportfishing vessels. One of the common problems today, for example, is the squealing that can occur when trolling at low speeds. This is typically due to the use of rubber bearings in the propeller shaft.

As any sports fishing enthusiast knows, a high pitched noise will reverberate for miles under water, chasing the big game away—especially marlins. What's the solution? For a growing list of yacht builders, refitters, and suppliers, the answer is Thordon COMPAC Propeller Shaft Bearings.

Grease-free and, thus, environmentally friendly, Thordon COMPAC is fast becoming the bearing of choice in a multitude of vessels from yachts to ocean liners...

When writing an article that features your company's product or service, follow these tips:

- *Read the target publication.* What is its editorial style? What topics do the magazine, journal, or newsletter typically cover? Who is the audience?

- *Write a compelling headline.* It has to impress the editor as well as the readers. The headline should be consistent with others in the target publication. For example, if the headline is usually short, yours should be too.
- *Open with a captivating lead.* A lead is the opening paragraph. The two best ways to write a lead is to highlight a pressing problem or issue, or begin with a compelling story.
- *Use word pictures.* Tell stories. Give examples. Illustrate the facts. Help the reader visualize the product being promoted.
- *Be specific.* Use facts, statistics, reviews, quotes from studies, research results.
- *Use quotes.* Quote customers, experts, research statistics, or company executives.
- *Avoid promotional blather.* If your article appears to be a long-winded ad, the editor will quickly delete it.

Even if an article doesn't get picked up by a business or industry publication, the company can still use it in its own newsletter, as a handout to prospects and customers, or on its Web site. So the investment in writing an article will always pay off to some degree.

## Speeches

There are some company executives who can stand in front of an audience and, with just a few notes, give an effective speech. This is a rare breed. Most people need, at a minimum, a detailed script before they hit the podium. That's why even the most experienced executive speakers use a speechwriter.

Writing a speech is one of the most challenging projects a copywriter can handle, but it can be one of the most fulfilling. It's difficult to describe the feeling of listening to a speaker deliver your words to a live audience. Every laugh, every accolade, every applause seems like it's for you, too.

**How many words are in a speech?**
The average speaker talks at a rate of 100–125 words per minute. So if you're writing a fifteen-minute speech, you can expect your script to be 1,500 to 1,875 words. However, if you know your speaker talks at a faster or slower pace, adjust your target word count accordingly. Many speak faster when they are nervous.

## The Speaker's Ghost

Most keynote speeches—those where there is little interaction with the audience and few, if any, visual aids—are usually ten to fifteen minutes long. This is sometimes referred to as a "classic speech." It is often written out word for word, unless the speaker is confident and skilled enough to speak from notes.

If the speech is longer, and more like a presentation or educational session, then the speaker will probably be using visual aids such as PowerPoint slides. In this case, notes associated with each slide may be preferable over a word-for-word script. But check with the speaker first to make sure.

Go over the speech with the speaker before you sit down to write it. Learn what she wants to say, and how she wants to say it. Also, listen to her speaking patterns and mannerisms. If you're going to put words in a person's mouth, get to know the person.

## Speechwriting 101

Entire books have been published on speechwriting. But if you follow these tips, you'll be on track to writing an excellent speech.

- *Write for the ear, not the eye.* Make the speech highly conversational. Read it out loud. Make sure it sounds natural.
- *Avoid humor.* A joke falling flat is one of the most embarrassing things to happen to a speaker. Don't risk it.

- *Use lots of examples and stories.* Create word pictures. This will make it easier for the audience to get involved with the speech and understand what is being said.
- *Don't cover too much territory.* Even in lengthy speeches there should only be three to five major points to make. Anymore and the audience's focus fades.
- *Stay focused.* It's easy to ramble when writing a speech.
- *Repeat important facts and points.* Don't be afraid to say some things over and over again. In a brochure, the reader can go back and forth to review information. During a speech, the audience doesn't have this advantage.
- *Know the audience.* Tailor the speech to their specific level of interest and knowledge of the topic. You wouldn't write the same speech about software to an audience of IT executives as you would a group of sales managers.
- *Summarize all the key points at the end.* Don't assume the audience will have retained everything the speaker said. They won't. So make sure they walk away knowing the most important key points.

If you're also writing copy for the presentation slides, make sure they don't upstage the speech. If there is additional information on a slide, or a funny or fascinating image, the audience may focus on it and tune out the speaker! Also, keep the points made on the slides brief.

# Chapter 14
# Writing Customer Communications Copy

Most of the copywriting techniques and projects described in this book are all about getting new customers. In this chapter you'll learn how to keep them. As the saying goes: A customer who buys once can make you money, but a customer who buys again and again, perhaps for a lifetime, can make you rich. That's why companies invest heavily in communications that keep their customers informed and satisfied.

## Customers for Life

Companies don't just want you to buy once. They want you to purchase their products and services again and again and again. That's why creating a pleasant and rewarding customer experience is so important to them. The hope is that, with a little placating and nurturing on their part, you'll become loyal to the brand—even if a competing product or service is superior.

So what "placating and nurturing" are we talking about here? To help ensure you become a repeat customer, companies dedicate a considerable amount of resources to communicating with you in a variety of ways. The idea—assuming you're happy with the product or service—is to keep the honeymoon going forever. There's no hiding their intentions. Often the very first letter or e-mail a company sends you begins with "Dear Loyal Customer."

**FACT**

A growing niche in the customer relations field is loyalty marketing. This involves programs that provide tangible rewards for customer loyalty. For example, many airlines have frequent flier programs, essentially offering the chance for free travel. As a copywriter, you could be asked to write a variety of loyalty marketing pieces: program brochures, in-store posters, ads, and more.

All of this is, of course, a good thing. As a customer, you deserve and appreciate the attention. Companies *should* thank you for your ongoing decision to support their products and services, and not take you for granted.

This is also a good thing for copywriters. Companies need a wide variety of customer communications written, everything from letters and e-mails to newsletters and flyers.

## More Than Just Repeat Business

There is much more at stake for a company than just keeping a customer happy and buying. When customers become delighted with a product or service, even loyal, they tend to spread the word, recommending it to others. Studies have shown that people make an average of twenty to thirty product recommendations or endorsements to friends and colleagues every year. Companies know this. They also know that a strong customer communications program leads to good word of mouth—or "buzz" as it's called in the public relations field.

Sometimes a community of loyal customers becomes a marketing force all on its own, sustaining and increasing sales of the brand over the long term. The level of loyalty among customers of Apple Computers borders on the religious. A big reason for this is the company's ability to communicate with their customer communities successfully.

## Expand Sales

Finally, companies also know that satisfied customers are more likely to purchase other products or services from the same company. A music lover who falls in love with his Bose sound system is likely to be interested in other products and accessories available in that brand category, especially if the company has stayed in touch.

## Cross-selling and Up-selling

A customer is not just a customer. He or she is also a hot prospect for many other products and services that a company sells. This isn't surprising. If you buy a hammer and a box of nails at ABC Home Improvement, chances are you're going to return to that store when you need lumber for your new deck.

There are two techniques that a company uses to sell more stuff to its customers: cross-selling and up-selling.

Cross-selling involves getting you to buy other products associated with the one you're already buying. If you have a favorite brand of shampoo, it makes sense for that company to persuade you to purchase their conditioners, mousses, and other hair products. (That's why you'll often see coupons for related products inside product packaging.)

**ALERT!**

Automotive dealerships actually cross-sell you all the time. The new car is the big-ticket purchase. But servicing that vehicle during your years of ownership is where the real money is made. That's why soon after your new car is delivered you begin to receive letters, flyers, e-mails, and even phone calls from your dealership announcing "spring tune-up" specials and other deals.

Up-selling is a little different than cross-selling. It involves persuading you to buy a more expensive version of the same product, or add on to a current product. For example, if you move into a new home and call the telephone company to activate your service, the operator might say something like, "Would you like to add our voice-mail service for just $8 extra per month?" That's up-selling. Even McDonald's uses this technique when they ask if you would like to supersize your order.

So just because your target audience is existing customers doesn't mean you can let your hair down and relax. Especially when cross-selling and up-selling, you need to be as determined as ever to craft copy that connects with the customer and persuades him or her to buy.

## *Newsletters*

Newsletters are one of the most popular and effective ways that companies stay in touch with customers. The main reason for this is that people tend to react more favorably to newsletters then they do to direct mail, flyers, e-mails, and phone calls. They expect to find useful articles and other information, and are willing to accept some promotional pitches intermixed with the content so long as it's not excessive.

A newsletter can also be sent out more frequently because, like a magazine, it is a type of periodical. People expect it to arrive at scheduled intervals. A company can get away with sending a newsletter to its customers once a month but would probably get complaints if they did a promotional mailing or telemarketing campaign with the same frequency.

**FACT**

Newsletters can be published in two formats: print and online. Which is better? That depends on the customer base. For business people and others who are active on the Internet, online is best. For other consumer markets, a print newsletter may be the best choice because those people may not be regular Internet users.

As a consumer, you may receive newsletters from your dentist, chiropractor, real estate agent, bank, or many of the other companies you deal with on an ongoing basis. Business people receive plenty of free newsletters as well from companies and professionals.

## What's Inside

In print format, customer newsletters are typically four pages in length. (Often, they are produced on 11" × 17" sheets folded to make four panels.) Of course, there are lots of variations. Some can be as short as a single page, while others can be several pages. E-mail newsletters are not restricted to any particular paper size. However, most e-mail and other online formats for newsletters are typically shorter than their print cousins, usually containing no more than three short articles. That's because it's generally easier to read on paper than on screen.

If you get involved in writing a customer newsletter, part of your job will likely be planning the articles. This involves playing the role of chief editor and deciding what topics to cover. Here are some thoughts to keep in mind:

- *Keep it reader-focused.* Select topics based on what customers want to read, not what you want to tell them.
- *Let the customers decide.* Survey customers to discover the kinds of topics they'd be interested in reading. This doesn't have to be a

complex process. In an e-mail newsletter, for example, you can simply ask readers to e-mail their topic suggestions.

- Be *careful with company news.* Think about it. Do customers really want to read about the antics at the latest company picnic? Or learn that Fred from Boston is the new VP of finance? This may be good fodder for an employee newsletter, but not for one aimed at customers.
- *Include people profiles.* Customers like to learn more about the people they deal with on the phone or via the Internet, especially those in customer service, technical support, and sales.
- *Make it fridge worthy.* Include articles that are so helpful they get clipped and posted on a refrigerator door or office wall. No one ever gets tired of a good how-to.
- *Reprint case studies and other success stories.* These work very well. Customers love to read them. And they are often already in article format.
- *No fluff, please.* Resist the temptation to use quotes from famous people, jokes, cartoons, or other fillers just to use the space.

So where do you put the promotional stuff? The news about new products? Accessories? Upgrades? Discount programs? Holiday sales? There are two ways to integrate this information into a newsletter while still maintaining an informative style and tone.

The first way is to write the promotional pitch in the form of an article. This can work well only if the promotion or campaign is, in fact, news. Take a look at this example:

**DAYTON CUTS THE CHEESE**

Dayton Cheese has being selling its product in standard block sizes for more than 75 years. This month, for the first time ever, Dayton Slices will be available for order. You can count on the same great quality and long-lasting freshness—now in convenient slices. And here's more good news. Customers who order before January 15th receive a 25% introductory discount!

The second method of weaving a promotional message into your newsletter is to actually place an advertisement. After all, magazines and many other publications contain ads. So customers will not be surprised when they see one in yours.

## *Article Writing Tips*

There are plenty of great article writing tips in Chapter 13. In addition, here are some more strategies that are particularly applicable to customer newsletters:

- *Short articles work best.* Use no more than 400 words.
- *Mix it up.* If a full-length article for your customer publication is 400 words, include some much shorter articles that are only 150–200 words.
- *Use a caption for every picture.* Captions have one of the highest readerships on a newsletter page. So take advantage of this fact.
- *Make it eye friendly.* Use plenty of subheads, sidebars, text boxes, and other text elements to make the newsletter look more inviting and easy to read.
- *Make it look like a newsletter.* If your newsletter looks too much like a sales brochure or flyer, few customers will read it.
- *Put your most captivating article on the front page.* This is the most important page to the customer, so use this space to target the customer, not just announce company news. For example, the opening of a new plant in China, as important as that may be to the company, may not be all that interesting to a shopper.
- *Use plenty of quotes.* Instead of saying that the new SML Fluid Monitoring System is 22 percent more accurate than the previous model, get someone to quote it. "John Smith, technical manager of development had this to say about the new SML Fluid Monitoring System. 'It is 22% more accurate than the previous model.'"

Place yourself firmly in the customer's shoes when planning a newsletter and researching and writing the articles. Ask yourself: "Would I read this article? Would I appreciate the company providing this information? Is this information useful to me?" If you can say yes to these questions, you're on the right track.

# *Customer Letters and E-mails*

In addition to newsletters, e-mails and snail-mail letters are an equally popular means of staying in touch with customers. You have no doubt received countless letters from your bank, credit card company, insurance company, and other companies you deal with regularly.

John Smith
123 Forth Street
New York, NY 32165
Account # BN-364552
ATT: Important News For Buyers of the XPZ-16 Voice Recorder

Dear John:
I hope you're enjoying your XPZ-16 recorder. When you registered the product, you indicated that you'd like to be informed of new upgrades and accessories, as they become available…

Companies will correspond with a customer for a variety of reasons:

- To follow up on a complaint or problem
- To notify customers of important news and information
- To announce sales, special discounts, and other promotions
- To alert customers that new versions of their current products are now available
- To survey customers so the company can better understand their needs and preferences
- To collect on overdue accounts

Clearly identify your letter or e-mail as customer communications. Otherwise, it might be confused with advertising mail or spam. Be sure to mark your correspondence with customer identifying information, such as customer ID numbers, account numbers, full name and address, and even the type of products they buy.

## *Promotional Announcements*

A letter or e-mail is an ideal way to announce sales, special discounts, or other tantalizing deals. Amazon.com does this all the time with their customers. You can even sign up for customized alerts that let you know when your favorite types of books become available.

Writing these types of announcements are very similar to writing sales letters and promotional e-mails, as described in Chapter 10 and Chapter 11. However, the tone is more familiar and informative. You're trying to build the relationship, not start one. If you come on too strong and forceful, even when you have a fantastic offer to make, the customer will be resistant. Worse, he might think, "These people are always trying to sell me something. I'll never buy from them again!" Ouch.

## *Problems and Complaints*

Dealing with problems and complaints from customers can be a challenge. The customer is usually—and perhaps understandably—angry and frustrated. A warehouse manager may have received a product shipment only to discover that a critical part was backordered. A trucking firm may have requested a repair, but the crew did not arrive as scheduled. An oenophile might have purchased an expensive new cork puller only to discover that it crumbles bits of cork into the wine.

**QUESTION?**

**Why are settling customer complaints so important?**
Some studies suggest that an unhappy customer will tell up to ten people about his dissatisfaction with a company or its products and services. So you not only risk losing a customer, but that customer may also prevent other potential new customers from buying your product or services. As the saying goes, "Bad news travels fast."

The biggest mistake that writers make in crafting a response to customer problems and complaints is being defensive. Sometimes legalese from the warranty fine print is sternly quoted in the letter or e-mail reply. This is a big mistake. It makes the customer even more agitated.

Dear John:

Regarding your request for a refund dated September 15, 2007. Please note that according to our warranty statement, which is printed clearly on the product packaging, we do not allow refunds on this product. Instead, you must send it in for repair to the following location...

How would you feel if you received a letter like that one? Like no one at the company cares?

Use some persuasive copywriting techniques to rewrite it:

Dear John:

I received your note that your XPZ-16 Voice Recorder isn't operating properly. All of us at XPZ are sincerely sorry for the frustration this must have caused you. Please give us a chance to make things right!

Send in the product to the service location listed below. If our repair technicians can't fix the problem immediately, we will replace the unit with a new one. That's a promise...

The second letter has exactly the same message as the first. But, as a customer, don't you feel better reading the second letter? There's a sense that someone—a real human being—is on your side, advocating for you. That's exactly the tone your complaint response reply must achieve.

## Collection Notices

Sending a letter or e-mail to collect on an overdue account can be tricky. That's because you are being pulled by two seemingly opposing objectives. On one side is the need to collect the money that is owed. On the other side is the desire to maintain customer satisfaction so that the customer will purchase from you again. (Assuming, of course, that you want him or her to.)

Even when they are in the wrong, customers feel insulted when receiving a collections letter. It's just human nature. So your challenge is to write it in such a way that it gets the job done without creating further ill will.

Here's an example:

RE: Invoice Number 23435-9

Dear John:

During the busy holiday season, it's easy for some things to fall through the cracks. It happens to the best of us! That's why we thought you'd appreciate this friendly reminder—to let you know that the above invoice is past due.

If you haven't done so already, would you please send your payment today? If there is any problem with the invoice that you would like to discuss, please call our customer service at…

Collections letters are often written as a series of three or four. The first is a friendly reminder, stating simply that the bill is past due. Subsequent letters are progressively sterner, reminding the customer of the consequences if he does not pay the invoice promptly. The final correspondence typically will feature the threat of legal action. If it gets to that point, persevering the customer relationship takes a backseat to getting paid.

## *Product Information*

If you ask any marketer or copywriter to rank project types in order of importance, product documentation would probably be at the bottom of the list. This is unfortunate because the information you receive with a product or service acts as a welcome kit. It is often the first written communication with the new customer, and it lays the foundation for all the other objectives that a company wants to achieve with that person—such as brand loyalty, recommendations, referrals, cross-selling, and up-selling.

Product information comes in many forms, including:

- User manuals
- Welcome letters and e-mails
- Autoresponders
- Instructions
- How-to CDs and videos

This area of customer communications creeps into the domain of technical writing and user-manual writing (both of which are unique specialties). As a copywriter, you will likely not be involved in writing the detailed documentation that comes with a product or service. However, you may be—and should be—involved in writing the welcome letter and other materials that greet the new customer.

You copy should reinforce that the company wants the customer to have a positive experience with the product or service. It should be friendly and personal rather than formal and aloof, which, unfortunately, is how most of this type of material is written.

## *Online Customer Communities*

The newest kid on the block in the field of customer communications is the online community. This is typically a special section of the company Web site that is reserved exclusively for customers. It often contains a lot of valuable free information and resources accessible only with a user name and password.

Online customer communities can include:

- A forum where customers can ask questions and get answers
- Online support or help from experts
- Articles
- Checklists and other stuff that can be downloaded
- Contests
- Newsletter archives

As the copywriter, you can be asked to write a wide variety of copy for an online customer community, including e-mails and letters inviting customers to participate, brochures explaining the community, and content for the site itself. As with other forms of customer communications, the basic writing objective is the same: To get customers to feel good about their decision to buy the product, so much so, in fact, that they'll buy more and tell others.

## Chapter 15

# Writing Marketing Communications Copy

Most of the how-to writing advice in this book is aimed at narrowly defined categories such as advertising or public relations. However, there are a few projects that just don't fit neatly into any particular camp. These projects, such as point-of-sale copy, corporate brochures, annual reports, trade show exhibits, and white papers, are included in this chapter.

15

## The Busy Marcom Department

As discussed in Chapter 2, marketing communications—or marcom as it is known in the industry—is a broad term. It refers to the creation and production of brochures, Web pages, e-mail campaigns, newsletters, advertising, press releases, virtually anything involving marketing and publicity, online or in print.

So don't assume that the projects featured in this chapter represent the entire spectrum of marketing communications. Not even close! They are only listed here to prevent them from slipping through the cracks. A white paper, for example, has become one of the most popular documents produced in business-to-business marketing. But is it advertising? Public relations? Sales communications? The answer is all of the above and none of the above. But there is one thing for certain: it is marketing communications.

**FACT**

Marketing communications is a huge field. Most large companies have a marketing communications manager, or even an entire marcom department complete with writers, designers, and production coordinators. There are also agencies that are referred to as marketing communications firms.

## Get to the Point with POS Copy

Go to any retail store and pick a product off the shelf. Chances are it will be covered with promotional copy on the front, back, and even the top and bottom! This packaging copy is part of a small niche in marketing communications called point-of-sale (POS) marketing.

The purpose of POS marketing—also known as merchandising—is to motivate you to buy the product when it's right there in front of you. It's designed to defeat your hesitation, overwhelm you with benefits, and get you to take the product to the cash register and pull out your wallet. Look at the text on the front and back cover of this book. That is a form of POS copy.

As a consumer you're familiar with this type of promotional copy. You see it everyday. It's on the side of the cereal box you stare at each morning, and on just about every item that has a package around it at your local grocery store, home improvement center, electronics shop, or other retailer.

**QUESTION?**

**Why is POS copy so important?**
Have you ever picked up an item from a store shelf and then stood there wondering whether you should buy it? This is the moment of truth in retail shopping. What POS copy attempts to do is transform your hesitancy into a purchasing decision by reminding you of all the great features and benefits of the product.

POS marketing might seem like it's primarily targeting consumers. But it plays a surprisingly significant role in business-to-business marketing as well. Business software, for example, utilizes intensive POS copy packaging. Some software product packages contain more than 1,500 words of text! You'll also find motivating POS copy hard at work at industrial and commercial supply stores (farm supply depots, plumbing supplies), computer and office supply retailers, and even at trade shows.

## Packaging and More

Packaging is the most common form of POS marketing, but it certainly isn't the only one. There is a wide spectrum of promotional pieces that are developed for in-store merchandising purposes. Any of which you may be asked to write as a copywriter.

- *Signage*—including posters, window stickers, banners, and pole signs
- *Coupons*—usually located with the product, or at least close by
- *Displays*—used not only to hold the product but also to promote it, often located on a floor, shelf, or counter

- *Product sheets*—a list of features and benefits, popular in computer, electronics, home improvement, and other stores that carry products where more information is required than can fit on a package
- *Aisle violators*—signs that stick out at a 90-degree angle directly into the aisle so they can't be missed
- *Shelf runners*—signs that are tucked under a product and fold down to expose the promotional copy

## *Pen Your POS Copy*

POS copywriting is very much like writing an ad. The only tangible difference is that the product is right in front of the customer. So your copy doesn't have to be introductory or descriptive. Instead, you can focus immediately on the key features and benefits, those sales messages that motivate an already interested prospect to buy.

**ALERT!**

In most promotional pieces the rule is to focus on the benefits. However, in POS copy, features can be equally important. If you're shopping for a new office printer, you need to know specifics about the print quality resolution, pages per minute, and other features. If 2,400 dpi is what you need but you can't find that information on the box, you may not buy the product.

The copy on product packaging and other in-store promotional pieces should be persuasive enough to sell the product then and there. You might not get another chance! So make sure that the information presented is complete, clear, and persuasive.

Here are some copy elements found in most POS marketing pieces:

- Quotes from glowing product reviews
- Testimonials from satisfied customers
- Special offers
- A free giveaway or bonus inside

- Comparison chart of the product versus the competition's
- Summary of top features and benefits
- Information on warranties or guarantees
- A list of applications for the product

If the product is an upgrade, or a new and improved version, be sure to highlight the new features and benefits on the packaging. Make these stand out to ensure that previous customers of the old version will be motivated to buy the new one.

If practical, write copy for every surface of the package, including the top and bottom. After all, you never know which part of the packaging the customer may be looking at.

## Corporate Brochures

While a sales brochure helps to sell a specific product or service, a corporate brochure focuses on promoting the company itself—its history, management, capabilities, innovations, and ideals—in addition to its current lineup of products and services.

The overriding objective of a corporate brochure is to persuade the general public—especially the investors, media, partners, and customers—that this is a great company with a bright future. Corporate brochures are also known as capabilities brochures, corporate profiles, and corporate histories.

When writing a corporate brochure, follow these guidelines:

- Just because it's called a corporate brochure doesn't mean the copy should be stiff and formal. It's okay to use a casual, even fun, tone.
- Use plenty of facts, statistics, and other evidence to support the claims made in the copy. A corporate brochure isn't the place to paint rosy descriptions of benefits you can't really prove.

- Be careful with anything that might date the brochure. Things can change quickly in a company. A new product due to be launched in the fall could very well be canceled. If that happened, the full-page spread you dedicated to it would become embarrassingly obsolete.
- Put your key messages in headlines, subheads, callouts, and text boxes. People often scan rather than read corporate brochures cover to cover.
- Answer the question "Why this company?" throughout the piece. Why should the reader invest in, support, or believe in this company?

There's a lot of scrutiny when you write a corporate brochure. Because it's about the company as a whole, senior management will likely review every word you write. Expect a lot of feedback and requests for changes and revisions. Here is an excellent example of effective corporate brochure writing.

**FACT**

Because they cover so much ground, corporate brochures often run several pages. Since the company is promoting itself, no expense is spared. These types of brochures are often printed on glossy stock featuring expensive photography and illustrations and sophisticated graphics and layout.

### Conquering the complexities of Canadian sales taxes

There are many definitions of innovation. But perhaps the most apt is that it's an idea whose time has come.

Bob Brakel had such an idea just over three decades ago. Recognizing how difficult it was for financial managers to cope with Canadian sales taxes, he pioneered a groundbreaking solution built on a novel contingency fee model that virtually eliminated the problem.

It was an innovation that gave birth to an industry.

Today, Robert Brakel & Associates is the recognized authority on Canadian sales taxes. In an age where tight budgets, scarce resources and crushing deadlines are the norm in most accounting departments, RBA clients tap a wealth of resources that make it easy to:

- Stay on top of tax issues,
- Get fast answers to tough questions, and
- Generate and sustain significant sales tax savings.

The toughest challenge in writing a corporate brochure is to avoid being too narcissistic. It's not easy talking about yourself without coming off as a braggart. The trick is to position the company's attitudes, ideals, achievements, and capabilities as benefits to the target audience. It's the same as in any promotional piece you write. You have to answer the question every reader asks: "What's in it for me?"

# Annual Reports

An annual report includes a lot of the same information as a corporate brochure, but with some key differences.

First of all, an annual report contains the company's financial statements for the year. In fact, that is technically what an annual report is: the financial statements that public companies must file with the Securities and Exchange Commission. All the promotional stuff singing the company's praises is extra and not required. However, companies can't resist an opportunity to promote themselves.

Because of this unique duality, an annual report is often divided into two sections. The first section features information about the company—very much like a corporate brochure but focused primarily on the year's achievements. The second part contains the auditor's report and financial statements. As a copywriter, you don't have to worry about the latter. (What a relief!) If you're asked to write an annual report, your job is limited to the first section only—basically everything before the section called Management Discussion & Analysis (MD&A). Unlike a corporate brochure, which can be organized any number of ways, the structure of an annual report is much more standardized:

- A front cover, often with a tagline or theme that relates to that given year.

- A page that highlights the year at a glance, often with lots of charts and graphs. Sometimes five- or even ten-year summaries are featured to show a trend.
- A one-page company profile, including a mission or vision statement. Timelines with key milestones may also be included. Again, this is to show a trend that the company is growing and has a track record of success.
- A letter from the president or chairperson. This is often called "Letter to Shareholders" and is usually one to four pages.
- Several other pages of content that is similar to what you would expect to find in a corporate brochure.

Annual reports are categorized as investor relations, which is a distinct communications field. Sometimes an investor relations agency will handle the annual report project, or someone inside the company may take on the job. Investor relations is all about keeping shareholders happy with the company they have a stake in, as well as attracting new investors to the fold.

## Creating the Book

The most challenging aspect of an annual report is writing the opening letter from the company president or chairperson. Since you're ghostwriting for the big boss, a lot of people will be vetting your copy. You may also have to interview the president or chairperson to determine what he or she wants to say to the shareholders. If you're not used to dealing with senior management, this can be a little intimidating. Don't worry. Just ask your questions and take good notes. Most executives are surprisingly down to earth.

Here are some useful annual report writing tips to follow:

- When ghostwriting the president's or chairperson's letter, don't make him or her sound distant, formal, or aloof. Make the tone friendly, open, informative and, most importantly, confident.

- Don't dance around controversial issues, such as poorer than expected financial results or being involved in labor strife. Present the facts clearly and directly. Show that the company is dealing with issues openly and with an intelligent plan of action.
- Avoid inadvertently predicting the future. For example, don't say in an annual report that "This new product is certain to seize substantial market share when it is launched next year." That statement may be misleading. Instead, position any forward-looking statements—the term the investment community uses—as plans rather than predictions. For example, "This new product is designed to meet a growing demand in the marketplace."

Annual reports are prestigious projects within the realm of marketing communications. Writing one will definitely be a feather in your cap. So enjoy the experience!

## Trade Show Exhibits

Since medieval times people have been selling their products and services at trade fairs. Amazingly, this method of reaching prospects and customers is more popular today than ever before.

**FACT**

Thousands of trade shows are produced each year throughout North America catering to just about every industry or special interest group. There are shows for wedding planners, gardening enthusiasts, cottage owners, boat lovers, golfing nuts, plumbers, real estate brokers, and more, plus shows for just about every industry, from chemicals to industrial equipment to pharmaceuticals.

To promote their products and services, companies often rent space at trade shows, put up lavish booths, and spend days exhibiting their wares. In some industries, attendance at the annual show is practically a necessity. (People will think you're out-of-business if you're not there!)

Companies spend a fortune participating in trade shows. When you take into account the costs of designing and building the exhibit, transportation, airfare, hotel and meals for the exhibit staff, and fees paid to the trade show producer, it's not unusual for a company to invest tens of thousands of dollars into a single show. That's often much more than would be spent on even the most lavish advertisement or direct-mail campaign.

Imagine the frustration, and waste of money, when few potential customers visit the booth. Ouch!

No wonder companies are so careful when creating their trade show booths and exhibits. They want to attract as many visitors—potential customers—as possible.

## Writing On Walls

As a copywriter, especially if you work for a business-to-business company or client, you can expect to handle a variety of projects related to getting prospects to attend a show and visit an exhibit. These can range from invitations sent by direct mail and e-mail to banner advertising and telemarketing campaigns. "Visit us at the Pet Owners Show and get a free bag of organic doggie treats!"

One of the most interesting copywriting tasks is writing copy for the trade show exhibit itself.

Most trade show exhibits are primarily dimensional and visual. Most have no words at all. But for some exhibits, well-crafted words and phrases positioned on the panels of the exhibit can play a major role in attracting visitors and holding their attention.

Trade show exhibit copy can range from just a headline to several short promotional blurbs to even full paragraphs.

When writing copy for the trade show panel, follow these important guidelines:

- All the techniques you've learned for writing a great headline apply to trade show exhibit copy. So use them!
- Your primary goal is to gain and hold attention. The salespeople in the exhibit will take care of the rest. So you don't need to have a strong close or call to action.

- Client testimonials and quotes from case studies and success stories can be very effective.
- Use short words, short phrases, or bullets, not full sentences or paragraphs.
- Focus on the biggest, most important benefit to the exhibit visitor. Often that's all you have room for.

Being concise is the key. You must distill your sales message to just a few powerful phrases, or even just words. Don't worry about conveying detailed product information. The handouts and salespeople at the booth will take care of that for you.

## *White Papers*

A white paper is an educational piece used primarily in business-to-business marketing. It typically explains a new or best way to solve a specific problem.

For example, a company that offers corporate training seminars in business writing skills might produce a white paper titled "How Ineffective Writing Can Cost You Sales." The document would explain the effect that bad writing can have on customer service, sales, marketing, and public relations.

Is a white paper always called a white paper? Not necessarily. For the sake of variety and distinctiveness, some are labeled as executive briefs, special reports, or overviews. Many don't have labels at all, just the document title. So the term *white paper* is often just a descriptive term.

White papers are used extensively by business-to-business companies to hand out at trade shows, add oomph to sales presentations, get known in a niche market, and enhance credibility. They are often made available as a download on company Web sites and used in lead-generation programs. In fact, business people are constantly being inundated with invitations via direct mail, e-mail, and advertising to download a company's latest white paper.

## What Does It Look Like?

A white paper is typically five to ten pages in length. Some can be as short as just two pages, while others—especially in the IT and pharmaceutical sectors—can have dozens of pages, approaching the length of a short book.

White papers are usually not as glossy as a brochure. Often they are simply designed and laid out to complement the nonpromotional style and tone of the piece. Most of the visuals used are charts and illustrations to support the content. The idea is to make the white paper seem unbiased, with solid information that the reader can truly benefit from. But make no mistake. Ultimately a white paper is designed to help the company get sales. That's why the conclusions drawn at the end of such a document almost always tie directly to the company's own products or services.

Here's an example of the opening few paragraphs of a typical white paper:

Title:
The Power of "Factory Thinking" in Sales Lead Generation

Subtitle:
How leading companies are using management techniques, traditionally applied to manufacturing, to optimize and accelerate sales lead generation

Overview:
Can the lead generation process really be like a factory? Can the cost-control, predictability, and overall rigor of goods manufacturing be applied to the seemingly tumultuous world of sales and marketing?

The answer is "yes" – but with some important exceptions.

This paper discusses how leading companies are using "Factory Thinking" to optimize and accelerate demand generation. The results? Lower costs, predictability, higher sales–*sooner*, and, in many cases, a significant competitive advantage.

In the following pages, we take a closer look at how factory thinking works, the limits of this analogy, what management techniques from manufacturing can be applied to sales and marketing, the steps to take, and recent examples of how companies are benefiting…

Writing a white paper is a major project. Often, you're expected to do extensive research, conduct interviews, and submit a detailed outline for review by your boss or client before you even type the opening sentence. It's like writing a little book. A white paper is usually structured as follows:

- A cover with a captivating title and perhaps two or three subheads.
- A one page (or less) executive overview that gives the reader the gist of the issues that the white paper will cover.
- An introduction to the problem or issue.
- The explanation of the solution—what it is, how it works.
- Supporting evidence, including statistics, charts, graphs, research results, and authoritative opinions from outside experts.
- The benefits of implementing the solution—results in terms of cost savings, revenue gains, productivity gains, new markets, or sales increases. Often case studies are integrated here.
- A summary, or next steps, which tells the reader what to do next to implement the suggestions in the white paper. (This is usually a thinly veiled pitch for the company's products and services.)

Take another look at the white paper excerpt above. Notice the extensive use of facts, statistics, and other information from authoritative sources. This is what makes or breaks a white paper. To be successful—which means to be taken seriously by the target audience—it must build a solid argument based on unbiased evidence and opinion. If your white paper doesn't, it will be seen as nothing more than a sales brochure in disguise.

## Proven Writing Strategies

Writing a white paper can be a challenge, simply because it is so different from most promotional pieces. You really can't compare it to a brochure, Web site, or anything else. Here are some proven tips that will help:

- *Be a relentless researcher.* Dig for all the facts and other evidence you can find to support the theme of the white paper.
- *Write an attention-grabbing title.* Your target audience is exposed to a lot of white papers, so make sure your title will stand out in the crowd.
- *The writing style and tone should be highly informative, descriptive, and educational—not promotional.* You're not trying to sell something. You're trying to influence the reader's thinking which, hopefully, will lead him or her logically to your company's product or service.
- *Readers may not have the time to read the entire document.* So make sure you summarize all the salient points in your first page or executive summary. This is like the abridged version of your white paper.
- *White paper expert Gordon Graham advises, "No one likes TLA that MTFD.* In other words, no one likes Three Letter Acronyms that Make Them Feel Dumb." Unless you are certain that the audience will understand a particular term, buzzword, or acronym, be sure to explain it at least once in the document.
- *If possible, include case studies and other real-world examples of success.* These help build belief, which is especially important in white papers because the topic is often a new technology or methodology that may be yet unproven to the reader.

It can be difficult to sustain the nonpromotional style of a white paper, especially when you're used to writing more aggressive sales copy for such projects as advertising and direct mail. What do you do if you're in doubt? Err on the side of being too educational rather than promotional. The number one complaint among prospects who read white papers is, "I've been duped! This thing is nothing more than a long-winded sales pitch." That's an impression you don't want to make.

Chapter 16

# Writing Branding Copy

IBM. McDonald's. Wal-Mart. Each of these names conjures up a distinct set of images and feelings for you. This is no accident. These companies spend a significant chunk of their marketing budgets trying to influence how you think about their products and services. Companies not only want you to recognize and remember their particular brands, they want you to prefer them. And, as a copywriter, you play a significant role in that effort.

# What Copywriters Need to Know about Branding

Just a few decades ago, branding was purely a creative advertising technique. Unless you were in the industry, you might have thought of branding as something that makes cows yelp.

These days, however, a brand is a serious corporate asset. You may make the best cereal in the world, but if it doesn't have Kellogg's printed on the box, you're at a serious disadvantage. After all, that's the brand that persuaded people to eat corn flakes!

Companies like Virgin use their well-known brands to sell everything from music to cell phones to airline tickets. People trust that brand so much that they're willing to purchase just about any product or service associated with it.

**FACT**

One of the oldest brands in the world is Chiquita. The company, in its earliest incarnation, began exporting bananas into North America in the 1870s. Today, it's one of the most recognizable brands in the food industry.

In the case of Virgin, MGM, Apple, and many others, the brand name has taken on a life of its own. A popular brand can be as valuable to a company as its physical assets, such as office buildings, manufacturing plants, and transportation networks. Companies are even bought and sold on the strength of their brands.

## What Is a Brand?

A brand is a combination of all the good things you associate with a company or product name—images, feelings, opinions, ideas, and attitudes. When you hear the word Sunkist you probably think of fresh, great-tasting oranges or juices. When you drive by the Lincoln dealership, the first image that comes to your mind might be that of a wealthy businessman.

In order for a brand to become valuable to a company, it has to get the RAP, which stands for:

- *Recognize*—the company or product name is instantly recognizable, even when all you see is the logo or tagline.
- *Associate*—the company or product name elicits predictable thoughts and feelings. For example, you probably associate the Mr. Clean brand of household detergents with a clean and bright kitchen or bathroom.
- *Prefer*—the company or product is not only recognized by its target audience, who associate it with good things, but is also preferred by those people. They will tend to select the brand over its competitors, even when the competing brand has more desirable features.

There is a fourth stage in brand development, although marketers don't focus on achieving it. This is when a brand becomes part of the popular culture or everyday vernacular. For example, if you have a stuffy nose, do you ask for a tissue or a Kleenex?

## The Selling Power of a Brand

Why do companies and their ad agencies spend so much time and money building a brand? A recognized and preferred brand helps sell the product. It makes all the marketing pieces that are developed—advertising, direct mail, e-mails, Web pages, and other promotions—work even better.

Think about it. If you received two flyers in the mail, one from Dell and the other from an unfamiliar brand, which one would you order a new $2,500 laptop computer from? Chances are Dell would get the sale.

And branding isn't just for big companies. Some businesses and even independent professionals can—and should—build their own brands. Even a deck contractor in your neighborhood could be so well-known for his workmanship and honest pricing that he becomes a powerful local brand. The neighbors know his name (*recognize*), feel good about the work he does and what he charges (*associate*), and select his deck building services over all others (*prefer*).

## *Where the Copywriter Comes in*

It's true that branding is primarily the domain of marketing strategists. However you, as the writer, can play a significant role whether it's for your own business or your client's.

Copywriters often participate in brand building activities, such as developing positioning statements and brainstorming taglines. (A tagline can, in fact, make or break a brand.) And there are many writing projects that are specific to branding. In addition, you need to understand the personality of the brand as you write other projects promoting the product or service. You need to know when to weave key brand messages into your copy and when to leave them out.

## *Build the Brand Identity*

A lawn care company turns to you write some copy for them. It's a new business so they want you to help them build their brand. Where do you start?

An effective brand is more than just the words and images you might find in a logo or tagline. It implies a unique benefit that the customer can only get by purchasing that particular product or service. So your first job is to find out exactly what it is that makes your client's lawn care service unique and meaningful to its customers. You then have to capture that essence in all the marketing materials you subsequently create.

**QUESTION?**

**Isn't the brand just the logo?**
When we think of a brand, one of the first things that comes to mind is the logo. This can be represented as an image, a stylized word or phrase, or a combination of both. But this is just the tip of the spear in the overall brand strategy. A brand is actually a whole series of images and messages that convey what is special about a product or service to its target audience.

Where do you begin? The best place to start is to use one of the following tools to determine what it is about the brand that makes it special—or could make it special—to customers.

- USP
- Positioning Statement

## Stand Out with a USP

The unique selling proposition, or USP, was first coined by advertising legend Rosser Reeves in his 1961 book *Reality In Advertising*. According to Reeves, a USP has these three characteristics:

1. The marketing message makes a proposition to the prospect. It says that if you buy the product or service, you will get this specific benefit in return.
2. The proposition must be one that the competition either cannot, or does not, offer.
3. The proposition must be so strong that it will motivate a significant amount of the target audience to buy the product or service. (In other words, it will motivate more than just the low hanging fruit.)

Reeves' insights into a successful USP gives copywriters a handy tool for creating a powerful brand message—or just about any other type of sales message for that matter.

For our lawn care company, the number one benefit—the unique proposition—might be a weed-free lawn without the use of dangerous pesticides or herbicides. If the local competition doesn't offer organic lawn care services, then this would satisfy both the first and second conditions of our USP.

But what about the third requirement? Is chemical-free lawn care enough of a benefit to convince a lot of people to sign up for the service? It could be. Especially if the neighborhood has a lot of families with small children and pets. Homeowners might be concerned about the effect of pesticides and herbicides. So organic lawn care could be a desirable alternative.

So the USP could be: "A healthy, green, weed-free lawn without using pesticides or herbicides that may harm your family or pets."

Connecting healthy lawns to family health and safety, the major theme of the brand could be: "Healthy lawns. Healthy families."

## Get CAT-y with Positioning Statements

Another strategy you can use to build the foundation for a strong brand is to use a positioning statement. A positioning statement is like staking a claim. It's often about getting there first. When M&M's claimed that their candies "melt in your mouth, not in your hand," the company was staking a claim. It's not like other candies don't have the same characteristic. Many do. But M&M's got there first. They struck a nerve with coated candy eaters everywhere who were sick of sticky hands!

There is a simple formula for creating an effective positioning statement. It's called CAT.

- *Category*
- *Advantage*
- *Target audience*

This formula is very simple to use. When writing a positioning statement for a company or product, begin with the category, state one or two key advantages—preferably something that the competition doesn't do—and then focus on the target audience.

For our lawn care company, our positioning statement could be: "Our lawn care service [*category*] is the only one in town that offers chemical-free lawn care [*advantage*] to families that care about health, safety, and the environment [*target audience*]."

## How Branding Affects Writing Style

How exactly do we integrate what we know about the brand into the sales letters, ads, e-mails, and other promotional pieces we create? The primary effect that brand has on copywriting is the personality or tone of the copy. Like people, most brands have a personality—a way of communicating that is distinctive. Ever notice how Apple Computer commercials always seem fun, creative, and playful? That brand's personality is centered around the core theme that Mac's are easy to use. And this theme is carried over into the copy for their commercials, Web pages, brochures, and advertising.

A law firm brand, on the other hand, might be stern and serious—a threat to any other law firm that opposes them in court. As the copywriter, your writing style and tone would then be authoritative and decisive; consistent with the brand.

Wouldn't all law firms be marketed this way? Not necessarily. The USP of a different law firm might be: "The divorce law specialists who guide individuals and families through tough times." The brand personality here is more supportive and caring than the previous example. Your copy would need to have a caring tone. "We're here to help you through this crisis while protecting your rights."

Look at some of the advertising and other promotional materials for products you know well. A sunny travel destination may be described as fun, adventurous, and exotic. The words used in a real estate agent's ad might emphasize speed and proficiency. An ad for a carpet cleaning company might emphasize care, thoroughness, and modern equipment.

All of these companies probably went through some strategic exercise, like the USP or positioning statement tools featured earlier, to try to work out what is distinctive about their products or services. "What's so special about us?" they asked. "And how can we communicate that effectively to our target audience?"

That's the advantage of a strong brand message. It acts as both a theme and a touchstone to guide the writer through the creation of the promotional materials. It helps you stay on message.

# Taglines and Slogans

How long does it take to dream up the perfect slogan for a new product? Five minutes? Five hours? Five days!?

The answer is…there is no answer! That's the nature of developing taglines and slogans. You could come up with a catchy phrase right away or agonize for hours or days, brainstorming dozens or even hundreds of alternatives.

At first glance you might think that writing taglines and slogans is a pure act of inspiration, that there are no formulas, techniques, or other strategies to help you. Fortunately, this isn't true. There are proven brainstorming techniques you can use that will make the whole process a lot easier.

But first you need to know the difference between these often confused terms. Because taglines and slogans are not exactly the same.

## Close Cousins

A tagline is a line of copy, usually just a few words, that is connected with a company or product name. For example, the famous tagline for Nike is "Just do it." It is meant to encapsulate the essence of the brand in a way that has a significant impact on its target audience. "Just do it" says that Nike is a serious athletic-wear company for active, energetic people. There are no excuses. Just do it!

A tagline is often positioned next to or integrated with the logo. Many professionals consider the tagline the written equivalent of the logo.

A slogan is very similar, but this term is not exactly a synonym. It may also be used with the company or product name, but slogans are most often developed as temporary themes for advertising campaigns, conferences, product launch events, and marketing-related activities

## Dream Up a Winner

Developing a good tagline or slogan requires a combination of strategy, inspiration, and luck. There's not much you can do about the last ingredient. If it happens, it happens! But you have a remarkable influence on strategy and inspiration. Sometimes it can come quickly. The copywriter working with software developer AutoDesk dreamed up "Tools for 3D Minds" within just a couple of minutes of receiving the assignment. Sometimes, however, putting together that perfect combination of words can take a lot longer than you expect.

What makes a winning tagline or slogan? The very best have the following characteristics:

- *It's easy to remember.* A slogan or tagline that cannot be easily recalled by your target audience isn't much use. You want the words to stay with prospects or customers, and even be repeated by them to others. If you hear "Hey, honey, let's have some finger lickin' good chicken tonight!" someone's going to KFC.
- *Contains a key benefit.* Great slogans and taglines don't always express a benefit directly. But the words often hint at or imply one.
- *Differentiates from the competition.* Some of the most effective taglines and slogans immediately set the company or product apart from the competition. This is usually done by emphasizing a USP or positioning statement (as explained earlier in this chapter).

Notice a pattern to the above? Despite the fact that they might be highly creative or clever—seemingly pure acts of inspiration—a successful tagline or slogan follows the basic rules of good copywriting. So there is really no mystery. It has to gain attention, be benefit focused, and set the product or service apart from the competition.

## Brainstorming Techniques

The next time you're asked to develop a tagline or slogan, follow these steps:

1. Look at the USP or positioning statement for your product or service. Get clear about the key benefits, advantages over the competition, target audience, and the one thing about the product or service that makes it distinct.
2. Brainstorm a list of keywords and phrases that are related in any way to the product or service. Don't be judgmental. Don't hold back. Write down as many options as comes to mind. The longer the list the better.

3. Expand on your brainstorm list by using word tools. Dig out your dictionary, thesaurus, synonym finder, and rhyming dictionary. Use an unabridged dictionary, as the origin and history of a word can be a great source of ideas. Most of these reference books are available online, making searching and compiling results even faster.

4. Play with all the words and phrases on your list. Move them around. Discover interesting ways you can put them together. Often, two seemingly unrelated phrases can be effective, such as "Healthy lawns. Healthy families" in our earlier lawn care example. If potential taglines or slogans jump off the page, highlight them. But don't make any final decisions yet.

5. Create a list of your top ten to twenty possibilities. Don't worry if a phrase is not fully developed yet. You can polish it later.

6. To narrow your list, focus on those candidates that represent benefits and results for your target audience. For a courier company, that might be those words and phrases that describe speed, accuracy, timeliness, and reliability. For a coffee machine, it could be style, speed, ease of use, convenience, and great taste. By this point you should have a handful of potential taglines and slogans.

7. Get opinions. Circulate your list to friends, colleagues, or those at your clients' location. Don't explain anything. Don't tell them your favorites. What you want to get is their first impression. Once you do, ask if the slogan or tagline is memorable, implies a meaningful benefit, and is distinctive from the competition.

8. By this stage you probably have two or three good candidates. Which one is easier to say? Which one lingers in your mind? Which one fits the personality of the brand? Sometimes the choice isn't easy. It may come down to a flip of a coin.

You can work through these steps on your own. But it's far more effective, not to mention less stressful, to collaborate with others. If you work at an ad agency or as a staff writer in a company, get some colleagues to go through this process as well. This can be a fun assignment. Chances are others will come up with ideas and options that you would have never discovered on your own. Tagline and slogan development is one of those rare copywriting tasks where too many cooks in the kitchen is actually a good thing!

# Copywriting Projects Most Affected by the Brand

Remember the famous line in George Orwell's *Animal Farm*? "All animals are equal, but some animals are more equal that others." You're probably wondering what that has to do with branding and copywriting. Well, everything you create for a product, from ads and direct mail to Web sites and in-store promotions, are affected by the brand identity.

In the following project types, you have to take special care to meld the key brand messages with the copy you're writing. In many ways, these projects are long-form expressions of the tagline or slogan. So they have to be consistent.

## Product Boilerplate Descriptions

Just about every product or service has a succinct paragraph that describes it. This is often referred to as the boilerplate. Here is an example:

**Checkup Toothpaste**
Fluoride-free Checkup Toothpaste fights cavities, plaque, tartar and bad breath, naturally. The proven formulation of myrtle, tea tree, and grapefruit thoroughly cleans and refreshes your teeth, your gums—your whole mouth! Finally … a toothpaste safe for the whole family. So go ahead. Show us your smile. Checkup can help it last a lifetime.

Boilerplates are handy things to have at your fingertips as a writer. You can plug them into brochures, press releases, trade show panels, just about anywhere that a short, explanatory blurb about the product is required.

The product boilerplate is often developed during the product launch phase and is often updated frequently throughout a product's time on the market. A boilerplate can even be tailored to various market segments.

An accounting software product, for example, may have multiple boilerplates: one for the small business market, another for IT professionals, and still another for corporate finance managers. So, depending on the product, you may need to write a whole fleet of boilerplates, ready to deploy in any target market or situation that arises.

One thing is for sure: the boilerplate must be consistent with the brand identity. In fact, next to the tagline, it is the written representation of the brand.

Writing a boilerplate is a lot like crafting a good elevator speech. Imagine that you're in an elevator with a potential customer. You have about ten seconds to describe your product as completely and persuasively as you can. Once those elevators doors open, your time is up. What would you say? Your answer would probably make an effective boilerplate.

## Company Profiles

In business-to-business marketing, where a customer can spend tens of thousands of dollars on a product or service, the company behind the brand matters. This can also be true when marketing to consumers. Wouldn't you want to learn more about the company you are going to trust with your retirement savings? That's why the About Us section of the Web site, brochure, and other promotional materials can be so important.

**FACT**

Company profiles are often produced in two versions: short and long. Press releases use the short version, which is usually just a paragraph. Lengthy brochures, corporate folders, and Web sites tend to use a more expansive version, often a page long.

The biggest mistake that copywriters make when writing a company profile is making it too narcissistic. Remember that prospects and customers are primarily interested in themselves. What's in it for them? You have to connect the dots and describe how the history, people, resources, and unique characteristics of the company is important to the reader.

Here is an excerpt from a company profile used in the About Us section of the company Web site:

> Established in 1929, Morris Real Estate Marketing Group has been active in many aspects of marketing and communications.
>
> Since 1991, we have focused exclusively on marketing solutions that build referrals and repeat business for real estate professionals.
>
> Why?
>
> Because we've done the research. And discovered that no other marketing approach—*not* mass advertising, *not* geographic farming, *not* cold calling, *not* anything—drives your business to the top with more certainty than Referral & Repeat Marketing.
>
> And that excited us.
>
> So we decided to commit to this marketing approach…an approach that elevates your status as a professional, and builds your business to a level where your clients respect you as a trusted advisor, rely on you whenever they move, refer you to friends and colleagues and, most importantly, are loyal to you.
>
> And if the success stories we hear from the thousands of real estate professionals we work with is any indication, we made the right decision…

Two things are clear from the Morris Real Estate example. This is a company with a definite brand personality. It isn't just a staid or boastful profile. You get a sense that these are real, honest people. And the profile conveys how the unique characteristics and resources of the company is a benefit to customers—in this case, real estate agents.

## When the Brand Gets in the Way

An effectively developed brand identity, complete with key messages, taglines, boilerplate descriptions, and slogans, can help make the copywriting of other materials much more effective. However, there are some circumstances where strict branding guidelines will get in the way of achieving the results you need.

This is especially true of direct-marketing projects, such as direct-mail, telemarketing, and e-mail campaigns. Direct marketing is much more concerned with getting sales than in trying to influence the way people think or feel about a product. The very success of a direct-marketing campaign is measured by how many clicks, replies, leads, or orders are generated. As a result, direct-marketing writers tend to rely on proven sales copy techniques to get the job done. And these aren't always compatible with the brand writing guidelines.

For example, product style guides or brand guides (explained in Chapter 8) may require a copywriter to use the boilerplate product description when the product is first mentioned in the copy. But can you imagine the impact on a telemarketing campaign if the telemarketer was forced to read a one paragraph blurb before proceeding into the pitch? Most people would just hang up. The same is true for sales letters, and even ads.

## Negotiation Is Key

It's understandable that the marketing department of a company wants to do everything possible to build the brand. And requiring consistent messages in all communications seems like a good way to accomplish this. It is, in most cases. But when it gets in the way of campaign success, some compromises need to be made.

If you feel restricted by brand writing guidelines that are impeding the success of a promotional piece, don't be afraid to bring this up with your boss or client. Explain your case and negotiate an exception or compromise. Ultimately, everyone wants the promotional piece to be successful. So bending the rules a little is usually not a problem.

# Chapter 17

# Special Copywriting Situations

There are some copywriting topics that don't fit neatly into any particular category. This chapter covers the projects that don't always follow the standard rules of copywriting and special situations that you're bound to run into from time to time. There is nothing mysterious or even difficult about these tasks. They just require some additional tips and strategies to get the job done successfully.

## *Business-to-Business*

Imagine you're writing two brochures to promote a new brand of house paint. The first targets homeowners, the second professional painting contractors. Would you write the second brochure in exactly the same way as the first? Probably not. The contractors will have a different set of needs and desires, as well as a more sophisticated knowledge of paint. While quaint descriptions of family dinners in a beautifully painted dining room might captivate a homeowner, a contractor will respond more to such technical facts as the square-foot-yield per gallon or the drying time required between coats.

The second brochure belongs to a category of marketing called business-to-business. As the term implies, this refers to businesses selling products and services to other businesses rather than to consumers. (As you've probably guessed, the other main category in marketing is business-to-consumer.)

**FACT**

Business-to-business goes by many other terms and acronyms. The most frequently used are B-to-B, B2B, and business marketing. For some strange reason, even B@B is sometimes used. So when someone asks if you can write B2B copy, don't mistakenly think they mean for a bed-and-breakfast!

Most of the general rules of effective copywriting apply to business-to-business communications. You need to explain the features carefully, bring the benefits to life, build belief—everything you learned in Chapter 3. However, you need to be aware of some crucial differences.

### *What Makes B2B So Different?*

Business people tend to have split personalities. That doesn't mean they're psychotic. It's just an expression of the tug-of-war that goes on in their minds when making a buying decision. On one hand, they want to address the needs of the business. On the other hand, they have personal quirks and preferences, too. Usually, the result is a compromise. That's why you'll see an expensive marble table in a boardroom, even though the company doesn't really need something so extravagant. The VP just likes it.

Business people also tend to make buying decisions based on a need rather than a want. For example, a consumer might buy new shoes just because she wants them—even though she has a closet full of shoes. By contrast, a businessperson will tend to buy only things that the business needs. A warehouse manager, who likes flowers, will have trouble getting a purchase order approved to decorate the warehouse with geraniums. But a new forklift truck? Probably not a problem.

Finally, business buyers may know a lot more about the products than you do. If you're writing a brochure to promote an air-conditioning system to HVAC contractors, these professionals are going to know air-conditioning systems inside and out. Your job, as the copywriter, is to present all the technical features and applications clearly, accurately, and persuasively. Lofty platitudes about a cool, comfy home just won't cut it.

## Writing Tips for B2B

Here are some tips for writing powerful business-to-business copy:

- *Stress the business benefits.* Business buyers act on behalf of a company. So highlight how your product or service will reduce costs, increase sales, avoid liabilities, gain a competitive advantage, improve quality, boost productivity, or accelerate cash flow.
- *Stress the personal benefits.* Business buyers are individuals. So explain how your product or service will save them time, make their job easier, make them look good to their superiors, get them promoted, advance their career, or get them home in time for dinner.
- *Features are important, too.* Don't rely on benefits alone to sell a product or service to a business audience. You must fully explain all the features of what you are selling. A human resources manager will want to know the dry research statistics behind the success of a new management training program. A plant engineer will need detailed technical specs before she orders a new pump bearing.
- *Write to the job title.* Not all business buyers have the same beliefs, interests, and desires—information you need to know to sell your

target audience. A financial manager will have very different purchasing habits than a sales manager. The first will want to keep costs down and buy only if you demonstrate a solid payback. The second may be willing to spend just about anything to reach her sales targets.

- *What's the payoff?* A business buyer often thinks of a product or service in terms of the potential return on investment. By saving time, reducing costs, or improving performance, how long will it take for the product to pay for itself? There's no bluffing your way through it. Your copy must present a solid business case.

- *Highlight the track record.* Unlike consumers, business buyers don't want to be the first to try something. They're not about to jump on board the latest trend too quickly. Instead, they want products and services that already are working well at other companies. So be sure to include plenty of customer testimonials, product reviews, client lists, success stories—anything that establishes a track record of success.

- *Get to the point quickly.* The main challenge in business-to-business communications is to write short, effective chunks of copy. Business buyers have no patience for long-winded puffery. They're too busy! So you must quickly explain what your product or service is, what it does, and how it benefits—otherwise the business buyer will simply move on to something else.

- *Speak their language.* Every profession has its own buzzwords, acronyms, and colloquialisms. If you're writing copy aimed at IT managers, for example, be sure to use terminology they are familiar with. (A tip: Review the trade publications your audience reads to get a sense of the language. A warning: Be accurate; nothing will torpedo the credibility of your copy more than incorrectly using a term or acronym.)

## Complex Products

It's common, especially in business-to-business communications, for a copywriter to be intimidated by a product he or she does not immediately understand. You may be confronted with a lot of strange and unfamiliar information along with weird terms and acronyms you can't begin to decipher. You may think: "If I can't understand it, how the heck am I going to write about it?" Don't worry. There are some very simple steps you can take to get your head around even the most mystifying products and services.

Business-to-business copy doesn't have to be stiff and formal. In fact, some of the best copywriting in this market is casual in its style and tone. How casual? Text that sounds like you're chatting at a weekend BBQ is probably too laid back. Copy that sounds like a professional sharing important information and ideas to a group of colleagues is more like it.

## Read Everything

This is obvious. Ask your boss or client to provide you with all the relevant information available on the product or service—brochures, Web pages, advertisements, e-mail promotions, sales letters—the works. (See Chapter 3 for a suggested list.)

Review this material thoroughly. Make note of things you don't fully understand so you can ask for clarification later. In the movie *Philadelphia*, Denzel Washington's character says, "Explain it to me like I'm a two year old." It's a great line. Use it!

## Get the Glossary

There are specialized dictionaries and glossaries available for just about every conceivable topic, from insurance terms to software acronyms to even snowboarding colloquialisms.

Years ago, these guidebooks were found only in print publications. These days, the Internet is the best place to look. Just type in the industry or product into Google or some other search engine and then add the word "glossary." Chances are a number of free glossaries will come up.

## Buy the Children's Book

Want to learn about semiconductors? Don't buy a technical book. Get the fully illustrated children's book version instead, complete with pop-ups! Your learning curve will be much easier.

Nonfiction books for kids may keep things simple, but they certainly are not dumbed down. In fact, many children's science and technology books are written by experts. One copywriter once learned the basics of digital animation from a children's book while writing a Web site for a software company targeting this industry.

## Speak to Sales

Copywriters most often work with marketing, public relations, and communications managers. But no one knows more about how to explain and sell a product than the people who do it every day—the salespeople.

When writing about a product that you don't fully understand, consider asking your boss or client for permission to speak to a salesperson, preferably one who works in the field dealing with prospects and customers face to face. These professionals have a knack for explaining product features clearly and concisely, and they also know which benefits are most important to the target audience.

In fact, salespeople are often a treasure-trove of stories, examples, and ideas you can use when writing your copy.

## Get Pictures

Pictures really are worth a thousand words. Confused about how wicket valves fit inside a hydroelectric turbine? You won't be once you've seen photos of a typical installation. Writing a microsite promoting a resort in South Beach? Unless you've traveled there yourself, seeing the pictures is the only way to really bring the place to life in your copy.

Find out if there are any available pictures or illustrations of the product. If you're writing a Web site promoting a new time-management system, for example, then seeing screen shots and examples of the forms used will help you understand the system much better—and faster—than simply reading an explanation.

## Get the Real Thing

Nothing compares to actually seeing, touching, and even trying the product or service you're writing about. Writing a promotion for a seminar? Find out if you can attend it. Crafting copy for a new countertop water-purification system? Ask if you can try it out in your own home. Creating copy to sell a new line of unicycles? Take one out for a test drive!

Seeing and experiencing the product or service up close is not always possible. But when it is, you'll gain a much deeper understanding—much more quickly—than you ever would with just a picture or description.

# Fundraising Letters

You've probably received a fundraising letter. It could have been from a local church asking you to contribute an item to a yard sale. Or the college you attended requesting your financial support of an important alumni program.

Fundraising letters are used by nonprofit organizations as a means to raise money for their good work. Most people think of nonprofits as charities, and many are. However, there are several other types of nonprofits that conduct fundraising campaigns, such as advocacy groups, political parties, research institutions, arts groups, and more.

**FACT**

There are two types of fundraising letters: the acquisition letter, which is sent to people who have no history of donating to the charity; and the renewal letter, which is used to get past contributors to donate again.

There are few, if any, similarities between a traditional sales letter and a fundraising letter. In a sales letter, you're asking people to exchange their dollars for a specific product or service. In a fundraising letter, you're asking for money and offering nothing of substance in return.

That's what makes writing a fundraising letter so tricky. The classic copywriting rules concerning features and benefits, and making an enticing offer, just don't apply. That's why some copywriters focus on fundraising letters and related materials exclusively. It's a specialty that is difficult to master.

Here are tips for writing a winning fundraising letter:

## Write in the First Person

Unlike many other forms of business communications, you must give the reader a strong sense of the author. The voice of the person who has signed the letter at the bottom should shine through in the copy. This person can be a director at the charity, a well-known celebrity who supports the organization, or even someone who has personally benefited from one of the charity's programs.

The writing style should be candid, personal, and conversational. A "friend-to-friend" tone often works well. There is a deeper level of intimacy in a fundraising letter that does not exist in traditional sales letters. After all, you're asking someone for support. It's personal.

## Use Stories

Stories help the reader visualize and appreciate what the charity is doing, and how a donation will help the organization perform even more good work. Take a look at this example of the first paragraph of a fundraising letter:

I remember my first night being homeless. I was cold. I was hungry. I was terrified. Life wasn't supposed to be like this. I was educated—a master's degree. Yet, sitting on the street shivering, I didn't know where my next morsel of food would come from…

Notice how the first-person account of homelessness brings this issue closer to home for the reader? This isn't just a vague category of people you have no relation to. This is a real person you might have sat next to in a college class!

## Get Specific

Don't use generalities like "Your donation will help feed the poor." Be specific. Tell the reader exactly what their dollars will buy. Writing that a $25 donation will help feed starving children overseas is not nearly as compelling and motivating as "Your $25 will buy a basic well for a village that can provide desperately needed clean water for months...even years."

## Make It Urgent

Give the reader sound reasons why he or she should donate right now rather than waiting until some milestone like the end of the year or tax time.

Get into the field and talk to the people who are doing the day-to-day work for charity. Meet some of the program beneficiaries. Their stories and insights will give you a perspective that will help you write a more effective fundraising letter.

Here's a compelling line from a fundraising letter: "Five single moms die of AIDS each day in Africa's poorest nations, leaving children homeless and starving. But your $25 a month will change the destiny for one of these kids...if you act now."

## Use the "M" Word

Don't tiptoe politely around the issue by cloaking your request with such polite terms as *support* and *financial assistance*. If the charity needs the reader to send money, ask for it. Don't be afraid to use the words *money* and *dollars*. For example: "Would you please donate $100 this month to help us meet the needs of this urgent crisis? Your money will buy five refurbished blankets that will provide warmth to the suddenly homeless in this area."

## *Selling to Resellers*

A reseller is simply a distributor, retailer, agent, broker, or dealer who buys products and services for the purpose of reselling them. For example, when you buy a new VCR from your local electronics store, that retailer already will have purchased the product from the manufacturer. The marketing materials produced by the manufacturer convincing the storeowner to stock the product will be much different from the brochure, ad, or flyer that persuaded you to buy it.

Just like consumers, resellers need to know the product's features and benefits and other key information. They also want to know how best to sell the product, how quickly it will sell, and how much money they can potentially make.

There are three objectives to keep in mind when writing copy that targets resellers: educate, equip, and organize.

Marketing materials that target resellers are often referred to as alliance materials or channel marketing materials. They often include special Web sites, brochures, training guides, selling tools—anything that's needed to persuade a reseller to get behind the product and sell it.

## *Educate*

Obviously, educating resellers on the nuts and bolts of the product is essential. But educating isn't easy. (Just ask anyone in the training industry!)

To facilitate learning, your copy must be organized, insightful, interesting, and easy to read. Use plenty of numbered lists, points, charts, pictures, and illustrations. When a reseller has a question, make sure the answer can be found easily.

## Equip

Resellers need selling tools. These are letter templates, model proposals, presentation slides and scripts, brochures, sell sheets, checklists, demo kits, and anything else that makes it easier to explain and sell the product.

Some companies make the big mistake of producing a single brochure that does double duty—targeting both resellers and their customers. The truth is, you can never effectively speak to two disparate audiences simultaneously. What you end up with is a diluted, even muddled, sales message.

**ALERT!**

Some manufacturers produce special sales guides and other documents that help resellers explain their products to customers. If the guide is long, be sure to include a one-page summary of key product points. No store clerk wants to look bewildered flipping back and forth through pages when a customer is standing in front of him.

If you have any say in the matter as the writer, create a separate set of marketing materials that speak directly to resellers. Their interests and requirements are different. And your copywriting should reflect that.

## Energize

If resellers don't get excited about a product, then they won't sell it. It's that simple. So your copywriting must inspire and motivate. How do you accomplish this? There are two questions that a reseller asks when considering purchasing a particular product:

- *"Will it be profitable?"* Where applicable, use plenty of charts and graphs to illustrate income potential. Be sure to use realistic numbers and forecasts.
- *"Will it be popular?"* If the product has done particularly well in other markets or territories, be sure to emphasize this in your copy. Cite research studies and surveys that demonstrate why the product will fly off the shelves.

When writing copy that targets resellers, you should also follow the guidelines in the business-to-business section earlier in this chapter. After all, resellers are business people.

## Long-Copy Sales Letters

You've seen them in the mail or read them on the Internet: mammoth sales letters that run on for pages or scroll down your computer screen for what seems to be a vertical mile. Do people really read these things? Direct marketers wouldn't spend time and money creating these unique and often controversial promotions if people didn't read them. Direct marketers often use long-copy sales letters to sell information-based products, such as pricy newsletter subscriptions or expensive how-to audio/video programs, via direct mail and Web sites.

Direct marketers know long copy works for their particular products because they test promotions continuously. If a two-page letter performs better than a twelve pager, they're not about to waste paper and ink on the latter. Direct marketers use long-copy letters in their promotions for one simple reason: It works.

**ALERT!** There's a difference between long copy and long-winded. It's not easy to hold a reader's attention over a four-, six-, or even sixteen-page letter. You have to make sure every page is fresh and compelling. Write just one lazy, dull paragraph and you risk losing the reader—and the sale.

Long-copy sales letters are one of the most difficult copywriting skills to master. But those who do are among the highest-paid practitioners in the freelance market.

So how do you write one? In addition to the copywriting basics explained in other sections of this book, here are the essentials:

- *Make a big promise in the headline.* But not so big as to be completely unbelievable. Empty promises such as "Double Your Income" don't work. However, a headline that says something specific, "How to Lose 2 lbs. Per Week and Never Feel Hungry," can be effective. (So long as you can prove that claim.)

- *Write a great lead.* Because the copy is so long, your first two or three paragraphs must be extremely compelling. Your words here must pull the reader in and motivate him or her to stay with you through the rest of the letter.
- *Create vivid word pictures.* The sheer length of long-copy letters gives you plenty of room to paint scenarios, examples, and stories with your words. Take advantage of this!
- *Use descriptive subheads.* The reader should be able to get the gist of the most important key messages just by skimming the subheads. (And many readers will do just that.)
- *Summarize the benefits at the end.* Some readers will skip to the end of the letter. Others will forget details they read earlier. So on the last page, remind them of all the great reasons why they should respond to the offer.

In addition to these tips, be sure to follow all the other rules of effective copywriting. (See Chapter 5.) If you're weak in just one area—if you fail to prove a claim or bring some benefit to life—your copy may not have enough oomph to make the sale.

## Preparing a Copywriter's Rough

When writing copy, your primary concern is the words. However, there may be circumstances when you have to prepare a copywriter's rough. This is typically a simple drawing—done on paper or on a computer—that shows in a very general way what the layout should look like and how the text should be placed.

"Whoa, wait a minute!" You might balk. "I'm not an artist. I can't even draw a convincing stickman!"

Don't worry. Preparing a copywriter's rough isn't nearly as difficult as it sounds. You just need to be able to make a simple sketch. Even a rough pencil scribble is fine.

## *You Don't Have to Be an Artist*

Your assignment is to write an ad for a flower shop. You might have an image in your mind of a businessperson in her office with a beautiful bouquet of flowers on her desk. You might even imagine her leaning toward the flowers and enjoying the pleasant scent as she talks business on the phone.

How do you communicate all this? You could simply use words to describe the scene. But a more compelling way to present your idea would be to sketch out the desk, the businessperson, and the flowers. Then other people on the project—the designer, for example—can see what you mean.

Most computer programs used for writing, such as Microsoft Word, have tools that make drawing basic shapes very easy. In just a few clicks, and some practiced moves of the mouse, you can create convincing rough sketches of just about anything. You can also save your drawing as a computer file, which makes it easier to share with others.

Worried about your lack of artistic flair? It's not a problem. Most graphic designers can accurately interpret even the crudest scribble. You can draw something as simple as a circle on a page and put a note beside it that says, "A picture of a happy customer goes here." The designer will know exactly what you mean.

# Chapter 18

# Conquering Common Copywriting Problems

Not every copywriting project you handle will go smoothly. Some will make you feel like you've just crawled out from under the rubble of a train wreck! The very nature of trying to do creative work, often under strenuous deadlines, means that you're bound to encounter some challenges. It comes with the territory. Fortunately, there are solutions to the most common dilemmas you may face.

## *What to Do if Your Copy Doesn't Sell*

You write a search engine ad and no one clicks on it. You craft a landing page promoting an e-book and it doesn't generate any sales. You slave over a sales letter until you're certain that copywriting legend Bill Jamie would have been jealous and it doesn't get any response. What do you do?

**ALERT!**

Effective copywriting is a combination of proven strategies, inspiration, and just plain luck. Even when you write well, and empty everything that's in your copywriting bag of tricks onto the page or screen, your copy may still be a flop.

Copy that delivers less-than-expected results can be a difficult situation for you as the writer. You obviously want your boss or client to be pleased with the work you did. The discovery that a promotion did not go as well as everyone had hoped is never happy news. The most important thing is to not be hard on yourself. Even the big hitters in Major League Baseball strike out every once in a while. It happens.

### *Put It in Perspective*

First of all, many of the reasons why a promotional piece may fail are out of your control. The product may just not be appealing, no matter how tantalizing the copy is that describes it. The mailing, telemarketing, or e-mail list may be low quality or out of date. The target audience may be wrong. You can't sell penguin traps to an Eskimo no matter how hard you try. (There are no penguins in the Arctic.) The competition may also be so fierce that it's a struggle for your promotion to even get noticed, let alone persuade anyone.

In some cases, you are given an opportunity to analyze the results and rewrite your copy. This is often the case in online marketing where it is relatively easy to make changes to the promotion or even go entirely back to the drawing board.

What do you look for during a copywriting postmortem where you can identify what's working, what's not working, and what needs to be changed? Here are some ideas:

- *Look for the obvious.* Is there a key fact that's missing? Are the phone numbers and Web URLs correct? It's amazing what can be overlooked. A promotion for a free seminar didn't get any response because—as discovered too late—the writer neglected to say that the event was free!
- *Check for clarity.* Are there any sections that lack clarity, or seem muddled or confusing? Customers won't buy if they don't understand what you're saying.
- *Watch out for assumptions.* Not every Web site owner who wants to sell products online understands what a "payment gateway" is. If in doubt, spell it out.
- *Put yourself in the reader's shoes.* Is there any reason why the prospect would not buy the product or service? Look at your sales training brochure from the reader's perspective. You might discover that you didn't provide enough information.
- *Try a new headline.* A new headline can have a huge impact on the effectiveness of a promotional piece. In direct marketing it is generally known that changing the headline affects response rates much more so than altering the body copy.
- *Check the ingredients.* Review Chapter 5 and the ingredients of highly effective copy. Did you miss something? A proof? A benefit? An inspired call to action? If so, revise accordingly.
- *Did you misfire?* Did you take aim at the problems, needs, and desires of your target audience with the most appropriate sales messages? Or is your copy missing the mark? Selling to accountants is very different from selling to engineers—even when you're pitching the same product.

For additional guidance in revising your copy, use the copy review checklist in Appendix B.

If tweaking and revising your copy doesn't work, perhaps you need to completely rethink your promotion. Clear the decks and start over again from scratch. A completely new approach might be just what is needed to finally hit one out of the park.

## *Dealing with Conflicting Feedback*

Your boss or client reviews your copy and returns it to you with comments and suggestions scribbled all over it. You're able to deal with most of this feedback (an edit here, a revision there) fairly easily. However, there are a couple of comments that conflict. In the second paragraph, one reviewer says that the copy is too "salesy," while another reviewer writes, "This section isn't strong and motivating enough." Who's right? Who's wrong? And who decides?

Feedback from more than one person is normal on most copywriting assignments. If you are writing copy for even a small company, then your words are going to be scrutinized by a few people. The marketing manager might review your copy first, then the sales manager might take a turn, and finally the company president might run his eyes over it. By the time you get your copy back, it's bleeding with comments, and they will not always be in sync.

**FACT**

If you're freelancing or working for an advertising agency, public relations agency, or major design firm, a whole committee—everyone from the creative director to the account executive—vets your copy. And that's before it gets sent to the client for even more reviews. So be prepared for plenty of feedback.

There's a natural instinct to make comments and offer suggestions when shown a piece of writing. If Harper Lee's Nobel Prize–winning novel, *To Kill A Mockingbird*, was passed around an ad agency or marketing department, there would be a flurry of requests for revisions! So don't take it personally.

## *Get Clarity*

The best way to deal with conflicting feedback is to be proactive. Ask your boss or client upfront, before you begin writing, who will review the copy. Hopefully, it will be no more than two or three people. But if the review committee is large, be sure to ask who makes the decision should there be conflicts in the feedback. Then at least you'll know who has the final word.

And don't forget that your opinion counts, too. Speak up! If the art director wants to lose a headline because he thinks it will make the piece look nicer, and the marketing manager wants to keep it, don't be afraid to take sides. "In my opinion, we should keep the headline in," you might say. "It's a proven principle in direct marketing that a headline helps to gain attention and encourage readership."

But what do you do if you can't get anyone to make a decision regarding conflicting feedback? Not much, unfortunately. There is no practical way to integrate two opposing comments into your copy. So you must make it clear to your boss or client that a decision needs to be made. Make your best recommendation on which way to go. Then say, "That's my suggestion. What's your decision?"

## *My Client (or Boss) Hates My Copy!*

"I have a few concerns about the copy you wrote and we need to talk." Ouch! If there is anything that a boss or client can say that will send a shudder down even the most thick-skinned copywriter, that would be it.

No doubt about it. It can be distressing when someone is less than pleased with your work. It's hard not to take it personally, feel discouraged, or even get depressed.

So what do you do when your boss or client does not like what you wrote? Ideally, you want him or her to feel reassured that a prompt revision—by you, of course—will make it all better.

Here is a six-step strategy that works very well in these situations:

### Step One: Don't Be Defensive

You want feedback, not combat. Listen carefully to your boss or client and try to determine what went wrong. Be open to criticism, suggestions, and new ideas. Don't act angry or defensive, even if you disagree. Be the consummate professional.

### Step Two: Explain Your Approach

Sometimes a boss or client doesn't understand why you wrote something the way you did. You may need to explain your strategy, or justify a particular copy element.

For example, in a sales letter you wrote for a small company the owner noticed that you used a P.S. (postscript). He balks, "Is that really necessary? It looks kind of gimmicky to me." You can simply explain that using a P.S. is very effective (as you learned in Chapter 10) and that you recommend it be kept. The owner will likely take your advice.

### Step Three: Ask for Specifics

Never accept vague feedback like, "Paragraph three just doesn't work for me." Nail down specifics. Ask your boss or client such questions as:

- "Are all the facts correct?"
- "Am I missing anything?"
- "Is there any extraneous information I should delete?"
- "Are there any awkward passages or transitions?"
- "Did I explain all the features and benefits clearly?"
- "Does the style, tone, and vocabulary fit the target audience?"

Don't guess. *Know* what needs to be fixed before you revise the copy.

### Step Four: Confirm

Once you have gone through the copy and clarified the areas that need revision, confirm these details with your boss or client. Make sure you are both in agreement as to what changes need to be made.

## *Step Five: Set a Deadline*

Never say, "I'll turn this revision around in a couple of days." Always confirm exactly when you'll complete and submit the revised draft. Your commitment to an exact deadline is very reassuring to a boss or client.

## *Step Six: Complete the Revisions Exactly as Directed*

When revising the copy, you may be tempted to explore new angles or try new ideas. Don't. Complete the revisions exactly as requested. If you have a great idea, present it separately.

These six steps are very effective. It's not uncommon for a boss or client to quickly go from being critical of your copy to praising your writing skills! So the next time you receive the dreaded "I've reviewed your copy. We need to talk…" call, you'll know what to do. Keep your chin up. Follow the steps. Act professional. Then get to work on those revisions!

# Writer's Block

As a copywriter, writer's block can strike you in many different ways. A project may be tough and complex and you feel intimidated. Or you might have a clear idea of what to write but are struggling to do so creatively. You might feel stuck on a particular headline, paragraph, or section and, try as you might, just can't seem to fix it. Or you might not feel like writing at all, preferring instead to do something else—like, say, cleaning your window blinds with a toothbrush.

What's the cure? Try these treatments the next time you get stuck.

- *Don't try to get it perfect the first time.* Don't be afraid to write something that is so bad that you wouldn't show it to a six-year-old for fear of ridicule. The most important thing is to write something, anything, even if it is far from perfect.
- *If you can't fix it, go around it.* Stuck on a headline, sentence, or paragraph that you just can't get right? Just skip a problem section and move onto the next. You don't have to write everything in order. You can always go back and work on difficult sections later.

- *Look for inspiration.* Go back to the source. Review the creative brief, background materials, and other notes and information on the product or service you're writing about. Often this will be the catalyst for new ideas, or ideas that you thought about earlier but then forgot.
- *Take a break.* Grab a coffee or take a walk around the block to clear your head. Try to think of anything but the project. Sometimes clearing your head also clears the block.
- *Try mind mapping.* This is explained in more detail in Chapter 4. As you connect thoughts and ideas, often that elusive "aha" moment will arrive and, before you know it, your fingers are dancing on the keyboard once again.
- *Don't procrastinate.* Often writer's block is simply a reluctance to get in front of the computer and do the work. Here's an idea. Find a stopwatch. Say, "I'm going to work on this project for one hour, without interruptions, diligently." Then do so until the alarm goes off.

The worse thing about writer's block is that it tends to breed even more writer's block. So take action right away using one of the above techniques. Staring at a blank screen or notepad rarely works. Just start writing anything. Map out your ideas. Make notes. Write in bullet points. Whatever gets the words flowing. Once you start taking action, momentum will kick in and, before you know it, you're writing again.

## Too Much Information, Not Enough Space

This is a common problem that happens to most copywriters. You slave over your copy, writing powerful headlines and body copy that sizzles. You cover all the salient selling points and describe the product features and benefits in a compelling manner. Then, once you've completed your masterpiece, your client, boss, or graphic designer comes back to you and says, "The text doesn't fit into the layout. It's too long. Can you cut it?"

There is an old saying in the advertising industry that goes something like this: "Your copy should be as long as it needs to be to do the job." That's a wonderful ideal. Unfortunately, it's not always practical. There are limits to the copy length of any project that a copywriter needs to adhere to. So what do you do when you have to trim your copy? Here are a few tips:

- *Go through the text and highlight every word or phrase that is absolutely necessary for the prospect to know in order to respond to the promotion.* Then look at those sections that you did not highlight. Can any of this extraneous text be shortened or eliminated altogether?
- *Take a look at your leads.* Often the first few sentences are just introductory warm-ups, which can be deleted with little, if any, adverse affect on the copy. (These cuts often improve the copy.)
- *Look at your closing copy.* This is often just summary text that ties your promotional piece up in a nice, neat bow. But ask yourself if this text is necessary. If not, cut it.
- *Take a look at your explanations.* Do any of these seem long-winded or overly expansive? Sometimes this is necessary. But if it really isn't, condense these sections.
- *Check for puffery.* Are you laying it on thick in some passages in your copy? Puffery happens when we abandon the use of solid features and benefits in favor of empty phrases. So cut the puff.

If all of the above fails to trim your copy down to a reasonable size, you have some tough decisions to make. If the promotion revolves around five key product benefits, maybe you can knock it down to the top three. Or you could emphasize the most important benefit in your copy and give the others second billing.

## Making It Happen Under Impossible Deadlines

What do you do when your boss or client hands you a great project but with a daunting deadline? If you're a freelancer, you may not want to turn down good paying work. If you're a staff writer at an agency or company, you may not have any choice. The job has to get done. And it's on your desk.

## *First Step: Negotiate*

When you are assigned a project deadline, ask why that particular date is so important. There may be a very good reason for a given deadline. Perhaps a trade show date is looming and the salespeople need a new brochure to hand out to visitors. Or a seminar date is coming up and the direct-mail invitations have to be in the mail by a certain date.

However, some deadlines are more arbitrary. Busy managers understandably want to get completed work in from their employees or freelancers as early as possible. In this case, you can often negotiate a more realistic deadline that fits both your schedule and your boss's or client's. For example, you could say: "This deadline is very tight for me. What would happen if I delivered the copy to you by next Wednesday at noon?"

## *Second Step: Do It*

Sometimes a deadline is a deadline and you just can't negotiate. What do you do? Usually your only choice is to just do it. Here are some tips that will make it easier.

- Clear your schedule. Tell your employer that you will have to put all else aside to get the job done.
- If possible, find a private office you can use, or ask if you can work from home so there are no further distractions.
- Write a draft as quickly as possible, no matter how terrible it is. Then clean it up. Revise it a few times. And polish.
- If it's a long project, divide the task up into smaller chunks. It will seem less intimidating.
- Get help. Is there another writer or editor who can assist you?

Deliver the best copy you can on the deadline. Surprisingly, the work writers do under pressure, even when the timelines seem impossible and a detriment to quality, is often very good.

## Chapter 19

# Getting a Job as a Copywriter

Imagine earning a great paycheck doing what others just dream of doing: writing. If you have a way with words, and a desire to work in marketing or public relations, there are a lot of job opportunities available. Many top professionals in these fields began as writers before progressing into senior management or creating their own successful businesses. Getting that first job, however, isn't easy. This chapter covers what you need to know to get your foot in the door.

19

## *Breaking in*

"So what do you do for a living?" someone asks you at a house party. "I'm a writer," you answer. A hush falls over the room. Heads turn. Suddenly, you're the center of attention. There is a fascination that many people have with writers. But, obviously, impressing people at social occasions isn't the best justification for getting a job as a copywriter. There are other more practical reasons why this employment opportunity can be so desirable.

**ALERT!**

Never discard a sample just because you think it's not suitable for your portfolio. Keep everything you write. You never know when a potential employer might have a nontraditional requirement—and your unsuitable sample suddenly becomes the ideal one to show.

As a copywriter or staff writer, you get to work with a team of creative professionals. In the morning, you're discussing layout with the design artist. At noon, you're meeting with a client during a working lunch to present your concepts for a new advertising campaign. In the afternoon, you're editing and polishing a new Web site. It's quite a day!

And here's the best part: You get a steady paycheck. No paying your dues as a starving artist. Even entry-level writing positions at agencies and corporations pay reasonably well. If your work is solid, you can expect to move up the ladder quickly. Eventually, you could be managing other writers, or even an entire communications staff of writers, designers, art directors, illustrators, and production coordinators.

The toughest part is breaking in and getting that first job. The competition can be fierce. A Help Wanted posting in the newspaper or on the Internet often generates a stampede of replies. There is no shortage of people who would love a job as a writer. But don't be discouraged. Someone has to get the work. And, if you follow the tips in this chapter, that someone could very well be you.

## Building Your Book

"Okay, let's see your book." That's one of the first things you'll hear during an interview for a job as a copywriter, especially at an ad agency or design firm. Your book is your portfolio of work—your writing samples. It demonstrates to potential employers your ability to plan and create the types of materials they may need you to write.

Typically, a book is put together in a large black portfolio case that, when open, takes up the better part of a conference table! Inside are several large plastic sleeves for holding and displaying your samples. You can buy a portfolio case at your local art or office supply store.

**FACT**

You can showcase your writing samples on the Internet, either on your own Web site or on special sites that offer online portfolio services, such as Elance (*www.elance.com*) and Portfolios.com (*www.portfolios .com*). This can be a great way to expose your credentials and talents to prospective employers. In fact, many will ask if they can review your portfolio online before they decide to interview you.

You'll definitely need a book to get a job at an ad agency, design firm, public relations firm, or other creative agency. It's considered the ticket to the industry. So it pays to spend time putting together the most effective portfolio possible.

Corporate marketing and PR departments work a little differently. You may be able to get a writing job without a fancy portfolio. However, you'll have a significant advantage over other candidates if you at least have some well-written samples to show. Think about it. If you're hiring a home improvement contractor to renovate your kitchen, wouldn't you want to see some pictures of his previous work?

## What to Put Inside

What types of samples should you include in your book? If you've only written a few published pieces, include all that you have. However, if you have lots of potential writing samples to choose from, you're lucky. You can pick and choose the most impressive ones to showcase in your portfolio.

Most portfolios feature ten to fifteen writing samples. Writers often will customize their books for each job interview to match the needs of that particular company or agency. If an ad agency creates mostly online work for its clients, it is not going to be impressed by your print brochure. It will want to see samples of your Web sites, banner ads, and e-mail campaigns.

## Ideal Copywriting Samples

When looking for a copywriting job, any sample is better than none. Yet there are some types of samples more suitable for a portfolio than others. These include just about anything involving sales, marketing, and public relations.

- Advertisements
- Advertorials
- Articles
- Brochures, sell sheets, other sales literature
- Case studies and product success stories
- Direct-mail packages
- E-mail campaigns
- Flyers and circulars
- Fundraising letters
- Inserts
- Landing pages and microsites
- Media kits
- Packaging and point-of-sale materials
- Postcards and other self-mailers
- Posters and billboards
- Presentations
- Press releases
- Print, banner, and e-zine advertisements
- Product names, taglines, slogans, and positioning statements
- Radio and television commercial scripts
- Sales letters

- Speeches
- Telemarketing scripts
- Trade show exhibits and handouts
- Web pages or complete Web sites

## *No Writing Samples? No Problem*

If you're just starting out as a copywriter, you might have few or no writing samples to show. This is a common catch-22 for writers trying to break into the field. You can't get a job if you don't have published samples to show, and you can't get published samples if you're not already working as a copywriter. What do you do?

First, ask yourself if you have written at least some type of business communications. Think about it. In your current or past jobs, you may have been involved in writing:

- Blogs
- Blurbs in newsletters
- Business letters
- E-mails to customers
- Employee communications
- Handouts
- Letters to the editor
- Magazine articles and other journalistic pieces
- Memos
- Proposals or requests for qualifications
- Reports
- Speaker notes for presentations
- Training materials
- Web pages

These may not be ideal samples for your portfolio, but they at least show that you have some writing experience. It's a start.

You can also create spec samples to fill your book. Spec samples are simply pieces you have written just to showcase your talents. They were not real assignments. For example, you could write a flyer "on spec" for an actual travel company or even a fictitious one.

Marketing and public relations firms respect spec books. After all, many of the top professionals at these firms probably started their careers exactly the same way. During an interview, just be sure to point out that the sample you're showing is a spec piece. Never pass off something you did on spec as real.

The best way to create spec writing samples is to use the "before and after" approach. Collect a few ads, flyers, or Web pages that you think you can improve. Then rewrite them, showing the actual piece on one side and your improved version on the other.

If you take a course in copywriting at a college or professional training program, building a spec book of writing samples will likely be part of the curriculum. Student portfolios look impressive because they have been vetted by experienced instructors who often are industry professionals.

But spec isn't the only way to quickly produce some writing samples. Here are some other proven strategies:

- Volunteer to write copy for a local charity.
- Help a small-business owner with a brochure or sales letter in exchange for copies of the published pieces and a testimonial or recommendation.
- Offer to intern at a small design firm for a few weeks at a low salary.
- Contact a local freelance designer and offer to edit or revise copy. (Freelance designers typically receive copy from their clients that is poorly written.)
- Write articles for a small publication, such as a church bulletin or e-mail newsletter.
- Write your own materials to promote yourself to prospective employers. (Some writers get hired on the strength of their own self-promotions.)

Use your imagination. Think of ways to demonstrate your writing abilities. Often, all it really takes is one impressive writing sample for an employer to say, "Okay, we'll give you a try. Can you start next Monday?" In fact, one copywriter once got a job offer based primarily on the persuasive letter he wrote to get the interview!

## Agency Jobs

Tom Hanks. Cary Grant. Lee Majors. Lauren Graham. Even Gonzo (one of the Muppets). All have portrayed ad agency copywriters in movies or on television.

Working at an agency often is perceived as exciting and glamorous. And in many ways it is. There are a lot of fascinating projects you can be involved in—everything from glossy ads in magazines to major television commercials. You also get a chance to work with a team of other creative professionals. The camaraderie among agency staff is often tight. Friday nights at the pub is a common ritual.

However, there is a downside. As a copywriter at an ad agency, you can expect a lot of stress and late nights as you try to crank out client-pleasing copy under increasingly tight deadlines. It's not uncommon for the creative director—your boss—to bring you a cappuccino at five in the afternoon and ask, "We're pitching a new account tomorrow morning. Would you mind working late tonight on some concepts?" He's just being polite. You're expected to say yes.

**FACT**

There are many types of agencies. Advertising agencies manage advertising and marketing for their clients. Public relations agencies help generate publicity. Investor relations agencies produce annual reports and other materials that target shareholders and investors. Direct marketing agencies produce direct-mail, telemarketing, and infomercial campaigns.

Still, many writers love the frenetic pace and excitement of an ad agency environment. It's a great place to learn the ropes—and fast. If you get an entry-level job at an agency, you'll work with experienced professionals who will review your copy and help develop your talents. In addition, you'll be exposed to the full spectrum of communications development, everything from strategy and planning to production and distribution. You'll learn a lot in just a few months.

## Getting Your Foot in the Door

How do you get a job at an agency? The best place to look for opportunities is in major industry publications. (See Appendix C.) They often feature Help Wanted ads by agencies looking for writers and other creative professionals.

However, the best jobs often are never advertised. So take the initiative and contact agencies directly. Give them a call or write a great pitch letter explaining why you're a writer worth hiring. Most agency executives will respect your approach.

At large agencies, writers are usually hired by the creative director or copy chief. At smaller agencies, it's usually the senior partner or owner.

Salaries for agency writers vary widely, depending on experience and track record. If you're just starting out, don't be too disappointed by an entry-level salary of $30,000. It will increase quickly as you gain more experience and get a few projects under your belt. If you write a few very successful campaigns, other agencies may even woo you. You'll be in demand. Top copywriters can earn as high as $135,000, with the average for those with five or more years' experience being about $65,000.

## *Corporate Jobs*

While being an ad agency copywriter is filled with late nights, client meetings, brainstorming sessions, and fancy award shows, working as a staff writer for a corporation is a little more sedate.

**FACT**

As a staff writer at a company, ad agencies consider you to be working on the client side. To them, you're playing for the other team! That's not a bad thing. It's just their way of distinguishing you from copywriters on the agency side—those employed at or freelancing for an advertising, marketing, or PR firm.

As a staff writer in a company, you can expect to be an important part of the marketing, communications, or PR team. While the more glamorous projects usually get handled by the ad agencies, you'll be asked to write things that are equally interesting, such as brochures, Web pages, customer letters, press releases, e-mails, landing pages, articles, speeches, newsletters, and more.

Even though writing may be your primary task, the word "writer" may not necessarily appear in your job title. Staff writers are considered entry-level positions at companies and are expected to move up the ladder to more managerial positions involving other aspects of the communications function. So even though you're the resident wordsmith, your business card may say something like marcom coordinator, marketing intern, or communications manager.

Compared to ad agencies, the hours for a corporate staff writer are more sane. Sure, you'll put in the occasional late night or weekend. But on the whole, you can expect your schedule to be similar to other corporate employees—essentially an eight-hour day. And here's more good news: Corporate staff writers tend to earn more than their agency counterparts.

So what's the downside? Corporate staff writers often complain of getting bored or stale because they are writing about the same types of products or services each day. However, many writers also like the fact that they become the writing expert in the corporation and, as a result, become indispensable.

## Get the Job

Ad agencies are on the constant lookout for good writers. But this isn't necessarily so for corporations. Some companies may prefer to outsource all copywriting work to an agency or freelancer. Others may have a manager on staff who has a way with words and is the de facto writer, even though he or she has other responsibilities. (Corporate public relations managers, for example, are often skilled writers.) So the best way to get a corporate job as a writer is to watch for Help Wanted ads.

You'll find these ads in industry publications as well as Internet job boards. (See Appendix C.) Typically, an ad will say something like:

### Marketing Writer Wanted

Join the marketing communications team at an exciting, fast-growing company. Experience in the travel industry a plus, but not essential. Great starting salary with a review in three months. Send your resume along with your three best writing samples to…

Don't worry if you don't meet all the criteria listed in the ad. Apply anyway and give it your best shot. Companies often create employment ads with their ideal candidate in mind, but that person may not be available or even exist. So even if you fall a bit short of the qualifications, you might still get the job.

## Nonprofit Jobs

Nonprofit doesn't mean no profit. On the contrary, this sector represents one of the largest industry groups in North America, spending billions of dollars each year. There are tens of thousands of nonprofits across the country, ranging from small local charities run strictly by volunteers to larger multinational organizations employing hundreds of people.

Although the size of the nonprofit market is huge, only a small percentage of these organizations employ staff writers on a full-time basis. Larger national organizations can afford to keep a writer on staff to handle such projects as fundraising letters, grant proposals, Web pages, brochures, advertising, educational materials, and donor communications.

The midsized and smaller nonprofits tend to rely on volunteers and freelancers to write the copy they need. In fact, many freelance copywriters specialize exclusively in the nonprofit market. (See Chapter 17.)

**FACT**

When most people think of nonprofits, they think of charities. But that's just the tip of the iceberg. Nonprofits encompass a wide range of organizations including professional trade groups, symphony orchestras, advocacy groups, hospitals, colleges and universities, and research institutes.

Working as a writer for a nonprofit can be very satisfying, especially if you support the cause. For example, if you're an environmentalist, then writing copy for an organization dedicated to saving rainforests can blend your passion with your vocation. Every day you get to write on a topic that you care deeply about. The vast majority of working writers cannot make the same claim.

## Networking Is Key

Nonprofit is a close-knit sector. Everybody knows each other, and a lot of jobs are filled through referrals and recommendations. Writing positions are rarely advertised. So try to get to know the people at the major nonprofits that you are interested in. Volunteer. Network at local gatherings of nonprofit and fundraising professionals. (See Appendix C.) Writers typically are hired by executives with titles like fundraising director, executive director, and marketing director.

## Climbing the Ladder

You can be a happy camper for many years writing for a great company or agency. However, there is going to be a time when you want to—or have to—spread your wings. Either you'll have the desire to take on more responsibility or your boss, in recognition of your experience and track record, will want you to do so.

On the agency side, the career track for copywriters is fairly well defined. After a few years as a copywriter—or even just a few months if you're a fast-rising star—you can expect your pay to increase and your job title to change to something like senior copywriter. Eventually, you may become the copy chief managing a team of writers. If you're really ambitious, you might even climb to the top of the agency heap and become the creative director—a senior executive supervising an entire creative staff of writers, designers, art directors, producers, and production coordinators.

Creative directors are among the highest paid professionals in the ad agency world, typically earning more than $100,000 annually.

The career track for agency and corporate writers often involves getting into managerial positions where you are supervising others. However, many writers don't want to be managers and prefer to stick to writing copy. The option for them is freelancing. See Chapter 20 for more information.

In the corporate world, the career path is a bit more muddled. You can begin as a staff writer, but where you end up next is not always predictable. Usually, the ladder to success involves rising into managerial positions with titles like marketing manager, public relations manager, and marketing communications manager. These positions often involve less writing and more strategy and coordination. Eventually, you could be promoted to the top of the department, say, the VP of marketing.

That being said, corporate staff writers have been known to migrate from their original departments and find success somewhere else entirely. For example, you might start as a staff writer in the PR department, move over to the technical department to write user manuals, get promoted to marketing coordinator, and then end up in employee communications!

That's the exciting thing about getting a job as a copywriter. It can lead you on an exciting, and sometimes unpredictable, career path. Enjoy the ride!

## Chapter 20

# Hanging Out Your Own Shingle

Are you self-motivated? Want more control over the hours you work and the type of projects you handle? Does the idea of working from home, full-time or part-time, and earning a good income appeal to you? Then freelancing may just be your ticket! Self-employment is a popular option for both aspiring and established copywriters. It allows you to chart your own course and set sail toward a career where you are firmly at the helm.

20

# *Going Freelance*

Freelancing is simply another word for self-employment. The term is used primarily in creative communications fields such as journalism, public relations, marketing, graphic design, editing, illustration, and copywriting.

When you freelance, you are working for one or more clients on a temporary or per project basis. For example, the marketing manager of a restaurant chain may hire you to write a series of newspaper advertisements. When that job is complete, you send her an invoice for your services and, eventually, receive your payment.

Then it's on to the next project, and the next, and the next. Assuming, of course, that you have an effective marketing plan in place to attract a steady stream of new business. This topic will be covered later in the chapter.

**ALERT!**

The idea of being your own boss is actually a myth. As a successful freelancer, you'll have plenty of bosses. They just go by a different name: clients. And clients can be just as demanding to work for as any traditional employer.

Why freelance? There are many reasons why copywriters decide to hang out their own shingle. For example, you might be:

- A stay-at-home parent who wants to earn a part-time income on a flexible schedule.
- An entrepreneur who yearns for the freedom and challenges of being self-employed.
- An independent spirit who prefers to work alone rather than as part of a team at a busy office.
- A job seeker interested in copywriting who needs to freelance for awhile to gain experience and build a portfolio.
- An established copywriter who wants to earn a higher income. (Freelancers can earn much more than staff writers.)

Regardless of your reasons for considering freelancing, like any business, there are pros and cons you need to consider.

## The Pros

There are many advantages to being a freelance copywriter. For example:

- *Working from home.* No more rush-hour traffic. No more business suits. No more cranky bosses looking over your shoulder. There are a lot of comforts when working from home. You can even work in your pajamas!
- *High-income potential.* Freelance copywriting can be very lucrative. It's common to earn more than $50,000 in your first year working full time. Many established practitioners make a six-figure income.
- *Low start-up costs.* As home businesses go, freelance copywriting ranks among the cheapest to launch. All you need to get started is a place to work, business cards and stationery, and an Internet-connected computer.
- *Control over your schedule.* You can work when you want. Quit for the day when you want. Schedule vacations when it's most convenient for you and your family. Walk the dog. Do the laundry. Take an hour off and read a book at your favorite café (as long as you get your clients' projects done on time!).
- *Plenty of work.* The demand for freelance copywriting services is huge. There are hundreds of thousands of advertising agencies, design firms, marketing companies, corporations, associations, government departments, and small businesses throughout North America. These are all potential clients.
- *Interesting projects.* Sure, you'll get your share of tedious writing gigs. But for the most part, copywriting projects are as fascinating as they are challenging. One week you're writing a Web site for a investment advisory firm, and the next week it's an ad for a trendy spa!

## The Cons

Freelance copywriting is not without its downside. Here are the most common issues that working freelancers often contend with:

- *Solitude.* If you enjoy the energy of a busy office environment—the meetings, the power lunches, the water-cooler chats—then working from home may seem lonely at times. The cure for this is to stay connected with friends and colleagues via phone and e-mail.
- *Distractions.* There are many distractions and temptations when working from home—the kids, the television, the refrigerator. It can be tough to stay focused. It's amazing how a fifteen-minute lunch break can mysteriously stretch into an hour. When this happens, you might fall behind on urgent client projects. That's why self-discipline is so important for the work-at-home crowd.
- *No steady paycheck.* In the first few months, or even years, as a freelancer, the work flow will be uneven. One week you're buried in work. The next you're chewing your nails wondering if the phone will ever ring again. This feast-and-famine rollercoaster ride is common in freelancing. But if you stick with it, things will eventually smooth out.
- *Lack of support.* When you're employed at a company, what happens when you get sick or go on vacation? Someone fills in for you. As a freelancer, however, there is no one else who can take your place. If there is a problem with a project, you have to solve it. If you're out of office supplies, you have to place the order. That's the nature of freelancing. You wear every hat.

Weigh the pros and cons of freelancing carefully. If freelancing still appeals to you, give it a try. Many copywriters enjoy freelancing immensely, despite the drawbacks. To them, the freedom, control, and, in many cases, higher income they gain far outweighs the shortcomings.

# Services You Can Offer

As a freelance copywriter, you can offer a variety of services to clients. Your services will depend on your skills, preferences, and what the market is demanding.

As you'll see below, some freelancers do quite well teaching others how to write copy. But if you dislike speaking before groups, or leading discussions in learning situations, then this option is probably not for you.

Take a look at all the possibilities below. Which of these fit you best?

## Copywriter Extraordinaire

Most freelance copywriters do very well just writing copy for their clients. They don't deal with strategy, they don't handle design, they don't teach—they just write.

"I enjoy writing ads, Web pages and other promotions for my clients," one long-time freelancer said. "I have no desire to get involved in any other aspect of the project. I prefer to keep things simple."

The vast majority of freelance copywriters feel the same way. They offer writing services. Period. If they are asked to develop a marketing plan, or handle the artwork, or offer some other service related to the project, they either recommend another qualified professional or simply say no.

## Makeover Maven

In addition to writing services, there is a growing demand for analyzing, editing, and rewriting copy that already has been written by someone else.

Here's a typical example: A small-business owner writes a sales letter to promote her company. However, she recognizes that she is not a professional copywriter. She doesn't know all the tips and tactics required to make her letter successful. So she asks you, the copywriting pro, to review and revise it for her.

Many copywriters offer this kind of copy consulting service. It also is known as a copy critique, copy review, or copy makeover. Sometimes the service is limited to just analyzing the copy and making suggestions for improvement. More often it includes a complete rewrite.

Here is an example of how one copywriter promotes this kind of service on his Web site:

A Copy Review is an expert analysis and rewrite of your marketing promotion, which can either be finished or in draft form.

During the process, I go over everything with a fine-toothed comb—including the copy, design, strategy, and offer—and identify ways to make it better.

I look for what's working, what isn't, what needs to be changed and how. Then, after discussing my ideas and suggestions with you, I rewrite the copy.

You end up with a fresh, new, more effective draft ... one that is significantly more likely to generate the results you need.

**FACT**

Be careful. Clients expect to pay less for revising than they do for writing. The problem is some revising jobs can take just as long as writing the document from scratch. The solution? Be sure to read the draft you're being asked to revise before you quote a price.

## Training

Do you like to teach? If so, there is a small but growing niche for teaching others how to write effective copy.

You can put together a course or class on copywriting skills and then offer it to corporate training directors, seminar companies, membership organizations, and schools and colleges (as part of their continuing education programs).

If you're ambitious, you can even produce and promote your own live seminars. These days, teleclasses and Internet-based courses are very popular. So you can teach a class to students located all over the world but never leave your home!

## One-Stop Shop

Most of the documents you'll write as a copywriter require design work, at least to some degree. If you write a brochure, for example, it's probably going to need pictures, illustrations, layout, and other artwork. So the idea of offering both copy and design is enticing. You can make more money! However, this is easier said than done.

Design is a much more complex process than writing. There are many elements to juggle, from developing and presenting concepts to agonizing over sizes, shapes, and colors to even picking the paper stock.

If you are not trained or experienced in graphic design, you'll have to subcontract the work to a professional. This can lead to complications. You'll have to deal with the client, coordinate revisions for both copy and design, pay the designer, and make sure that everything is completed on time.

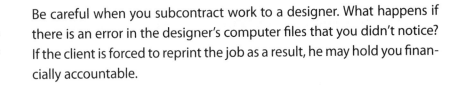

Be careful when you subcontract work to a designer. What happens if there is an error in the designer's computer files that you didn't notice? If the client is forced to reprint the job as a result, he may hold you financially accountable.

Don't assume the designer you subcontracted the work to will handle all the details. If the client is getting both the copy and design from you, you're the one who has to make sure everything goes smoothly. Expect to spend a lot of time on project management.

With that being said, some freelancers do very well offering both copy and design services to their clients. Some are even accomplished designers themselves.

## Consulting

Many freelance copywriters offer various types of consulting services or handle special consulting projects. Here are a few examples:

- Developing a program to get more articles published in trade magazines.
- Creating a plan to generate more leads for the sales force.
- Analyzing a Web site to maximize its chances of being listed high in search engine rankings. (This is called search engine optimization, or SEO, and is discussed in Chapter 11.)
- Developing concepts for a direct-mail piece.
- Interviewing customers to develop a list of testimonials.

One copywriter, who specializes in writing case studies (customer success stories), also offers a consulting service to help her clients plan their annual case study strategy.

## *Where to Find Clients*

Hanging out a shingle isn't enough. If you want to persuade clients to hire your copywriting services, you have to do much, much more. In your first few weeks, or even months of freelancing, you can expect to spend most of your time selling yourself.

If you have never promoted your own services before, it can be a little intimidating. Don't worry. There really is no mystery to getting clients. It just takes a few simple techniques, some discipline, and good old-fashioned hard work.

The number one reason why freelance copywriters fail to get enough clients is that they give up too soon. Marketing and self-promotion takes time. Success doesn't happen overnight, especially when you first launch your business. But if you keep at it, and do the right things, the clients will come.

Who hires freelance copywriters? Not every business is a potential client. To make the best use of your time and marketing budget, you need to narrow your focus to those organizations that are most likely to use free-lance copywriting services.

## Creative Services Agencies

These include ad agencies, design firms, public relations firms, market-ing consultants, and other firms involved in creating communications for their clients. Virtually all these firms outsource creative work from time to time, so this is a big market for freelancers. The best people inside to contact include the creative director, copy chief, account executive, and, at small agencies, the owner.

## Midsized to Large Companies

The marketing or public relations department of just one big company can generate enough work to keep you busy full time. Even if the company already has an ad agency or design firm on retainer, they will still outsource writing projects to freelancers. The best people to contact have the words "marketing," "communications," or "public relations" in their job titles.

## Small Businesses

The mere size of this market makes this a lucrative opportunity for copy-writers. There are tens of millions of small businesses throughout North America. However, small-business owners will often want you to provide additional services, such as coordinating design or distributing a press release. The best person to contact is usually the owner.

## Nonprofit Organizations

This is a big market for freelance copywriters. Some copywriters special-ize exclusively in writing for nonprofits, cranking out such vital communica-tions as fundraising letters, ads, grant proposals, newsletters, and speeches. Contact the executive director or fundraising director.

### Direct Marketers

Some companies sell primarily through direct mail, television infomercials, and the Internet. They usually don't have stores or salespeople. So their marketing has to do all the work. That's why direct marketing (also known as direct response) is the highest-paying copywriting specialty. If you can craft a direct-mail letter, ad, or other marketing piece that actually generates sales, you can do very well indeed.

## Getting the Word Out

Once you know who hires copywriters—and you have business cards, letterhead, and a basic Web site put together—your next step is to let as many potential clients as possible know about your copywriting services. There are many ways to get the word out. Here are some of the most effective strategies:

### Write Articles

Most trade and professional publications will publish articles written by experts. If you write an article on copywriting for a local marketing newsletter, potential clients may notice your byline and give you a call! Focus your efforts on publications—print and online—related to advertising, marketing, communications, and public relations.

### Speak at Meetings

There are numerous business groups and professional associations located within driving distance from your home. Contact the person responsible for meetings or educational events and ask if you can speak. Your topic will be, of course, copywriting.

These days you don't even have to attend in person. Many organizations hold teleseminars—mini seminars conducted on a teleconference line—for their members. They often invite special guest experts to participate.

## Networking

Business meetings and events also are ideal for mingling and meeting potential clients. You don't even have to leave your home to do it. Many professional associations have forums, blogs, and discussion boards where you can chat with members online.

## Pitch Letters

Mailing letters to potential clients is a very effective way to promote your services. You can build a list of company names and contacts that represents your ideal clients using business directories and the Internet. Write a letter introducing your services and describing how you might be able to help them achieve their sales, marketing, and PR goals.

Here is an excerpt from an effective pitch letter written by Pam Magnuson, a copywriting expert for the nutraceutical industry. (It's not shown here, but on the actual letter a bag of green tea is attached.)

Dear Friend,
As a busy marketer myself, I understand how occupied you are, and perhaps a bit stressed. You're invited now to sit back and relax with a nice cup of tea while you read my letter.

My name is Pam Magnuson. I'm a freelance copywriter specializing in nutraceutical and herbal marketing.

I've noticed that a great many websites for nutraceuticals and herbal products are missing a huge opportunity for profit. Many are not using powerful lead-generating (or order-generating) copy or techniques.

This has lead me to create a very informative report about how to easily have a dynamic, hard-working website…

Pam's pitch letter goes on to offer a free report for those prospects who visit her Web site. This is a very powerful lead-generating technique for freelancers.

## Telephone Prospecting

Cold calling doesn't have to be frigid. Simply pick up the phone and politely introduce yourself and your services to potential clients. Say that you're available for freelance work and ask if you can e-mail them your contact information and link to your Web site. If you're friendly and not pushy, chances are most people will respond positively.

## Watch for Opportunities

There are many other ways to reach out to potential clients. These are just the most common—and effective. Use your imagination. Always be on the lookout for opportunities to let people know about your freelance copywriting services. Never give up. It may take a lot of time and effort to get that first client. But once you do, you'll be in business!

# Pricing Your Services

A potential client who's interested in your copywriting services calls and asks how much you charge to write a four-page Web site. How are you going to respond?

Most freelance copywriters, even those with a lot of experience, find quoting and pricing to be a nerve-racking experience. And for good reason! If you quote too high, you may price yourself out of that project. If you quote too low, you risk looking like an amateur—and still not get the project!

That's why quoting a client a realistic price is key to getting the job.

## Hourly Rate or Project Fee?

The first thing you need to decide when pricing your services is whether to quote an hourly rate or a project fee. Quoting an hourly rate means you bill the client for the amount of hours you spent working on the project. Quoting a project fee means you quote and are paid an agreed-upon fixed price regardless of how long it takes you to complete the job.

A hourly rate seems like a simple, safe, and fair way to quote. However, this method of quoting is fraught with problems.

First, many clients don't like to hire freelancers this way. It's too much like writing you a blank check. They're going to insist that you at least commit to an estimated number of hours for the project (which isn't much different than quoting a project fee).

Secondly, when you charge by the hour, you actually get paid less the faster and better you get. For example, if a sales letter normally takes you five hours to write, but in a surge of productivity you finish the job in three hours, you can only bill for three hours of work. That's a 40 percent cut in pay!

That's why most freelance copywriters prefer to charge a project fee rather than an hourly rate. Clients prefer it. And it's usually better for the bank account, too.

## *Quoting the Job*

Before you can estimate your fee for a project, you have to ask the client several questions. You goal is to find out as much as you can so that you fully understand the work that is required as well as the client's expectations.

Here are some typical questions you should ask:

- What is the size of the project? How many pages or screens does it have? What is the size of a page?
- When is the deadline? Do you require an outline to be approved first? If so, when is that due?
- How do I learn more about the product and target audience? What background materials are available? Who should I contact if I have questions?
- Do we need to meet in person? Or can we exchange project information by phone, e-mail, and the Internet?
- How many people will be reviewing the copy? If revisions are required, how quickly will you need these completed?

There may be several other questions you need to ask depending on the nature of the project. Once you're confident that you understand everything completely, then you're ready to prepare a quotation.

Move quickly. If possible, prepare and send the quotation the same day the client contacts you with the request. You want to take advantage of the momentum and the client's desire to get the job done. Also, you don't want to wait too long or the client might get a quotation earlier by another copywriter—and then hire that person for the job.

## How Much to Charge

Unfortunately, there is no generally accepted rate schedule published in the copywriting industry. There are, however, typical fee ranges that clients expect to pay for certain types of projects. For example, most clients are willing to pay $500 to $1,000 for a one-to-two page sales letter. So if you quote within that range, you're pretty safe. Of course, there are many inexperienced copywriters who will charge much less, and a few superstar practitioners who can get away with charging much more.

Here are estimated fee ranges charged by full-time freelance copywriters. Some professionals charge more, others less, depending on their experience and track record.

**Estimated Copywriting Fees**
Full page print advertisement … $500–$2,000
Advertorial … $500–$1,000 per page
Sales letter (1–2 pages) … $750–$2,000
Direct-mail package, to generate leads … $1,500–$3,500
Direct-mail package, to generate sales … $2,500–$7,500
Postcard or other self-mailer … $750–$2,000
Teleselling script … $750–$2,000
Web site, home page … $750–$1,500
Web site, other pages … $500–$750
E-zine ad … $500–$750
Banner ad … $500–$750
Landing page … $750–$1,500
Microsite … $750–$1,000 per page
E-mail marketing … $500–$750
Brochure … $500–$750 per page
Catalog … $250–$750 per item

Press release … $500–$750
Article … $750–$1,000
Case study … $750–$1,500
White paper … $2,000–$5,000
Presentation slides … $75–$150 per slide

How do you decide where to price a specific job within the above fee ranges? That will depend on your experience, track record of success with the type of project you're quoting, the deadline ("Is this a rush job?"), and the volume of work you can expect from the client in the future.

Quoting isn't easy. It's one of those things in the freelancing business that you get better at over time. If you're just starting out, you're bound to make some mistakes when pricing jobs. When that happens, use what you learned to quote the next project more accurately. Before long, you'll be quoting with confidence.

## Get It in Writing

Never start work on a copywriting project without a written agreement. If you do, you risk misunderstandings and other issues occurring and won't have anything in writing to back you up.

For example, a client calls you to ask for your price to write a newsletter advertisement. On the phone you say, "$350." He agrees and says, "Go ahead." So you get to work. Once the copy is approved, you submit your invoice. The client balks, "Wait a minute. You said the price is $250. I'm not paying a cent more!" If you didn't get anything in writing, you're in a tough position to defend yourself.

Disagreements over pricing and terms can occur even with long-standing clients. Don't assume that just because you've known a client for years that you can rely on a handshake agreement. Always get things in writing.

How do you avoid situations like these? Make sure that both you and the client are on the same page by using a written agreement. This can be as simple as a one-page letter or e-mail that details your understanding of the project, pricing, and terms.

Your agreement should answer such questions as:

- What is the project?
- When is the deadline?
- What is the copywriting fee?
- How many rounds of revisions are included in this fee?
- What are the payment terms?
- What happens if the project is canceled by the client before completion?

Here is an example of a typical letter of agreement:

Letter of Agreement
ATT: John Smith
Thank you for considering my services!
The project, as I understand it, is to write a one-page print advertisement for your New Gizmo.
I will deliver the draft copy of this ad to you on or before Friday, June 16th.
My fee for this project will be $1,200.
Should you request any revisions to the copy, I will complete these promptly and for no additional charge. This is provided the revisions are assigned within 30 days of you receiving my initial draft copy.
Please note the following:

- The quoted fee is for copy only; it does not cover design and production.
- Regarding proofreading, I do check each draft carefully for errors. However, I strongly advise that you have the copy proofread at your end before production.
- I will take care to write copy that complies with the law, but I am not a lawyer. It is your responsibility to submit all copy for legal review.

I look forward to working with you. If this project is a "Go," simply let me know by return e-mail that you agree to these terms, and forward any required purchase order documents.

**QUESTION?**

### What if the client cancels the project?

If the client cancels a project after you've begun working on it, you're entitled to a "kill fee." This is usually calculated as a percentage of the total project price. So, if you've completed 25 percent of a $1,000 job, you can bill the client $250. Make sure you explain your kill fee policy to your client before you take the job.

To save time, the best way to handle a letter of agreement is by e-mail. Simply send your client the letter within an e-mail and ask him to read and approve it. He can just reply to the e-mail to indicate his agreement.

# Appendix A
# **Glossary**

**account executive:**
The person at the ad agency, public relations firm, or design firm who is in charge of the account. Often referred to as the AE, the account executive acts as the liaison between the client and the agency, and makes sure that projects run smoothly.

**art director:**
The person at the agency or company that is in charge of the design of a promotional piece. He or she is typically responsible for the layout, text placement, photos, illustrations, and other visual elements. Art directors often work closely with copywriters. In some cases, they are a defined team.

**AV or A/V:**
Abbreviation for audio-visual, it typically refers to videos, presentations, and multimedia CDs. Copywriters often script storyboards, dialogue, and text for AV projects.

**awareness:**
Also known as brand awareness, it's how well-known a product or service is or a promotion designed to get a product recognized rather than solicit a direct sale.

**big idea:**
The theme of an advertisement or how that theme will influence potential buyers. It's what scrutinizing creative directors or marketing managers look for when critiquing concepts for ads and direct-mail packages.

**bleed:**
A term used in print communications, a bleed is a photo, illustration, or background color that goes to the edge of the page, beyond the expected border or margin. Promotional pieces that have a bleed are usually more expensive to print.

**body:**
The main text of a promotional piece, as opposed to the headlines, sidebars, subheads, and other elements. So when someone says, "the body of the ad," he or she is referring to the text below the main headline.

**boilerplate:**
A block of text, often describing the company or product, that is used over and over again in multiple promotional pieces. Press releases, for example, often end with a boilerplate paragraph on the company.

**book:**
See portfolio.

**boutique agency:**
An agency that is not full service. They may handle graphic design, for example, but not market research or production. A freelance copywriter is, technically, a boutique agency.

**brand:**
The name of the product, along with all the taglines, slogans, images, and other identifiable features associated with it. In the advertising world, brand is also used in reference to a product's popularity and success. To "build a brand" is to increase its recognition and preference among buyers.

**brand awareness:**
See awareness.

**BRC:**
Abbreviation for business reply card. This is used in direct mail as a means for the recipient to reply to the offer. ("Just fill in the reply card and drop it in the mail.")

**BRE:**
Abbreviation for business reply envelope, it's the same as a BRC except that it's an envelope rather than a card.

**budget:**
The money allocated for the creation, production, and distribution of a promotional piece. This is a big concern for marketing managers.

**business-to-business:**
Selling products and services to other companies rather than consumers. It's considered a specialized field, and there are many professional associations, events, books, and periodicals dedicated to business-to-business sales and marketing. Also known as B2B or B-to-B.

**business-to-consumer:**
The selling of products and services to consumers rather than businesses. Also known as B2C or B-to-C

**buzz:**
Excitement that is generated about a product or service, which hopefully translates into sales. Buzz is often generated by public relations campaigns and word-of-mouth.

**call to action:**
The section of a promotion that asks the reader to do something. It may be to visit a store, go to a Web site, fill out a form, or place an order. A call to action is a necessity in any piece that is meant to generate a lead or sale, such as a mail-order package, catalog, sales letter, or e-mail promotion.

**campaign:**
A coordinated effort to accomplish a specific sales, marketing, or public relations goal.

**collateral:**
Printed pieces—brochures, sell sheets, case studies, and other literature—used primarily by salespeople.

**concept:**
An idea for a promotional piece that is developed to a point where it can be presented to others. An ad agency, for example, might prepare several concepts for an ad campaign and ask the client to choose one.

**consumer:**
Someone who buys for him or herself rather than on behalf of a company. A grocery store is frequented mostly by consumers. But an office supply store caters to both consumers and business buyers.

**copy chief:**
The person at an agency or company that is responsible for the copywriting of all promotional materials. He or she usually supervises other writers.

**copy platform:**
Common in direct marketing, it is a plan for how the copy will be structured and written, with a description of the basic strategy and theme of the piece. It's a cross between a creative brief and an outline.

**copywriter's rough:**
A rough sketch used by a copywriter to communicate an idea for a layout or visual. A copywriter's rough can be as basic as a pencil scribble or as sophisticated as a detailed drawing done on computer.

**corporate brochure:**
A brochure that promotes all the features and positive aspects of the company rather than any specific product or service; same as a corporate profile only longer. Corporate brochures are often used in public relations and investor relations to help "sell" a company.

**corporate profile:**
A description of a company that often appears in Web sites, brochures, and other corporate materials, usually two or three paragraphs long.

**creative:**
All the activities involved in creating a promotional piece, such as copywriting, graphic design, illustration, and photography. Creative doesn't typically include research, strategy, production, or distribution.

**creative director:**
The person at the ad agency or design firm who is responsible for all aspects of the creative. This is the top rung on the creative ladder. He or she will typically supervise a team of designers, writers, producers, and others.

**cross-selling:**
The attempt to sell unrelated products and services to existing customers. The fact that you bought a Honda means you might be a good prospect for a Honda lawnmower.

**demographics:**
Statistics that describe a particular segment of the population, covering such identifiable characteristics as age, sex, and income. Marketers use this information to more accurately target their campaigns.

**direct mail:**
Promotional pieces delivered by mail, including postcards, flyers, envelopes, and catalogs.

**direct marketing:**
Any marketing effort that is directed at a specific list of people rather than the general population. An ad in a magazine isn't direct marketing, but a sales letter sent to your home is.

**direct-response marketing:**
A promotional piece that directly solicits a lead or sale. It wants you to respond to it. Direct-response ads, direct mail, and other promotions typically include a call to action and instructions on how to reply or buy.

**farm out:**
Work that is done by an agency or freelancer rather than in-house.

**flash:**
Computer software used to create Web site graphics, and sometimes the entire site. Flash images can be animated.

**FPO:**
The short version of for position only. When a designer mocks up a promotional piece, he or she might mark certain images, such as drawings or photos, as placeholders only, or for position only (FPO). The real drawing or photo will be developed and placed later.

**full-service agency:**
An agency that handles all aspects of marketing or public relations, including research, strategy, creative services, media buying, and more.

**greek:**
The text equivalent of an FPO, greek is the name give to dummy text that is used by designers in a layout as placeholder copy until the real stuff is written.

**HTML:**
Abbreviation for Hypertext Markup Language, the computer language used to create most of the Web sites you see on the Internet.

**landing page:**
A special Web page, usually an order form, that is usually part of a larger campaign. For example, clicking on a banner advertisement might take you to a landing page where you can learn more about the product and, hopefully, order it.

**lead:**
Also known as a sales lead, this is the name of a person who has expressed interest in a product or service, and a willingness to learn more. Lead generation is an important task for copywriters in business-to-business marketing.

**mail order:**
Direct-mail packages and catalogs that offer products you can order through the mail or online.

**marcom:**
Short for marketing communications, which is anything that the marketing department produces, such as press releases, sales brochures, and advertisements, to reach out to prospects and customers.

**microsite:**
A Web site dedicated to a specific product or campaign. It's often different from the company's main Web site. A microsite is often used in conjunction with another promotional piece. For example, a link within an e-zine ad might take the reader to a microsite that provides more detailed information on the product.

**PDF:**
Abbreviation for Portable Document Format. This is the standard way that mockups and design concepts are shared. A designer, for example, might e-mail a copywriter a draft of a layout as a PDF file. The software you need to view a PDF file, Adobe's Acrobat Reader, is available at *www.adobe.com*.

**portfolio:**
Also known in the industry as a book, this is a collection of copywriting samples used to promote your talents to potential employers and clients.

**psychographics:**
Similar to demographics, except the information also includes needs, interests, preferences, annoyances, and other psychological insights into a particular segment of the marketplace.

**PPC:**
Short for pay per click, this is a form of online advertising, such as a banner, where the advertiser only pays when someone clicks on the ad.

**premium:**
A gift offered to potential buyers as an incentive for buying the product. Premiums are often used in direct-mail and online promotions. ("Order today and you'll also receive this free gift.")

**prospect:**
A potential customer; someone who has the budget, authority, and desire to buy a product or service but hasn't done so yet.

**pull:**
The response generated from a promotional piece, such as a direct-mail package. ("The sales letter pulled a 5% response.")

**ROI:**
Short for return on investment, this is a popular term in business-to-business marketing. Business buyers often have to justify their purchases by the return in revenues and cost savings that a product or service can potentially generate.

**sales copy:**
Copy that attempts to sell the product or service rather than simply raise awareness or convey information.

**sell sheet:**
A specialized type of sales brochure that explains only a specific aspect or application of a product or service.

**space:**
The area in a publication that is reserved for advertising. ("We just booked space in *Lawn Care Monthly* for a half-page ad.")

**universe:**
The estimated number of potential customers for a product or service.

**up-selling:**
The attempt to get a customer to purchase extras or a better version of the product or service. "Would you like to supersize that meal?" is the classic example.

**USP:**
Short for unique selling proposition. According to the person who first coined the phrase, advertising legend Rosser Reeves, a USP has three characteristics: 1) the promotion must make a specific proposition to the prospect, 2) the proposition must be one that the competition either cannot, or does not, offer, and 3) the proposition must be strong enough to motivate the masses to buy the product or service.

**Webinar:**
A Web seminar; a presentation that you can listen to and view on a special Web site.

# The Copy Review Checklist

Use this checklist as a quality-control tool. It will help you review your copy and identify ways to make it more effective.

❏ Will the headline gain the reader's attention? (The average prospect sees dozens of headlines each day. Will yours stand out?)

❏ Is the copy focused primarily on the prospect? (His or her problems, needs, and desires.)

❏ Is the copy really persuasive or merely descriptive?

❏ Is there a clear connection made between each feature and benefit?

❏ Are the advantages of the product highlighted? (An advantage is something that the competition either doesn't do or can't do as well.)

❏ Are the benefits brought to life? (Using examples, stories, scenarios, and other word pictures.)

❏ Are all the benefits jumping off the page, or are some hard to find within the body copy?

❏ In a longer piece, are the main features and benefits summarized at the end?

❏ Are all claims proven, or at least supported with specific evidence? (Using testimonials, reviews, statistics, success stories, and research.)

❏ Has the risk of buying the product being reduced? (Is there a guarantee? A demo? A trial version?)

❏ Has the price been put in perspective? (Will a prospect understand why an expensive product is worth every penny?)

❑ Is there a call to action? (Will a prospect know what to do next?)

❑ Is the offer compelling enough to motivate the customer to buy?

❑ Does the copy differentiate the product from the competition? (Will the product stand out in a crowd of look-alikes?)

❑ Are there any mistakes or typos? (Did you check for the obvious, such as correct addresses, phone numbers, full product names and part numbers, and Web site URLs?)

❑ Are there any clichés?

❑ Does the copy primarily use an active voice? (Don't say: "Fuel consumption was reduced through the addition of a catalyst." Do say: "Adding a catalyst reduced fuel consumption.")

❑ If appropriate for the piece, is the tone friendly, authoritative, and conversational?

❑ Is the copy highly scannable? (Make sure there are plenty of bullets, subheads, captions, sidebars, and emphasized words and phrases.)

❑ Are there any overly long sentences or paragraphs?

❑ How does the copy sound when you read it out loud? Do any sections seem confusing or awkward? (The copy should sound as good as it reads.)

❑ Are all the facts accurate?

❑ Are all acronyms defined at least once in the copy? (Do this, even if you think a prospect will know the acronym.)

❑ Is the writing style consistent throughout?

❑ Are there any extraneous words or sentences that can be cut without damaging the effectiveness of the copy? (Make the copy as concise as possible.)

❑ Is there any missing information? (Is there anything a prospect needs to know to make a buying decision that is not covered in the copy?)

❑ Is everything clearly explained? Will the prospect understand what the product or service is, how it works, and why he or she should buy it?

❑ Has a sense of urgency been created? (Why should the prospect act now?)

❑ Would the prospect look forward to receiving similar promotions from you in the future?

# Resources

## E-mail Newsletters (e-zines)

### For Copywriters Only

This is a highly informative newsletter for both employed and freelance copywriters. It features copywriting tips and techniques, plus advice on project management and freelancing. Published by Steve Slaunwhite.

✑ *www.ForCopywritersOnly.com*

## Books

### Start and Run a Copywriting Business, 2nd ed., Steve Slaunwhite, 2005, Self-Counsel Press

This bestselling guide to becoming a successful freelance copywriter has been endorsed by many of the top professionals in the industry. It covers all the basics from setting up your business and finding clients to handling various copywriting tasks and getting paid. The books also includes a CD of ready-to-use checklists and forms.

### On Writing Well, 25th anniv. ed., William Zinsser, 2001, Harper Resource

Now a classic, this continually updated book is probably the bestselling nonfiction writing guide in history—with more than one million copies sold. Every copywriter needs to read this and absorb the lessons it teaches.

### How to Write Successful Fundraising Letters, Mal Warwick, 2001, Jossey-Bass

If you want to write fundraising letters and other promotions for charities and other nonprofits this book is a must. It is recognized as the definitive guide on the subject. Even if you don't write for nonprofits, you'll find Warwick's advice indispensable for any kind of copywriting task you handle.

**Tested Advertising Methods, 5th ed., John Caples and revised by Fred E. Hahn, 1998, Prentice Hall**

Caples is a pioneer in direct-response space advertising. He has written ads that have run for decades. This book is packed with tips, lists, and proven advice for writing headlines, that crucial first paragraph, body copy, and the close. It's the classic in creating promotions that sell. His chapter on headlines is priceless.

**Write On Target, *Donna Baier Stein and Floyd Kemske, 1997, NTC Business Books***

This book has become a standard in direct-mail copywriting. It covers all the basics of writing effective sales letters, envelope teaser, DM bro-chures, self-mailers, order forms, and more. Perhaps the most helpful aspect of this book is that it contains dozens of real-world examples.

## *Courses*

### *Steve Slaunwhite's Copywriting Workshop*

This comprehensive two-day workshop is held two or three times each year in Toronto and Vancouver. Designed for marketing and publicity professionals, as well as freelance writers, it's a great way to learn copywriting techniques and strategies that really work. For more information, visit *www.ForCopywritersOnly.com*.

## *Industry Web sites*

Inside Direct Mail
*www.insidedirectmail.com*

Advertising Age
*www.adage.com*

B-to-B
*www.btobonline.com*

Direct Marketing News
*www.dmn.ca*

DM News
*www.dmnews.com*

Target Marketing
*www.targetmarketingmag.com*

Marketing Magazine
*www.marketingmag.ca*

Marketing VOX
*www.marketingvox.com*

Sales & Marketing Management
*www.salesandmarketing.com*

Selling Power
*www.sellingpower.com*

# Index

# THE EVERYTHING SERIES!

## BUSINESS & PERSONAL FINANCE

Everything® Accounting Book
Everything® Budgeting Book
Everything® Business Planning Book
Everything® Coaching and Mentoring Book
Everything® Fundraising Book
Everything® Get Out of Debt Book
Everything® Grant Writing Book
**Everything® Guide to Personal Finance for Single Mothers**
Everything® Home-Based Business Book, 2nd Ed.
Everything® Homebuying Book, 2nd Ed.
Everything® Homeselling Book, 2nd Ed.
**Everything® Improve Your Credit Book**
Everything® Investing Book, 2nd Ed.
Everything® Landlording Book
Everything® Leadership Book
Everything® Managing People Book, 2nd Ed.
Everything® Negotiating Book
Everything® Online Auctions Book
Everything® Online Business Book
Everything® Personal Finance Book
Everything® Personal Finance in Your 20s and 30s Book
Everything® Project Management Book
Everything® Real Estate Investing Book
**Everything® Retirement Planning Book**
Everything® Robert's Rules Book, $7.95
Everything® Selling Book
Everything® Start Your Own Business Book, 2nd Ed.
Everything® Wills & Estate Planning Book

## COOKING

Everything® Barbecue Cookbook
Everything® Bartender's Book, $9.95
**Everything® Cheese Book**
Everything® Chinese Cookbook
Everything® Classic Recipes Book
Everything® Cocktail Parties and Drinks Book
Everything® College Cookbook
Everything® Cooking for Baby and Toddler Book
Everything® Cooking for Two Cookbook
Everything® Diabetes Cookbook
Everything® Easy Gourmet Cookbook
Everything® Fondue Cookbook
Everything® Fondue Party Book
Everything® Gluten-Free Cookbook
Everything® Glycemic Index Cookbook
Everything® Grilling Cookbook

Everything® Healthy Meals in Minutes Cookbook
Everything® Holiday Cookbook
Everything® Indian Cookbook
Everything® Italian Cookbook
Everything® Low-Carb Cookbook
Everything® Low-Fat High-Flavor Cookbook
Everything® Low-Salt Cookbook
Everything® Meals for a Month Cookbook
Everything® Mediterranean Cookbook
Everything® Mexican Cookbook
**Everything® No Trans Fat Cookbook**
Everything® One-Pot Cookbook
**Everything® Pizza Cookbook**
Everything® Quick and Easy 30-Minute, 5-Ingredient Cookbook
Everything® Quick Meals Cookbook
Everything® Slow Cooker Cookbook
Everything® Slow Cooking for a Crowd Cookbook
Everything® Soup Cookbook
**Everything® Stir-Fry Cookbook**
Everything® Tex-Mex Cookbook
Everything® Thai Cookbook
Everything® Vegetarian Cookbook
Everything® Wild Game Cookbook
Everything® Wine Book, 2nd Ed.

## GAMES

Everything® 15-Minute Sudoku Book, $9.95
Everything® 30-Minute Sudoku Book, $9.95
Everything® Blackjack Strategy Book
Everything® Brain Strain Book, $9.95
Everything® Bridge Book
Everything® Card Games Book
Everything® Card Tricks Book, $9.95
Everything® Casino Gambling Book, 2nd Ed.
Everything® Chess Basics Book
Everything® Craps Strategy Book
Everything® Crossword and Puzzle Book
Everything® Crossword Challenge Book
**Everything® Crosswords for the Beach Book, $9.95**
Everything® Cryptograms Book, $9.95
Everything® Easy Crosswords Book
Everything® Easy Kakuro Book, $9.95
**Everything® Easy Large Print Crosswords Book**
Everything® Games Book, 2nd Ed.
Everything® Giant Sudoku Book, $9.95
Everything® Kakuro Challenge Book, $9.95
Everything® Large-Print Crossword Challenge Book

Everything® Large-Print Crosswords Book
Everything® Lateral Thinking Puzzles Book, $9.95
Everything® Mazes Book
**Everything® Movie Crosswords Book, $9.95**
**Everything® Online Poker Book, $12.95**
Everything® Pencil Puzzles Book, $9.95
Everything® Poker Strategy Book
Everything® Pool & Billiards Book
**Everything® Sports Crosswords Book, $9.95**
Everything® Test Your IQ Book, $9.95
Everything® Texas Hold 'Em Book, $9.95
Everything® Travel Crosswords Book, $9.95
Everything® Word Games Challenge Book
**Everything® Word Scramble Book**
Everything® Word Search Book

## HEALTH

Everything® Alzheimer's Book
Everything® Diabetes Book
Everything® Health Guide to Adult Bipolar Disorder
Everything® Health Guide to Controlling Anxiety
Everything® Health Guide to Fibromyalgia
**Everything® Health Guide to Postpartum Care**
Everything® Health Guide to Thyroid Disease
Everything® Hypnosis Book
Everything® Low Cholesterol Book
Everything® Massage Book
Everything® Menopause Book
Everything® Nutrition Book
Everything® Reflexology Book
Everything® Stress Management Book

## HISTORY

Everything® American Government Book
**Everything® American History Book, 2nd Ed.**
Everything® Civil War Book
Everything® Freemasons Book
Everything® Irish History & Heritage Book
Everything® Middle East Book

## HOBBIES

Everything® Candlemaking Book
Everything® Cartooning Book
Everything® Coin Collecting Book
Everything® Drawing Book
Everything® Family Tree Book, 2nd Ed.
Everything® Knitting Book
Everything® Knots Book
Everything® Photography Book

Everything® Quilting Book
Everything® Scrapbooking Book
Everything® Sewing Book
**Everything® Soapmaking Book, 2nd Ed.**
Everything® Woodworking Book

## HOME IMPROVEMENT

Everything® Feng Shui Book
Everything® Feng Shui Decluttering Book, $9.95
Everything® Fix-It Book
Everything® Home Decorating Book
Everything® Home Storage Solutions Book
Everything® Homebuilding Book
Everything® Organize Your Home Book

## KIDS' BOOKS

**All titles are $7.95**

Everything® Kids' Animal Puzzle & Activity Book
Everything® Kids' Baseball Book, 4th Ed.
Everything® Kids' Bible Trivia Book
Everything® Kids' Bugs Book
Everything® Kids' Cars and Trucks Puzzle & Activity Book
Everything® Kids' Christmas Puzzle & Activity Book
Everything® Kids' Cookbook
Everything® Kids' Crazy Puzzles Book
Everything® Kids' Dinosaurs Book
Everything® Kids' First Spanish Puzzle and Activity Book
**Everything® Kids' Gross Cookbook**
Everything® Kids' Gross Hidden Pictures Book
Everything® Kids' Gross Jokes Book
Everything® Kids' Gross Mazes Book
Everything® Kids' Gross Puzzle and Activity Book
Everything® Kids' Halloween Puzzle & Activity Book
Everything® Kids' Hidden Pictures Book
Everything® Kids' Horses Book
Everything® Kids' Joke Book
Everything® Kids' Knock Knock Book
Everything® Kids' Learning Spanish Book
Everything® Kids' Math Puzzles Book
Everything® Kids' Mazes Book
Everything® Kids' Money Book
Everything® Kids' Nature Book
Everything® Kids' Pirates Puzzle and Activity Book
**Everything® Kids' Presidents Book**
Everything® Kids' Princess Puzzle and Activity Book
Everything® Kids' Puzzle Book
Everything® Kids' Riddles & Brain Teasers Book
Everything® Kids' Science Experiments Book
Everything® Kids' Sharks Book
Everything® Kids' Soccer Book
**Everything® Kids' States Book**
Everything® Kids' Travel Activity Book

## KIDS' STORY BOOKS

Everything® Fairy Tales Book

## LANGUAGE

Everything® Conversational Japanese Book with CD, $19.95
Everything® French Grammar Book
Everything® French Phrase Book, $9.95
Everything® French Verb Book, $9.95
Everything® German Practice Book with CD, $19.95
Everything® Inglés Book
**Everything® Intermediate Spanish Book with CD, $19.95**
**Everything® Learning Brazilian Portuguese Book with CD, $19.95**
Everything® Learning French Book
Everything® Learning German Book
Everything® Learning Italian Book
Everything® Learning Latin Book
**Everything® Learning Spanish Book with CD, 2nd Edition, $19.95**
Everything® Russian Practice Book with CD, $19.95
Everything® Sign Language Book
Everything® Spanish Grammar Book
Everything® Spanish Phrase Book, $9.95
Everything® Spanish Practice Book with CD, $19.95
Everything® Spanish Verb Book, $9.95
Everything® Speaking Mandarin Chinese Book with CD, $19.95

## MUSIC

Everything® Drums Book with CD, $19.95
**Everything® Guitar Book with CD, 2nd Edition, $19.95**
Everything® Guitar Chords Book with CD, $19.95
Everything® Home Recording Book
Everything® Music Theory Book with CD, $19.95
Everything® Reading Music Book with CD, $19.95
Everything® Rock & Blues Guitar Book with CD, $19.95
**Everything® Rock and Blues Piano Book with CD, $19.95**
Everything® Songwriting Book

## NEW AGE

Everything® Astrology Book, 2nd Ed.
Everything® Birthday Personology Book
Everything® Dreams Book, 2nd Ed.
Everything® Love Signs Book, $9.95
Everything® Numerology Book
Everything® Paganism Book
Everything® Palmistry Book
Everything® Psychic Book
Everything® Reiki Book

Everything® Sex Signs Book, $9.95
Everything® Tarot Book, 2nd Ed.
**Everything® Toltec Wisdom Book**
Everything® Wicca and Witchcraft Book

## PARENTING

Everything® Baby Names Book, 2nd Ed.
Everything® Baby Shower Book
Everything® Baby's First Year Book
Everything® Birthing Book
Everything® Breastfeeding Book
Everything® Father-to-Be Book
Everything® Father's First Year Book
Everything® Get Ready for Baby Book
Everything® Get Your Baby to Sleep Book, $9.95
Everything® Getting Pregnant Book
Everything® Guide to Raising a One-Year-Old
Everything® Guide to Raising a Two-Year-Old
Everything® Homeschooling Book
Everything® Mother's First Year Book
**Everything® Parent's Guide to Childhood Illnesses**
Everything® Parent's Guide to Children and Divorce
Everything® Parent's Guide to Children with ADD/ADHD
Everything® Parent's Guide to Children with Asperger's Syndrome
Everything® Parent's Guide to Children with Autism
Everything® Parent's Guide to Children with Bipolar Disorder
**Everything® Parent's Guide to Children with Depression**
Everything® Parent's Guide to Children with Dyslexia
**Everything® Parent's Guide to Children with Juvenile Diabetes**
Everything® Parent's Guide to Positive Discipline
Everything® Parent's Guide to Raising a Successful Child
Everything® Parent's Guide to Raising Boys
**Everything® Parent's Guide to Raising Girls**
Everything® Parent's Guide to Raising Siblings
Everything® Parent's Guide to Sensory Integration Disorder
Everything® Parent's Guide to Tantrums
Everything® Parent's Guide to the Strong-Willed Child
Everything® Parenting a Teenager Book
Everything® Potty Training Book, $9.95
**Everything® Pregnancy Book, 3rd Ed.**
Everything® Pregnancy Fitness Book
Everything® Pregnancy Nutrition Book
Everything® Pregnancy Organizer, 2nd Ed., $16.95
Everything® Toddler Activities Book
Everything® Toddler Book

Everything® Tween Book
Everything® Twins, Triplets, and More Book

## PETS

Everything® Aquarium Book
Everything® Boxer Book
Everything® Cat Book, 2nd Ed.
Everything® Chihuahua Book
Everything® Dachshund Book
Everything® Dog Book
Everything® Dog Health Book
**Everything® Dog Obedience Book**
Everything® Dog Owner's Organizer, $16.95
Everything® Dog Training and Tricks Book
Everything® German Shepherd Book
Everything® Golden Retriever Book
Everything® Horse Book
Everything® Horse Care Book
Everything® Horseback Riding Book
Everything® Labrador Retriever Book
Everything® Poodle Book
Everything® Pug Book
Everything® Puppy Book
Everything® Rottweiler Book
Everything® Small Dogs Book
Everything® Tropical Fish Book
Everything® Yorkshire Terrier Book

## REFERENCE

**Everything® American Presidents Book**
Everything® Blogging Book
Everything® Build Your Vocabulary Book
Everything® Car Care Book
Everything® Classical Mythology Book
Everything® Da Vinci Book
Everything® Divorce Book
Everything® Einstein Book
**Everything® Enneagram Book**
Everything® Etiquette Book, 2nd Ed.
Everything® Inventions and Patents Book
Everything® Mafia Book
Everything® Philosophy Book
**Everything® Pirates Book**
Everything® Psychology Book

## RELIGION

Everything® Angels Book
Everything® Bible Book
Everything® Buddhism Book
Everything® Catholicism Book
Everything® Christianity Book
**Everything® Gnostic Gospels Book**
Everything® History of the Bible Book
Everything® Jesus Book

Everything® Jewish History & Heritage Book
Everything® Judaism Book
Everything® Kabbalah Book
Everything® Koran Book
Everything® Mary Book
Everything® Mary Magdalene Book
Everything® Prayer Book
**Everything® Saints Book, 2nd Ed.**
Everything® Torah Book
Everything® Understanding Islam Book
Everything® World's Religions Book
Everything® Zen Book

## SCHOOL & CAREERS

Everything® Alternative Careers Book
Everything® Career Tests Book
Everything® College Major Test Book
Everything® College Survival Book, 2nd Ed.
Everything® Cover Letter Book, 2nd Ed.
Everything® Filmmaking Book
**Everything® Get-a-Job Book, 2nd Ed.**
Everything® Guide to Being a Paralegal
**Everything® Guide to Being a Personal Trainer**
Everything® Guide to Being a Real Estate Agent
Everything® Guide to Being a Sales Rep
Everything® Guide to Careers in Health Care
Everything® Guide to Careers in Law Enforcement
Everything® Guide to Government Jobs
Everything® Guide to Starting and Running a Restaurant
Everything® Job Interview Book
Everything® New Nurse Book
Everything® New Teacher Book
Everything® Paying for College Book
Everything® Practice Interview Book
Everything® Resume Book, 2nd Ed.
Everything® Study Book

## SELF-HELP

Everything® Dating Book, 2nd Ed.
Everything® Great Sex Book
Everything® Self-Esteem Book
**Everything® Tantric Sex Book**

## SPORTS & FITNESS

Everything® Easy Fitness Book
Everything® Running Book
Everything® Weight Training Book

## TRAVEL

Everything® Family Guide to Cruise Vacations
Everything® Family Guide to Hawaii
Everything® Family Guide to Las Vegas, 2nd Ed.
Everything® Family Guide to Mexico
Everything® Family Guide to New York City, 2nd Ed.
Everything® Family Guide to RV Travel & Campgrounds
Everything® Family Guide to the Caribbean
Everything® Family Guide to the Walt Disney World Resort®, Universal Studios®, and Greater Orlando, 4th Ed.
Everything® Family Guide to Timeshares
**Everything® Family Guide to Washington D.C., 2nd Ed.**

## WEDDINGS

Everything® Bachelorette Party Book, $9.95
Everything® Bridesmaid Book, $9.95
Everything® Destination Wedding Book
Everything® Elopement Book, $9.95
Everything® Father of the Bride Book, $9.95
Everything® Groom Book, $9.95
Everything® Mother of the Bride Book, $9.95
Everything® Outdoor Wedding Book
Everything® Wedding Book, 3rd Ed.
Everything® Wedding Checklist, $9.95
Everything® Wedding Etiquette Book, $9.95
Everything® Wedding Organizer, 2nd Ed., $16.95
Everything® Wedding Shower Book, $9.95
Everything® Wedding Vows Book, $9.95
Everything® Wedding Workout Book
Everything® Weddings on a Budget Book, $9.95

## WRITING

Everything® Creative Writing Book
Everything® Get Published Book, 2nd Ed.
Everything® Grammar and Style Book
**Everything® Guide to Magazine Writing**
Everything® Guide to Writing a Book Proposal
Everything® Guide to Writing a Novel
Everything® Guide to Writing Children's Books
**Everything® Guide to Writing Copy**
Everything® Guide to Writing Research Papers
Everything® Screenwriting Book
Everything® Writing Poetry Book
Everything® Writing Well Book

---